Intellectual Property Law in Japan

日本知的財産法

CHAEN Shigeki(ed.)
茶園 成樹 編

発明推進協会

は　し　が　き

本書は，日本の知的財産法の基礎を解説するものである。

近時，知的財産は，社会においてその重要性を高めており，これに伴い，知的財産法に関する知識を備えた人材がますます必要となってきている。そのため，国立大学法人大阪大学は，2010年に，知的財産法の全学的な教育・研究拠点として，知的財産センターを設置した。

本書は，知的財産センターのスタッフにより，日本語で執筆された『知的財産法入門』（第1版：2013年，第2版：2017年）を英訳したものである。本書によって，多くの方々に日本の知的財産法を理解してもらうことを期待している。

本書の翻訳は，トランスユーロ株式会社の齊藤真由子氏，茂呂恵理子氏，井内由美氏，德永郁氏，高木健一氏，鈴木章浩氏，天野ローズマリーエルドレッド氏の協力を得た。また，本書の出版に際しては，一般社団法人発明推進協会の城水毅氏，神林宏美氏に大変お世話になった。

ここに記して，謝意を表したい。

2017年11月

茶　園　成　樹

Preface

This book explains the basics of intellectual property law in Japan.

Recently, intellectual property increases its importance in the society, and it enlarges the need for people who know about intellectual property law. Therefore, Osaka University established Intellectual Property Center as a base of education and research for intellectual property law in 2010.

This book is the translation in English from "Introduction to Intellectual Property Law", written in Japanese by the staff of Intellectual Property Center in 2013 [first edition] and in 2017 [second edition]. We hope that, through this book, many people will learn Japanese intellectual property law.

In translation of this book, we were helped by Ms. Mayuko Saito, Ms. Eriko Moro, Ms. Yumi Iuchi, Ms. Iku Tokunaga, Mr. Kenichi Takagi, Mr. Akihiro Suzuki and Ms. Rose Marie Eldred Amano in TRANSEURO, Inc. We are particularly grateful to them. Special words of thanks should be extended to Mr. Takeshi Shiromizu and Ms. Hiromi Kambayashi in Japan Institute for Promoting Invention and Innovation for publishing of this book.

Shigeki Chaen

Osaka, November 2017

About the Editor

CHAEN Shigeki [UNIT 1, 5, 7]
Professor, Osaka University Law School

About the Authors

AOKI Hiroya [UNIT 4, 12, 13]
Associate Professor, Graduate School of Law and Politics, Osaka University

CHEN Siqin [UNIT 2, 3, 15]
Associate Professor, Osaka University Intellectual Property Center (IPrism)

KATSUHISA Haruo [UNIT 8, 9, 11]
Assistant Professor, Osaka University Intellectual Property Center (IPrism)

MURAKAMI Eri [UNIT 6, 10, 14]
Associate Professor, Osaka University Intellectual Property Center (IPrism)

Law Reports

Chitekisaishu
Intellectual Property Law Cases Reports (Civil and Administrative Cases)

Gyoshu
Administrative Law Cases Reports

Hanrei Jiho
Law Cases Reports

Hanrei Times
Law Times Reports

Minshu
Supreme Court Reports (Civil Cases)

Mutaisaishu
Intangible Property Law Cases Reports (Civil and Administrative Cases)

CONTENTS

Preface ······ i
About the Editor ······ ii
About the Authors ······ ii
Law Reports ······ iii

UNIT 1 Introduction ··· 1

I Intellectual property law ······ 1

1 What is intellectual property law? ······ 1

2 Why is intellectual property protected? ······ 1

3 Various categories of intellectual property laws ······ 2

II Patent Law and Utility Model Law ······ 4

1 What is protected? ······ 4

2 Who is protected? ······ 5

3 What needs to be done in order to receive protection? ······ 6

4 Trials (*Shinpan*) and actions against trial decisions ······ 7

5 Patent rights and infringement of a patent right ······ 8

6 Utilization of patent rights ······ 9

7 Utility Model Law ······ 9

III Design Law ······ 10

IV Trademark Law ······ 11

V Copyright Law ······ 12

1 What is protected? ······ 12

2 Who is protected? ······ 12

3 What needs to be done in order to receive protection? ······ 13

4 Rights of an author ······ 13

5 Infringement on the rights of an author ······ 14

VI Unfair Competition Prevention Law ······ 15

VII Other ······ 16

CONTENTS

UNIT 2　Patent Law (1) ··· 17

I　General remarks ······ 17

  1　What is an invention? ······ 17

  2　Types of inventions ······ 17

II　Requirement (1): Utilization of the laws of nature ······ 18

  1　What is the utilization of the laws of nature? ······ 18

  2　The laws of nature *per se* is not considered to be an invention ······ 18

  3　A creation which is contrary to the laws of nature is not considered to be an invention ······ 19

  4　A creation utilizing something other than the laws of nature is not considered to be an invention ······ 19

  5　Software-related inventions ······ 21

III　Requirement (2): Technical idea ······ 22

  1　What is a technical idea? ······ 22

  2　The enablement requirement ······ 23

  3　Reproducibility ······ 23

  4　Incomplete inventions ······ 24

IV　Requirement (3): Creation ······ 25

  1　What is a creation? The difference between an invention and a discovery ······ 25

  2　Use inventions ······ 26

V　Requirement (4): Highly advanced ······ 27

UNIT 3　Patent Law (2) ··· 29

I　Overview ······ 29

  1　What is patentability? ······ 29

  2　Patentability requirements under the Patent Law ······ 29

II　Industrial applicability ······ 30

  1　Definition of industrial applicability ······ 30

  2　Medical invention ······ 31

III　Novelty ······ 32

  1　Definition of novelty ······ 32

  2　The term "publicly" ······ 34

v

CONTENTS

3　Publicly-known inventions ······ 35

4　Publicly-worked invention ······ 35

5　Description in publications ······ 36

6　Determination method ······ 37

7　Exceptions to the lack of novelty ······ 38

Ⅳ　Inventive step ······ 41

1　What is an inventive step? ······ 41

2　Technological level by which the existence of an inventive step is determined – Person skilled in the art ······ 41

3　Determination method ······ 42

4　Inventive step of a use invention ······ 43

5　Selection invention ······ 43

6　Numerically limited invention ······ 43

V　First-to-file system ······ 44

1　Outline ······ 44

2　Determination method ······ 45

Ⅵ　Secret prior art ······ 47

1　Outline ······ 47

2　Gist - why a secret prior art has exclusivity? ······ 48

3　Determination method ······ 48

Ⅶ　Unpatentable inventions ······ 49

UNIT 4　Patent Law (3) ·· 51

I　Right to obtain a patent ······ 51

1　What is the right to obtain a patent? ······ 51

2　Who is an inventor? ······ 52

3　Joint inventions ······ 52

4　Content of a right to obtain a patent ······ 53

Ⅱ　Misappropriated application ······ 53

1　What is a misappropriated application? ······ 53

2　Countermeasures to be taken by an entitled person ······ 55

Ⅲ　Employee inventions ······ 57

1　Outline ······ 57

CONTENTS

2 Requirements for an employee invention ······ 58

3 Effect of employee invention: statutory license of an employer ······ 60

4 Effect of employee invention: acquisition by an employer of a right to obtain a patent for an employee invention ······ 61

5 Effect of employee invention: reasonable benefit ······ 62

UNIT 5 Patent Law (4) ······ 65

I Overview ······ 65

II Filing of patent applications ······ 65

1 Overview ······ 65

2 Specification ······ 66

3 Claims ······ 67

4 Drawings and abstract ······ 69

III Examinations ······ 69

1 Overview ······ 69

2 Amendments ······ 71

3 Publication of application ······ 74

4 Patent oppositions ······ 75

IV Trials ······ 76

1 Overview ······ 76

2 Trials against a decision of refusal ······ 77

3 Trials for invalidating a patent (Trial for invalidation) ······ 78

4 Trials for correction ······ 78

5 Trials for invalidating the registration of extension ······ 80

UNIT 6 Patent Law (5) ······ 81

I Overview ······ 81

II Utilization of patent right ······ 81

1 Working of patented invention ······ 81

2 Transfer of patent right ······ 82

3 License by agreement ······ 83

4 Establishment of right of pledge ······ 89

III Statutory license (*hotei jisshiken*) ······ 89

vii

CONTENTS

Ⅳ Award granting non-exclusive license (*saitei jisshiken*) ······ 90

  1 What is an award granting non-exclusive license? ······ 90

  2 Award granting non-exclusive license where patented invention is not worked ······ 90

  3 Award granting non-exclusive license where the working of one's patented invention involves using another party's patented invention ······ 91

  4 Award granting non-exclusive license for public interest ······ 91

UNIT 7　Patent Law (6) ······ 93

Ⅰ Overview ······ 93

Ⅱ Patent right infringement ······ 94

  1 Literal infringement ······ 94

  2 Doctrine of equivalents ······ 95

  3 Indirect infringement ······ 96

Ⅲ Defense against a claim of infringement ······ 98

  1 Overview ······ 98

  2 Limitations on the effect of a patent right ······ 98

  3 Prior use right ······ 100

  4 Invalidity defense ······ 101

  5 Exhaustion of patent right ······ 103

UNIT 8　Copyright Law (1) ······ 105

Ⅰ Copyrightability ······ 105

  1 What is copyrightable? ······ 105

  2 Thoughts or sentiments ······ 106

  3 Expression ······ 107

  4 Originality ······ 108

  5 Falling within the literary, academic, artistic or musical domain ······ 109

Ⅱ Types of works ······ 109

  1 Overview ······ 109

  2 Literary works ······ 110

  3 Photographic works ······ 110

  4 Musical works ······ 111

CONTENTS

5 Choreographic and pantomimic works ······ 111

6 Artistic works ······ 112

7 Architectural works ······ 113

8 Diagrammatical works ······ 113

9 Cinematographic works ······ 113

10 Computer programs ······ 114

Ⅲ Works based on pre-existing works, etc. ······ 115

1 Derivative work ······ 115

2 Compilations ······ 115

3 Database works ······ 116

UNIT 9　Copyright Law (2) ······ 117

Ⅰ Definition of authors ······ 117

1 Overview ······ 117

2 Creator doctrine ······ 117

3 Determination of authors ······ 118

4 Joint works ······ 119

Ⅱ Works for hire ······ 122

1 Overview ······ 122

2 Requirements for works for hire ······ 122

3 Legal effect of works for hire ······ 125

UNIT 10　Copyright Law (3) ······ 127

Ⅰ What is a copyright? ······ 127

1 Overview ······ 127

2 Sub-divided rights (*shibunken*) ······ 128

Ⅱ Contents of sub-divided rights ······ 129

1 Overview ······ 129

2 Right to produce a copy ······ 129

3 Right to communicate an original work directly or with the use of its copy ······ 130

4 Rights to provide a copy ······ 133

5 Rights to create and exploit a derivative work ······ 135

ix

CONTENTS

Ⅲ **Term of protection** ······ 136

  1 General principle ······ 136

  2 Exceptions to the term of protection ······ 136

UNIT 11   Copyright Law (4) ······ 139

Ⅰ **Overview** ······ 139

  1 What are the issues? ······ 139

  2 Purpose of the limitations of a copyright ······ 139

Ⅱ **Provisions on the limitations of a copyright** ······ 140

  1 Overview ······ 140

  2 Key provisions on the limitations of a copyright ······ 140

Ⅲ **General provisions on limitations of a copyright** ······ 148

UNIT 12   Copyright Law (5) ······ 151

Ⅰ **Moral rights of an author** ······ 151

  1 Definition of moral rights of an author ······ 151

  2 Relationship with copyrights ······ 152

  3 Author's consent ······ 152

Ⅱ **Right to make an original work public** ······ 152

  1 What is the right to make an original work public? ······ 152

  2 Contents of the right to make an original work public ······ 153

  3 Limitations on the right to make an original work public ······ 154

Ⅲ **Right of attribution** ······ 155

  1 What is the right of attribution? ······ 155

  2 Contents of the right of attribution ······ 155

  3 Limitations on the right of attribution ······ 156

Ⅳ **Right to integrity** ······ 157

  1 What is the right to integrity? ······ 157

  2 Contents of the right to integrity ······ 157

  3 Limitations on the right to integrity ······ 159

Ⅴ **The exploitation of a work in a manner that is prejudicial to the honor or reputation of the author** ······ 160

  1 What is the exploitation of a work in a manner that is prejudicial to the honor or

reputation of the author? ······ 160

2　Honor or reputation ······ 161

Ⅵ　Protection of moral interests after the author's death ······ 161

1　Protection of moral interests after the author's death ······ 161

2　Contents of protection ······ 162

3　Who claims protection? ······ 162

UNIT 13　Design Law ······ 163

Ⅰ　Overview of the Design Law ······ 163

1　What is the Design Law? ······ 163

2　Difference and similarity with the Patent Law ······ 163

3　Protection under the Unfair Competition Prevention Law ······ 164

Ⅱ　What is a design? ······ 165

1　Form "of an article" ······ 165

2　"Form" of an article ······ 166

3　Visual observation ······ 166

4　Aesthetic impression ······ 167

5　Design of a graphic image ······ 167

Ⅲ　Requirements for design registration ······ 169

1　Requirements for registration ······ 169

2　Industrial applicability ······ 169

3　Novelty ······ 169

4　Not easily created ······ 171

5　First-to-file system ······ 171

6　A design of a later application which is identical or similar to a part of a design of a prior application will be excluded from protection ······ 171

7　Unregistrable design ······ 172

Ⅳ　Person who is protected ······ 172

Ⅴ　Application and examination / trial ······ 173

1　Application ······ 173

2　Examination ······ 173

3　Trial ······ 174

Ⅵ　Design right and exercise of it ······ 174

CONTENTS

1 Contents of design right ······ 174

2 Exercise of design right ······ 174

3 Infringement by utilizing a registered design ······ 177

4 Indirect infringement ······ 177

5 Defense ······ 178

Ⅶ Utilization of design right ······ 178

UNIT 14   Trademark Law ······ 179

Ⅰ Outline of Trademark Law ······ 179

1 Protection of trademarks ······ 179

2 Functions of trademarks ······ 179

3 Scope of protection ······ 180

4 Requirement of protection (requirement for registration) ······ 182

5 Similarity in trademarks and similarity in goods or services ······ 188

6 Filing an application for registration of trademark and opposition against registered trademark ······ 189

7 Trials and actions against trial decisions ······ 191

8 Trademark rights and infringement of a trademark right ······ 193

Ⅱ Defense against a claim of infringement ······ 199

1 Defense in an infringement litigation and procedures at the JPO ······ 199

2 Prior use right ······ 199

3 Invalidity defense ······ 200

4 Trials for invalidation ······ 200

5 Trial for cancellation of trademark registration which has not been used ······ 201

Ⅲ Protection under the Unfair Competition Prevention Law ······ 202

1 Outline ······ 202

2 Act which gives rise to confusion with a well-known indication of goods, etc. ······ 202

3 Act of unauthorized use of a famous indication of goods, etc ······ 203

UNIT 15   Unfair Competition Prevention Law ······ 205

Ⅰ Introduction to the Unfair Competition Prevention Law ······ 205

xii

1 Purpose of the Unfair Competition Prevention Law ······ 205

2 Characteristic of Unfair Competition Prevention Law ······ 206

3 Overview of unfair competition acts ······ 208

Ⅱ Unfair competition acts concerning trade secrets ······ 210

1 Overview ······ 210

2 Definition of trade secret ······ 210

3 Unfair competition acts ······ 213

4 Statute of limitations ······ 218

5 Exemptions ······ 219

Ⅲ Other unfair competition acts ······ 220

1 Provision of devices which disable technological restrictions ······ 220

2 Wrongful act in relation to domain names ······ 220

3 Misleading indication for quality, etc. ······ 221

4 Defamation of business reputation ······ 221

5 Unauthorized use of trademark by agent ······ 222

Index ······ 223

Introduction

I Intellectual property law

1 What is intellectual property law?

Intellectual property law is a field of law in which rules are stipulated in relation to the protection and utilization of intellectual property. Intellectual property generally means information with a proprietary value. It is especially noted that intellectual property is information. In other words, intellectual property is not a tangible object which occupies a part of physical space, but is an intangible object without a tangible presence.

There is no single law for the comprehensive protection of intellectual property. Instead, there are various laws which are intended to protect specific types of intellectual property. For example, as explained in Chapter II and thereafter, the *Tokkyo Hou* (Act No. 121 of April 13, 1959, as amended) ("Patent Law") is for the protection of inventions, the *Jitsuyou Shin-An Hou* (Act No. 123 of April 13, 1959, as amended) ("Utility Model Law") is for the protection of devices, the *Ishou Hou* (Act No. 125 of April 13, 1959, as amended) ("Design Law") is for the protection of industrial designs, the *Shouhyou Hou* (Act No. 127 of April 13, 1959, as amended) ("Trademark Law") is for the protection of trademarks, and the *Chosakuken Hou* ("Copyright Law") is for the protection of original works.

2 Why is intellectual property protected?

(1) To promote the activity of creating intellectual property

In the case of a tangible object, one must have possession of the object in order to use it. For example, a person who purchases a water purifier needs to have possession of it to purify water, and if another person takes it away from the purchaser, the purchaser would obviously not be able to use the water purifier. Thus, in order to protect a tangible object, ownership rights are stipulated in the law, and a person who has ownership rights for a certain object would have a right to claim the return of such object if it was taken away from him or her.

In contrast, since intellectual property is information and intangible, a person

UNIT 1   Introduction

who created intellectual property are not precluded from using such intellectual property, even if the other person uses it without permission. So the reason for protecting tangible objects would not be applicable to intellectual property.

However, there would be less motivation for creating intellectual property if intellectual property could be freely utilized by another person. The creator of intellectual property would find it difficult to enjoy any profit due to others using such intellectual property without permission, and would even find it difficult to recoup the expenses incurred for creating the intellectual property.

Therefore, in order to promote the activity of creating intellectual property, legal protection is necessary to prevent others from using intellectual property without permission.

(2)   Striking a balance between intellectual property protection for oneself and intellectual property utilization by others

To promote the activity of creating intellectual property, it is not enough to consider only the protection of intellectual property. New intellectual property is often created by building upon prior intellectual property. Therefore, if there is too much protection of intellectual property (e.g., if the scope of intellectual property protection is too broad), it would be difficult to create new intellectual property based on existing intellectual property as other individuals could not utilize the existing intellectual property. As a result, there must be an appropriate balance between the protection and utilization of intellectual property to ensure that the creation of intellectual property is not stifled.

As mentioned above, the field of intellectual property law consists of various laws to protect specific types of intellectual property. This is because the rules for promoting the creation of intellectual property are not the same for each type of intellectual property. Clearly, the rules for the active creation of technology such as inventions would differ from the rules for the active creation of novels, paintings and music. That is why there are a variety of laws in which rules have been stipulated that suit the nature of the specific type of intellectual property, such as the Patent Law for the protection of inventions, and the Copyright Law for the protection of original works such as novels.

3   Various categories of intellectual property laws

Based on various perspectives, intellectual property laws ("IP Laws") can be

I   Intellectual property law

categorised as follows.

(1)   From the perspective of "purpose for protection," IP Laws can be categorised as an industrial property law for the purpose of developing any industry; and a copyright law (in a broad sense) for the purpose of developing culture.

(2)   From the perspective of "subject matter for protection," IP Laws can be categorised as a "creation" law which protects the result of the creative activity of individuals; and an identification mark law which protects the identification mark with business reputation.

(3)   From the perspective of "method of protection," IP Law can be categorized as an "entitlement" law which grants certain statutory intellectual property rights to its holder; and a law which regulates the behavior of individuals to prevent a third party's improper and unfair use of an intellectual property.

(4)   From the perspective of "a method of generating rights," the aforementioned entitlement laws can also be categorized as a law where rights are generated by registration; and a law where rights are generated by creation itself without the need for any procedure.

For category (1), the Patent Law is an industrial property law because its purpose is to "encourage inventions, and thereby to contribute to the development of an industry" (Patent Law Art. 1). For category (2), the Patent Law is a creation law because an invention, which is a creation based on a technical idea, is protected under it.[1] With regard to category (3), the Patent Law is an entitlement law because an invention is protected by generating a patent right. Lastly, for category (4), the Patent Law is a law for generating a right by registration, because a patent right is generated by registration of its establishment.[2] All of these points also apply to the Utility Model Law which is for the protection of devices, as well as to the Design Law which is for the protection of industrial designs. Although the Trademark Law is identical to the Patent Law for categories (1), (3) and (4), since the object for protection is a trademark (i.e., an identification mark to distinguish between one's own products and services from those of others), the Trademark Law falls under the identification mark laws in the aforementioned category (2).

With regard to the Copyright Law, for category (1), it is a copyright law (in a broad sense) because its purpose is to "contribute to the development of culture."[3] For

---

[1] See Patent Law, Art. 29(1).

[2] Patent Law, Art. 66(1).

3

UNIT 1   Introduction

category (2), the Copyright Law is a creation law because it protects original works which are original expressions.[4] With regard to category (3), the Copyright Law is an entitlement law because original works are protected through the generation of a copyright. For category (4), the Copyright Law is a law which generates rights when the original work is created, and no formal requirements are necessary to enjoy the privileges of a copyright.[5]

In category (3), the entitlement laws protect IP by granting certain intellectual property rights to its holder. For example, there are patent rights for inventions and copyrights for original works. Compared to ownership rights for tangible objects, since intellectual property rights are intended for intangible objects, there are certain characteristics in intellectual property rights which are different, such as the scope of an intellectual property right being unclear, or the intellectual property right having a limited duration which will terminate after a fixed period of time.[6] There is also the *Fusei Kyousou Boushi Hou* (Act No. 47 of May 19, 1993, as amended) ("Unfair Competition Prevention Law") which would be a law that regulates the behavior of individuals to prevent improper and unfair use of an intellectual property as being referred to in category (3).

An overview of the laws included in intellectual property laws are explained as follows.

II   Patent Law and Utility Model Law

1   What is protected?

(1)   Subject matter for protection

The Patent Law is for the protection of inventions. An invention is defined as a "highly advanced creation of a technical idea utilizing the laws of nature."[7] Namely, an invention must satisfy the requirements of: (1) utilizing the laws of nature; (2) being a technical idea; (3) being a creation; and (4) being highly advanced (refer to UNIT 2).

---

[3] Copyright Law, Art. 1.
[4] Copyright Law, Art. 2(1)(ⅰ).
[5] Copyright Law, Art. 17(2). The author gets a moral right of an author, as well as a copyright, by the creation of an original work.
[6] However, the duration of trademark rights for a trademark can be renewed (Trademark Law, Art. 19 (2)).
[7] Patent Law, Art. 2(1).

II Patent Law and Utility Model Law

(2) Requirements for protection

Not any invention can be protected. The following requirements must be satisfied for an invention to be protected.

(1) Industrial Applicability[8]

(2) Novelty[9]

(3) Inventive step[10]

(4) Principle of prior application (i.e., first-to-file)[11]

(5) Expanded scope of prior application (i.e., quasi-known)[12]

(6) Not unpatentable invention[13]

As mentioned below, in order to acquire a patent right, a patent application must be filed for the relevant invention. Of the aforementioned requirements, for example, requirement (2) means that an invention for which an application was filed was not publicly known at the time of filing of that invention; requirement (3) would require that the invention could not have been easily developed from a known invention; and requirement (4) means that when several applications were filed for the same invention, the first applicant would be entitled to the patent right.

Since an invention is protected by a patent right, and since a patent right is generated by registration,[14] the requirements for protection mean the requirements for registration, which are generally called the requirements for patentability (refer to UNIT 3).

2　Who is protected?

Under Patent Law, the person who invents acquires a right to obtain a patent.[15] The right to obtain a patent is the status of being able to request a country that a patent be granted, and this right is transferrable.[16] Accordingly, a person who has the right to obtain a patent may file a patent application and acquire a patent right (refer to UNIT 4).

---

[8] Patent Law, Art. 29(1).
[9] Id.
[10] Patent Law, Art. 29(2).
[11] Patent Law, Art. 39.
[12] Patent Law, Art. 29-2.
[13] Patent Law, Art. 32.
[14] Patent Law, Art. 66(1).
[15] However, a company may have originally the right to obtain a patent for an employee invention, in which a company employee produces an invention in the course of his or her employment (Patent Law, Art. 35(3)).
[16] Patent Law, Art. 33(1).

UNIT 1   Introduction

3   What needs to be done in order to receive protection?

A patent right cannot be acquired merely by inventing something. In order to acquire a patent right, an application for a patent must be filed with the Commissioner of the Japan Patent Office (JPO). The name and domicile or residence of the applicant, and the name and domicile or residence of the inventor(s) are to be stated on the application form. Moreover, the specification, claims, and other items must also be attached to the application form.[17] In the specification, a "detailed explanation of the invention" must be stated,[18] where this explanation must be clearly and sufficiently described so that an average technical person involved in the technical field to which the invention belongs (i.e., a person skilled in the art) would be able to understand the invention. Also, this explanation must be clearly and sufficiently described to the extent that the person skilled in the art would be able to implement or use that invention.[19] The claims indicate the invention for which protection is to be obtained, and "must describe all matters regarded as necessary for specifying the invention for which the applicant intends to obtain a patent."[20]

When an application is filed, the JPO first conducts a formality examination to determine whether there are any deficiencies in the required formalities. If a request for examination is then made by the applicant or another, the examiner will conduct a substantive examination to determine whether there are any reasons for refusal as listed in the items under Article 49. Some of the reasons for refusal include: 1) the requirements for patentability are not satisfied; 2) the applicant does not have a right to obtain a patent; or 3) the necessary matters are not described in the specification or claims. The substantive examination is not automatically conducted, but is conducted only if a request for examination is submitted.[21] If a request for examination is not submitted within three years from the application filing date, the application will be deemed to have been withdrawn.[22]

If the examiner finds no reason for refusal in the application, he/she will render a decision that a patent is to be granted.[23] On the other hand, if a reason for refusal is found,

---

[17] Patent Law, Art. 36(1) and (2).
[18] Patent Law, Art. 36(3).
[19] Patent Law, Art. 36(4)(ⅰ).
[20] Patent Law, Art. 36(5).
[21] Patent Law, Art. 48-2.
[22] Patent Law, Art. 48-3.

II   Patent Law and Utility Model Law

a notification which states the reason(s) for refusal will be rendered to the applicant, where the applicant is given an opportunity to provide a written opinion.[24] The applicant may submits a written argument or an amendment in response to this notification, and depending on how the applicant has responded, the examiner will render a decision that a patent to be granted if he/she determines that the application no longer has any reason for refusal. On the other hand, a decision of refusal will be rendered if the applicant does not respond, or if the examiner determines that the reason(s) for refusal were not overcome despite the applicant's response. An applicant who objects to a decision of refusal may request a trial against that decision (refer to UNIT 5).[25]

4   Trials (*Shinpan*) and actions against trial decisions

A trial generally indicates a system in which an administrative agency makes certain decisions in accordance with quasi-judicial procedures, which are similar to litigation procedures. Generally, a trial is concluded with a trial decision, and a party who is not satisfied with a trial decision may file an action against such a trial decision. The exclusive jurisdiction for an action against a trial decision is with the Tokyo High Court, where a motion must be filed with the Intellectual Property High Court (IP High Court) which is a special branch of the Tokyo High Court.[26] Under the Patent Law, there are primarily four types of trials which are provided (refer to UNIT 5). They are:

(1) Trials against a decision of refusal (for lodging an appeal against an examiner's decision of refusal);[27]

(2) Trials for invalidating a patent (Trials for invalidation) (for retroactively extinguishing a patent right);[28]

(3) Trials for correction (for making corrections to the specification, claims, etc., attached to an application form);[29] and

(4) Trials for invalidating a registration of extension (for invalidating the registration of extension for a duration of a patent right).[30]

---

[23] Patent Law, Art. 51.
[24] Patent Law, Art. 50.
[25] Patent Law, Art. 121.
[26] Patent Law, Art. 178(1); Article 2(ii) of the Act for the Establishment of the Intellectual Property High Court.
[27] Patent Law, Art. 121.
[28] Patent Law, Art. 123.
[29] Patent Law, Art. 126.

UNIT 1   Introduction

A trial against a decision of refusal is for an applicant who wants to appeal a decision of refusal. A trial for invalidation is for retroactively extinguishing a patent right when there are reasons for invalidation, as listed under the items under Article 123(1). The reasons for invalidation are nearly identical to the reasons for refusal. For example, if an applied-for invention does not satisfy the requirements for patentability, then a decision of refusal should be issued. However, if a patent was granted in error and a patent right was generated for that invention, a trial for invalidation needs to take place. If the trial decision to invalidate such patent right becomes final and binding, then such patent right will be deemed to have not existed from the beginning.[31] Also, if the patent right holder finds that there are reasons for invalidation, then he/she may request a trial for correction in order to correct the specification, claims, etc., and thus remove possible challenges for invalidation.

5   Patent rights and infringement of a patent right

When a decision that a patent is to be granted is rendered, through the payment of patent fees, the establishment of a patent right is registered, and a patent right is generated upon registration of its establishment.[32] Moreover, the descriptive matter on the application form, as well as in the specification and claims attached to the application form, etc., are published in the patent gazette issued by the JPO, and are available to the public.[33]

The duration of a patent right ends 20 years from the application filing date.[34] However, in the case of pharmaceutical inventions, etc., a considerable time period is often necessary for dealing with matters such as obtaining approvals in accordance with relevant laws (e.g., in the case of pharmaceutical drugs, laws relating to the quality, effectiveness, and safety of drugs, medical devices, etc.[35]), and a patented invention cannot be worked during that period. In such a case, the duration of a patent right can be extended for up to 5 years.[36] The extension of the duration comes into force upon a

---

[30] Patent Law, Art. 125-2.
[31] Patent Law, Art. 125.
[32] Patent Law, Art. 66(1) and 66(2).
[33] Patent Law, Art. 66(3).
[34] Patent Law, Art. 67(1).
[35] Act No. 145 of August 10, 1960, as amended.
[36] Patent Law, Art. 67(2).

registration of extension. However, if a trial decision in a trial to invalidate a registration of extension becomes final and binding, then the extension of duration through such registration of extension will be deemed as having not been made from the outset.[37]

A patent right is an exclusive right to work a patented invention in the course of business.[38] Accordingly, another person who works a patented invention in the course of business without permission from the patent right holder infringes on the patent right. Even if another person did not imitate a patented invention, but independently created an identical one on his/her own, this would still constitute infringement on such patented invention. Article 101 would, in addition to a direct infringement described above, regard a preliminary act which is highly likely to give rise to direct infringement as an infringement (i.e., an indirect infringement).

A patent right holder can claim an injunction of infringement against a party infringing on his/her patent right,[39] and furthermore, can claim compensation for damages sustained due to the infringement.[40] An injunction may be claimed against a non-intentional or non-negligent infringer, whereas damage compensation can only be recovered from an intentional or negligent infringer. However, it is noted that Article 103 presumes the negligence of the infringer (refer to UNIT 7).

6 Utilization of patent rights

The ways to utilize a patent right include the patent right holder implementing his/her own patented invention, assigning the patent right, establishing a license or a patent pledge, etc. Types of licenses include exclusive or non-exclusive licenses, where a non-exclusive licensee (*tsuujou-jissiken*) only has the right to work a patented invention in the course of business, and an exclusive licensee (*senyou-jissiken*) has an exclusive right to work a patented invention in the course of business similar to the patent right holder (refer to UNIT 6).[41]

7 Utility Model Law

The Utility Model Law, similar to the Patent Law, relates to the protection of

---

[37] Patent Law, Art. 125-2(3).
[38] Patent Law, Art. 68.
[39] Patent Law, Art. 100.
[40] Civil Code, Art. 709.
[41] Patent Law, Arts. 78(2) and 77(2).

UNIT 1   Introduction

technology. Devices (*kouan*) are intended to be protected. Devices are defined as "the creation of technical ideas utilizing the laws of nature,"[42] and there is no requirement for it to be highly advanced.[43] The requirements for protection of devices are nearly similar to the requirements for patentability.

A device is protected by the creation of a utility model right. A utility model right is generated by registration, and the duration of a utility model right ends ten years from the application filing date.[44]

To acquire a utility model right, an application to register a utility model must be filed with the Commissioner of the JPO, similar to the case of a patent right. However, the Utility Model Law differs greatly from the Patent Law, in that although there is a formalities examination, the principle of non-examination has been adopted so that the utility model right can be generated at an early stage. Therefore, most of the requirements for protection are not examined prior to the generation of the right, and in most cases, any issues as to whether a requirement for protection has been satisfied is brought up after the generation of a utility model right.

III   Design Law

In the Design Law, an "industrial design" is intended to be protected, where a design is defined as "the shape, pattern or colors, or a combination thereof, of an article, ... which brings about an aesthetic impression through the eye."[45]

In order to have an industrial design protected, the following requirements must be satisfied.

(1)   Industrial Applicability[46]

(2)   Novelty[47]

(3)   Not easily created[48]

(4)   Principle of prior application (i.e. first-to-file)[49]

---

[42] Utility Model Law, Art. 2(1).
[43] Utility Model Law is often described as the law to protect "minor inventions".
[44] Utility Model Law, Arts. 14(1) and 15.
[45] Design Law, Art. 2(1).
[46] Design Law, Art. 3(1).
[47] Id.
[48] Design Law, Art. 3(2).
[49] Design Law, Art. 9.

(5) Exclusion of protection of a design of a later application which is identical or similar to, part of a design of a prior application[50]

(6) Not unregistrable design[51]

A design is protected by a design right, and a design right is generated by registration, similar to a patent right.[52] Hence, the requirements for protection mean the requirements for registration.

Similar to the Patent Law, the protected person is the person who created the design. Furthermore, as in the case of patent rights, an application for design registration must be filed in order to acquire a design right. After the application, the examiner will conduct a substantive examination as to whether the application for design registration has any reason for refusal, such as the requirements for registration not being satisfied, etc., as listed under the items of Design Law Art. 17. If there is no reason for refusal, the examiner will render a decision that the design is to be registered. Then a design right is then generated upon the registration of its establishment through payment of registration fees (refer to UNIT 13).

IV Trademark Law

A trademark is a mark which distinguishes one's own goods or services from another person's goods or services, and is the subject matter for protection under the Trademark Law. The Trademark Law, unlike the Patent Law and Design Law, is not a creation law to protect the results of creative activity, but is an identification mark law.

In order for a trademark to be protected, an application for a trademark registration must be filed on a trademark for which protection is to be obtained, similar to the Patent and Design Laws. The examiner conducts a substantive examination as to whether an application for a trademark registration has any reason for refusal, such as the requirements for registration not being satisfied, etc., as listed under the items of Trademark Law, Art. 15. If there is no reason for refusal, the examiner will render a decision that the trademark is to be registered. Then a trademark right is generated upon the registration of its establishment through payment of registration fees (refer to UNIT

---

[50] Design Law, Art. 3-2.
[51] Design Law, Art. 5.
[52] Design Law, Art. 20(1).

UNIT 1   Introduction

14).

V   Copyright Law

1   What is protected?

Original works are the subject matter to be protected under the Copyright Law. "Original works" are defined as "original expression of ideas or sentiments which belongs to the literary, scientific, artistic or musical scope."[53] The term "original" does not mean that creativity must be demonstrated in a strict sense, but rather it is regarded to be sufficient if some kind of individuality of the creator has been demonstrated. Generally, something is original if the creator produced that thing him/herself without imitating the work of another person. Examples of the types of original works include: (1) novels, theatrical scripts, essays, speeches and other literary works; (2) musical works; (3) choreographic and pantomimic works; (4) paintings, engravings, sculptures and other artistic works; (5) architectural works; (6) maps as well as drawings, charts, and models and other diagrammatical works; (7) cinematographic works; (8) photographic works; and (9) computer programs (refer to UNIT 8).[54]

The Patent Law can be viewed as a law relating to the technical realm, while the Copyright Law is a law relating to the cultural realm.

2   Who is protected?

The protected person is the author, that is, the "person who created the original work."[55] By creating a work, the author obtains rights of an author for such work. However, there are exceptions such as when a company employee produces an original work in the course of his or her employment. If a company employee, based on the instruction of a company, produces a work during the course of his or her employment, and the company publicizes the work under its own name, the company is the author unless otherwise stipulated by contracts, work rules, etc., at the time that the work was produced.[56] In such a "work for hire" situation, the company, as the author, would have

---

[53] Copyright Law, Art. 2(1)(i).
[54] Copyright Law, Art. 10(1).
[55] Copyright Law, Art. 2(1)(ii).
[56] Work for hire. Copyright Law, Art. 15.

12

V Copyright Law

the rights of an author, and the employee who actually produced the work would have no rights whatsoever (refer to UNIT 9).

3 What needs to be done in order to receive protection?

An author automatically obtains a copyright upon the creation of a work, and the author does not need to do anything to acquire a copyright.[57] This is the principle of "no formalities," which greatly differs from patent rights, utility model rights, design rights and trademark rights where an application needs to be filed and rights are generated by registration.

4 Rights of an author

An author, through the creation of a work, has rights of an author for that work. The rights of an author consists of two types of rights, a copyright and a moral right of an author.

The moral right of an author is for the protection of moral interest of the author, where he or she has: (1) the right to make an original work public;[58] (2) the right of attribution;[59] and (3) the right to integrity.[60] The moral right of an author is exclusively for the author himself or herself, and cannot be transferred (refer to UNIT 12).[61]

On the other hand, a copyright is for the protection of the proprietary interest of the author, and is composed of the following rights (called sub-divided rights) intended for specific acts of exploitation, such as rights with respect to the reproduction and public transmission of a work.

(1) Right of reproduction[62]

(2) Right of performance[63]

(3) Right of on-screen presentation[64]

(4) Right of public transmission, etc.[65]

---

[57] Copyright Law, Art. 17(2).
[58] Copyright Law, Art. 18.
[59] Copyright Law, Art. 19.
[60] Copyright Law, Art. 20.
[61] Copyright Law, Art. 59.
[62] Copyright Law, Art. 21.
[63] Copyright Law, Art. 22.
[64] Copyright Law, Art. 22-2.
[65] Copyright Law, Art. 23.

UNIT 1   Introduction

(5)   Right of recitation[66]

(6)   Right of exhibition[67]

(7)   Right of distribution[68]

(8)   Right of transfer of ownership[69]

(9)   Right of rental[70]

(10)   Right of translation, adaptation, etc.[71]

(11)   Rights of the original author in relation to exploitation of a derivative work[72]

Unlike the moral right of an author, a copyright can be transferred.[73] A copyright is generated by the creation of an original work, and in principle, the right survives for 50 years after the death of the author (refer to UNIT 10).[74]

5   Infringement on the rights of an author

Any act which falls under the aforementioned sub-divided rights that is carried out without permission of a copyright holder constitutes an infringement of a copyright. However, a copyright extends only to the case where a copyrighted work is imitated, and if the utilized work was independently created, there would not be a copyright infringement even if the independently created work is identical to the copyrighted work (this would also apply to the moral right of an author).

There are limitations on copyrights where another person can freely carry out specific acts of exploitation of an original work. There would be no copyright infringement if such copyright limitations are applied. For example, Article 30(1) stipulates that when the purpose of using an original work is for private use (i.e., "personal or family use or other equivalent uses within a limited scope"), a person who uses the work can reproduce it. Article 32 also stipulates the limitations on copyrights with respect to quotation of an original work (refer to UNIT 11).

An author or copyright holder may claim an infringement injunction against a

---

[66] Copyright Law, Art. 24.
[67] Copyright Law, Art. 25.
[68] Copyright Law, Art. 26.
[69] Copyright Law, Art. 26-2.
[70] Copyright Law, Art. 26-3.
[71] Copyright Law, Art. 27.
[72] Copyright Law, Art. 28.
[73] Copyright Law, Art. 61(1).
[74] Copyright Law, Art. 51.

party infringing on his/her moral right or copyright.[75] Furthermore, one can claim compensation for damages incurred due to such infringement.[76] An injunction can be claimed against a non-intentional or non-negligent infringer, but a damage compensation claim can only be recovered against an intentional or negligent infringer. Unlike the Patent Law, there are no provisions in the Copyright Law which provide for the presumption of negligence of the infringer.

VI Unfair Competition Prevention Law

The Unfair Competition Prevention Law is not an entitlement law such as the aforementioned Patent and Copyright Laws, but is a law which regulates behavior to protect intellectual property against specific acts of utilization, which is in contrast to laws which grants certain rights to a holder. Prohibited acts are called "unfair competition," and these are listed in Article 2(1) of the Unfair Competition Prevention Law, which are stipulated specifically as follows.

(1) an act which gives rise to confusion of an entity of a well-known "Indication of goods, etc." which means "something which indicates goods or business"[77]

(2) an act of unauthorized use of a famous Indication of goods, etc. [78]

(3) an act of imitating a certain form of goods[79]

(4) a wrongful act in relation to a trade secret[80]

(5) an act of providing devices and the like which disable technological restrictions used in businesses[81]

(6) a wrongful act in relation to domain names[82]

(7) an act which gives rise to misleading quality and the like[83]

(8) an act which defames business reputation[84]

---

[75] Copyright Law, Art. 112.
[76] Civil Code, Art. 709.
[77] Unfair Competition Prevention Law, Art. 2(1)(ⅰ).
[78] Unfair Competition Prevention Law, Art. 2(1)(ⅱ).
[79] Unfair Competition Prevention Law, Art. 2(1)(ⅲ).
[80] Unfair Competition Prevention Law, Art. 2(1)(ⅳ) to (ⅹ).
[81] Unfair Competition Prevention Law, Art. 2(1)(ⅺ) and (ⅻ).
[82] Unfair Competition Prevention Law, Art. 2(1)(ⅹⅲ)).
[83] Unfair Competition Prevention Law, Art. 2(1)(ⅹⅳ).
[84] Unfair Competition Prevention Law, Art. 2(1)(ⅹⅴ).

UNIT 1   Introduction

(9)   an act of using a trademark of an agent etc. without permission[85]

Among these, as (1), (2) and (6) relate to the Indication of goods, etc., there is a correlation with the Trademark Law.[86] Moreover, (3) relates to the form of goods, and thus there is a correlation with the Design Law.[87] Furthermore, since technological information is included in trade secrets of (4),[88] a person who developed a technology has a choice of obtaining protection under Unfair Competition Prevention Law as a trade secret or obtaining patent protection by filing a patent application for such technology.

A person whose business interests are injured by unfair competition can request an injunction.[89] Moreover, a person whose business interests have been intentionally or negligently damaged by unfair competition can claim for compensation under the Unfair Competition Prevention Law (refer to UNIT 15).[90]

Ⅶ   Other

Other key laws which are considered a part of intellectual property laws relate to plant varieties and to circuit layouts of semiconductor integrated circuits. New species of plants are protected under the *Shubyou Hou* (Act No. 83 of May 29, 1998, as amended) ("Plant Variety Protection and Seed Law"). Furthermore, as the title suggests, the circuit layouts of semiconductor integrated circuits are intended to be protected by the law relating to circuit layouts of semiconductor integrated circuits.[91]

Moreover, unlawful acts as defined in Civil Law, Art. 709, could be recognized for information which is not protected by the aforementioned various laws. Although injunctions cannot be requested in such cases, relief could be granted by claiming damage compensation.

---

[85] Unfair Competition Prevention Law, Art. 2(1)(ⅹⅵ).
[86] Refer to Part Ⅲ of UNIT 14.
[87] Refer to Section 3, Part Ⅰ of UNIT 13.
[88] Unfair Competition Prevention Law, Art. 2(6).
[89] Unfair Competition Prevention Law, Art. 3.
[90] Unfair Competition Prevention Law, Art. 4.
[91] Act No. 43 of May 31, 1985, as amended.

Patent Law (1)

● Inventiveness

I General remarks

1 What is an invention?

A person who creates an invention can obtain a patent for it if such invention satisfies the specific requirements as defined in Patent Law Art. 29 (refer to UNIT 3). The subject matter to be protected by the Patent Law is not any "invention" generally, but only inventions which are specifically defined.

Accordingly, Patent Law Article 2(1) defines an "invention" (*hatsumei*) as "a highly advanced creation of a technical idea utilizing the laws of nature." This definition of an invention is further broken down into the following four requirements:

(1) utilizing the laws of nature;
(2) being a technical idea;
(3) being a creation (*sousaku*); and
(4) being highly advanced.

These four requirements will be explained below, but first, the various types of inventions will be explained as background knowledge.

2 Types of inventions

Inventions are categorized into two types: the "product invention" and the "process invention." Moreover, the "process invention" is further categorized as a "pure process invention" and a "process invention by which a product is produced." Although the Patent Law does not directly define such categorization of inventions, this can be interpreted from the definition for the implementation of an invention.[1]

(1) The product invention (*Mono no hatsumei*)

In general, a product invention is a technical idea manifested in the form of an

---

[1] Patent Law Art. 2(3). In some translations, the "implementation of an invention" is translated as the "working of an invention."

UNIT 2   Patent Law (1)

object which does not require a chronological process. A mechanical device or a chemical substance are examples.

The Patent Law stipulates that a "computer program, etc." is also included in the definition of "product invention."[2] However, this definition means that a computer program could be a product invention, and certainly does not mean that any computer program would constitute an invention.

(2)   The process invention (*Houhou no hatsumei*)

Generally, a process invention refers to an invention which contains a chronological process. A process invention is further categorized into a "pure process invention" and a "process invention by which a product is produced."[3]

A pure process invention is not associated with the production of a product. Examples include a measuring process or an analytical process. Moreover, the processes of separating and/or dissolving a product are also not associated with the production of a new product, and therefore, such processes would be regarded as pure process inventions. On the other hand, a process invention by which a product is produced includes a specific process of producing a specific product – e. g., foodstuff processing methods, pharmaceutical preparation processes or chemical substance synthesizing methods.

II   Requirement (1): Utilization of the laws of nature

1   What is the utilization of the laws of nature?

The laws of nature are the physical, chemical and biological laws and principles which are empirically discovered in the realm of nature. The utilization of the laws of nature can be understood to be synonymous to the use of a natural force. Since the utilization of the laws of nature is a requirement in order for a creation to be an invention, any creation which does not utilize any law of nature is not deemed to be an invention.

2   The laws of nature *per se* is not considered to be an invention

Since the laws of nature need to be utilized in order for a creation to be an invention, even the discovery of the laws of nature *per se* would not regarded as an

---

[2] Patent Law Art. 2(3)(ⅰ).
[3] *See* Patent Law Art. 2(3)(ⅱ) and (ⅲ).

18

II   Requirement (1): Utilization of the laws of nature

invention unless that discovery was utilized in some form. For example, if a law of nature was discovered where a mixture of a substance A and a substance B is easily explosive at a specific ratio, the discovery of that law in and of itself cannot be regarded as an invention. However, an object such as an "explosive" which utilizes that law of nature, or a method of producing that object could be deemed to be an invention. Similarly, pure observation of natural phenomena also would not be considered to be an invention.

3   A creation which is contrary to the laws of nature is not considered to be an invention

A creation which is contrary to the laws of nature is problematic in that the creation cannot be implemented from the outset (refer to Section 2, Part III of UNIT 2), and thus is not regarded to be an invention in that the laws of nature are not utilized. A perpetual motion machine which is contrary to the laws of nature (namely, the law of conservation of energy) is a typical example.[4]

4   A creation utilizing something other than the laws of nature is not considered to be an invention

Since human mental activities, economic principles, mathematical formulae and man-made rules are not laws of nature, these laws, formulae and rules *per se*, or any creation which utilizes only these laws, formulae and rules, are not regarded to be inventions, because no laws of nature are utilized.

(1)   Human mental activities

Humans act with free will and self-determination, and human mental activities and decision-making *per se* do not utilize the laws of nature. Therefore, such activities and decision-making are not considered to be inventions. Having said that, any creation of a technical idea provides a means for supporting human activity (including mental activity), or a means for its replacement. Accordingly, the inventiveness of the creation of a technical idea should not initially be denied based only on whether human mental activity is included in, or intimately correlated with, the configuration of the creation of that technical idea. Instead, if the portion of the creation which utilizes the laws of nature is a primary means for solving the problem, then that creation would be regarded as an

---

[4] Tokyo High Court decision of June 29, 1973, *Hanrei Times*, No. 298, p. 255.

UNIT 2   Patent Law (1)

invention.

In a court precedent, the IP High Court reviewed an issue regarding a dental restorative network consisting of a database for accumulating information such as dental prosthetic material and a computer for browsing such information. The Court determined that even if this network relates to the mental activity of dentists for determining the necessary dental restorations and formulating treatment plans, the creation of the technical idea of the network, regarded as a whole, utilizes the laws of nature in that the creation provides a technological means by a computer to support dental treatment. Therefore, this dental restorative network was determined to be an invention.[5]

(2)   Economic principles and mathematical formulae

Since economic principles and mathematical formulae are academic theories and not laws of nature, any creation which utilizes only an academic theory is not considered to be an invention.

There is a court precedent in relation to this issue, which held that if a balance sheet for various funds were created where, for example, a company's financial standing, etc., could easily be learned, then such a creation would exclusively cover the mentally creative activity of humans while utilizing specific economic and accounting theories *per se*, and thus could not be a creation which utilized the laws of nature.[6] Moreover, in regards to the operation of a novel mathematical calculating method by means of an existing operating device, the IP High Court determined that a solution to a mathematical problem and a mathematical calculating procedure (algorithm) *per se* were purely academic theories which did not utilize any law of nature, and therefore, could not be considered to be an invention.[7]

(3)   Man-made rules

Since rules created by persons such as in sports or gaming are also not laws of nature, any creation which only utilizes such rules would not be considered to be an invention. There are court precedents, for example, where it was determined that the

---

[5] Intellectual Property High Court decision of June 24, 2008, *Hanrei Jiho*, No. 2026, p. 123 (As a similar case, Intellectual Property High Court decision of August 26, 2008, *Hanrei Jiho*, No. 2041, p. 123). On the contrary, the Intellectual Property High Court decision of December 5, 2012, *Hanrei Jiho*, No. 2181, p. 127 determines that the invention at issue mainly focuses on human mental activities and it is not an invention for the purposes of the Patent Law.

[6] Tokyo District Court decision of January 20, 2003, *Hanrei Jiho*, No. 1809, p. 3.

[7] Intellectual Property High Court decision of February 29, 2008, *Hanrei Jiho*, No. 2012, p. 97.

II   Requirement (1): Utilization of the laws of nature

process of producing an encryption code for telegraph by suitably combining roman alphabets, numbers, codes, etc., was not deemed to be an invention, as no means of utilizing a natural force was carried out.[8]

(4)   Not necessary to prove the laws of nature

Although a requirement of an invention as previously discussed is to utilize the laws of nature, it is not necessary to prove the laws of nature. The establishment of a creation as an invention will not be rejected if it is confirmed by experimentation and other similar means where empirical results are produced with a specific certainty and if the laws of nature are utilized, even if that law of nature still cannot be theoretically proven or was erroneously proven.

5   Software-related inventions

(1)   Inventiveness of software

There has been intensive debate in terms of whether software can conventionally utilize the laws of nature and be regarded as an invention, because software could be considered a certain type of process of operating a computer with man-made rules. In the current examination practice at the JPO, software will be considered to be the creation of a technical idea which utilizes the laws of nature if the software-based information process is specifically achieved by means of a hardware resource (e.g., a computer as the physical device, the constituent elements of which are a CPU, memory, input device and output device, or a physical device connected to a computer). In other words, if the unique information processing device or operating process specifically intended for a particular purpose use is built by the cooperative working of the software and hardware resources, such software is regarded as a creation of a technical idea which utilizes the laws of nature.[9] Since software can be an original work protected by the Copyright Law[10], protection can be sought for software in the form of a patent as well as a copyright.

However, not any software can be acknowledged to utilize the laws of nature and be regarded as an invention. In the case of software which executes a method of calculation which is merely displayed by the use of a computer only, the hardware

---

[8] Supreme Court decision of April 30, 1953, *Minshu* , Vol. 7, No. 4, p. 461.
[9] Section 2.1.1.2 in Chapter 1, Annex B of the JPO 'Patent and Utility Model Examination Handbook'.
[10] Copyright Law Art. 10(1)(ix)

UNIT 2   Patent Law (1)

resource would be considered only as a tool for calculation, and thus, this type of software would not be regarded as utilizing the laws of nature, nor be a patentable invention.[11]

(2) Types of software-related inventions

As mentioned above, the Patent Law clearly states that "computer programs, etc." are included as a "product" according to the product invention definition.[12] This new definition of a product invention was included in the 2002 revision to the Patent Law, which purpose was to extend patent right protection to software-related inventions provided via a network (e.g. internet downloads). It is also clear by this provision that a program *per se* can be a product invention, and not limited only to a program stored in a memory medium. Moreover, a software-related invention can be established not only as a product invention, but also as a process invention.

In examination practice, when a software-related invention can be expressed by several functions which are served by that invention, then it may be described in the patent application document as a "product invention" which is specified by those functions. Further, if a software-related invention can be expressed as a chronological series of processes or operations (i.e., if the invention can be expressed as a "procedure"), then it can be described as a "process invention" (including a "process invention by which a product is produced") by specifying the relevant "procedure."[13]

Ⅲ Requirement (2): Technical idea

1 What is a technical idea?

An invention protected by the Patent Law is a technical "idea" or notion. In other words, the Patent Law is for the protection of an idea *per se*, and not for the protection of an embodiment of an idea. In contrast, the Copyright Law protects not the idea *per se*, but the manifested "expression" of an idea, because an original work which is protected by the Copyright Law is an "original expression of ideas or sentiments."[14]

An invention is also a "technical" idea. A technique can be understood to be a specific and rational means for solving a certain problem which is able to be implemented,

---

[11] *See* Intellectual Property High Court decision of February 29, 2008, *Hanrei Jiho*, No. 2012, p. 97.

[12] Patent Law Art. 2(3)(ⅰ).

[13] *See* Section 1.2.1.1 of Chapter 1, Annex B of the JPO "Patent and Utility Model Examination Handbook."

[14] Copyright Law Art. 2(1)(ⅰ).

Ⅲ Requirement (2): Technical idea

with identical results obtainable when a person with ordinary knowledge in the relevant technical field (called "the person skilled in the art") carries out the technique. Namely, the technique must be implementable as well as reproducible, because there is no need for patent protection of a technique which cannot be replicated nor implemented.

Court precedents have also held that, taking into consideration the purposes of the patent system, the technical content of an invention must be embodied and objectified in the invention to the extent that a person with ordinary knowledge and experience in the relevant technological field would be able to implement, replicate and achieve the intended technological effect, where any such content which is not configured to this extent would be regarded to be incomplete as an invention, and thus not considered to be an invention.[15]

2 The enablement requirement

In order for a creation to be a technical idea, it must be implementable. If the creation cannot be implemented, it is not regarded to be an invention. For example, a process to cover the entire surface of the Earth with an ultraviolet-ray-absorbing plastic film in order to protect against the increase of ultraviolet rays, which is associated with the thinning of the ozone layer, obviously cannot be implemented and thus cannot be regarded to be an invention.

3 Reproducibility

A technical idea must also be reproducible. Accordingly, the same technical effect must be obtainable even when the idea is carried out by another person, and if this is dependent on the personal skill or technique of the creator, the idea would not be considered to be an invention. However, if technical content is devised such that it is not affected by personal skill, then this creation could possibly be acknowledged as an invention. For example, if a machine which reproduces a physics-based controlled kicking method is developed and configured into a device for training soccer goalkeepers by simulating free kicks, e.g. like a pitching machine, then such a device would be considered to be a product invention.

It is not always necessary that the probability of replication and implementation

---

[15] Supreme Court decision of January 28, 1969, *Minshu*, Vol. 23 No. 1, p. 54.

UNIT 2   Patent Law (1)

must be 100 % in order for reproducibility to be acknowledged. The required probability for such replication and implementation could change depending on the technical content of the invention. For example, the Supreme Court stated in relation to an invention for a method of breeding and proliferating a new breed of yellow peach, that a high probability of reproducibility is not required if a person skilled in the art is satisfied that such a plant can be scientifically reproduced while taking into consideration the characteristics of the invention.[16] This is because if the breeding of a new species is possible even though the probability is low, then such a new species, after breeding, can be produced again by conventionally employed proliferation methods, and therefore, the technological effect intended for the invention can be achieved. On the other hand, in the creation of a device, normally, such device is required to always demonstrate a certain effect.[17]

4   Incomplete inventions

An incomplete invention is not considered to be an invention. However, unlike a creation which absolutely cannot be regarded as an invention (e.g., a creation which does not utilize the laws of nature), there could be cases where an incomplete invention could be considered to be an invention in the future if the technical content were to be completed. Although the Patent Law does not clearly stipulate the reasons for refusing an application as being an incomplete invention[18], the Supreme Court has determined that an incomplete invention cannot be regarded as an "invention" according to Patent Law Article 2(1), and thus, patent applications for such inventions should be refused.[19]

There are many issues with incomplete inventions in relation to chemical substances. Since it is not easy to understand how chemical substances can be used based on their chemical structures, in order to establish an invention of a chemical substance, it is regarded to be insufficient to confirm only the existence of the chemical substance *per se* and that this substance can be produced. Instead, it is necessary to disclose the usefulness of the substance in the specification. Thus, if the usefulness or the specific use of a substance is not disclosed, then the invention of that substance will be regarded as an "incomplete invention" and cannot receive protection as an invention. The protection of

---

[16] Supreme Court decision of February 29, 2000, *Minshu*, Vol. 54, No. 2, p. 709.

[17] Patent Law Art. 49; *See* Intellectual Property High Court decision of November 29, 2007 (2006 (*Gyo-ke*) No. 10015).

[18] Patent Law Art. 49

[19] Supreme Court decision of October 13, 1977, *Minshu*, Vol. 31, No. 6, p. 805.

biological inventions (such as genes and micro-organisms, animals and plants) would similarly not be considered to be an invention if the usefulness of such biological inventions is not described in the specification or cannot be interpreted from any other descriptive content.

Incidentally, since the completeness or incompleteness of an invention is determined by how the specification is described, in many cases an incomplete invention appears as a deficiency in the description of the specification (refer to Section 2, Part II of UNIT 5). At the time of filing an application for a particular invention, it is often difficult to distinguish whether the invention is an "incomplete" one or the disclosure of the technical content in the specification for the (completed) invention is insufficient. In theory, the patent application of an incomplete invention should be refused for not satisfying the requirements of an invention, and the patent application of a complete invention should be refused for not satisfying the descriptive requirement of the specification as defined in Article 36 of the Patent Law. However, the "Examination Guidelines for Patent and Utility Model", which is actually used by the JPO examiners during the examination, does not mention the "completeness or incompleteness of an invention". Therefore, in the current patent examination practice, applications are not refused over incompleteness of an invention, but instead are dealt with as a problem with the descriptive requirement of the specification (in particular, the lack of the enablement requirement as set forth in Art. 36 (4)(i) of the Patent Law).

IV Requirement (3): Creation

1 What is a creation? The difference between an invention and a discovery

An invention is the "creation" of a technical idea, where the creation is a creation of something new which did not previously exist. Further, finding out for the first time about something which exists is also called a "discovery," and this would be distinguished from an invention. Therefore, the laws of nature *per se* differs from the utilization of the laws of nature, and thus, cannot be acknowledged as an invention. Also, the laws of nature *per se* cannot be regarded as an invention, because even if such law can be "discovered," it cannot be created.

However, there is a certain subtlety in distinguishing between inventions and

UNIT 2   Patent Law (1)

discoveries, as well as distinguishing between the utilization of the laws of nature and the laws of nature *per se*, and it is not easy to draw a clear boundary line between them. For example, a court precedent determined that although blue-green algae such as Spirulina platensis or Spirulina maxima imparts a colour enhancement effect (colour-developing effect) to a living body, that effect *per se* was merely a discovery. However, the Tokyo High Court determined that a breeding method for increasing the effect of enhanced dark spots and colour tones by feeding that algae to red-coloured Nishiki carp and goldfish, was considered to be an invention.[20]

2   Use inventions

A use invention is based on the discovery of an unknown attribute of a certain item, and then discovering that this item is suitable for use in new applications because of the newly discovered attribute. A well-known example is the discovery of a pesticidal effect in the already-known chemical substance DDT, and then the utilization of this attribute in inventions for a "pesticide comprising DDT as an effective component" and a "pesticidal process using DDT."

In use inventions there is no particular limitation on the "product" for which a new use was found. However, in most cases for mechanical inventions, the uses are decided from the beginning, although there are rare cases where a new use was later discovered. In contrast, the attributes of chemical substances are multi-faceted, as in the DDT example, and a chemical substance often can be implemented in uses that had not been previously known, and therefore, most use inventions are in the chemistry field.

There is almost no difference between the essence of a use invention and the "discovery" of an attribute of an item. However, by acknowledging the creative act in terms of utilizing the discovered attribute for a specific purpose, a use invention can be protected as an invention. Moreover, if there are new uses based on unknown attributes, then even if the item *per se* is known, the requirement for novelty could be satisfied (refer to UNIT 3). However, if those uses can be easily conceived by a person skilled in the art based on already-known attributes, then the requirement for an inventive step would not be satisfied (as also explained in UNIT 3).

---

[20] Tokyo High Court decision of February 13, 1990, *Hanrei Jiho*, No. 1348, p. 139.

V   Requirement (4): Highly advanced

A highly advanced creation of a technical idea is required for an invention. In other words, only a high-level creation of a technical idea can be acknowledged to be an invention. However, this requirement for a creation to be highly advanced was provided merely to distinguish such creation from "device" (Utility Model Law Art. 2(1)) which was meant to be protected under the Utility Model Law. In practice, the JPO does not typically determine that a creation is not an invention due to not being highly advanced. Instead, a creation which is not highly advanced would be regarded as lacking a requirement for patentability (namely, an inventive step) during the examination of the application.

Patent Law (2)

• Patentability

I Overview

1 What is patentability?

The Patent Law defines an invention in Article 2(1),[1] but such inventions cannot necessarily be patented. For an invention to be patented, the "patentability requirements" must be satisfied.

If a patent application does not satisfy a patentability requirement, there will be a reason for refusal, and a decision of refusal will be issued by the JPO for the application.[2] Even if the JPO erroneously registers a patent right for an invention where a patentability requirement is not satisfied, the registered patent invention would be regarded as having a reason for invalidation of the patent right,[3] and the patent right will be deemed to have never existed when a trial for invalidation has become final and binding.[4] When a patent right has a reason for invalidation, the patentee may not demand an injunction or claim damages based on the patent right.[5]

2 Patentability requirements under the Patent Law

Article 29 of the Patent Law sets forth the following patentability requirements:

"(1) An inventor of an invention that is industrially applicable may be entitled to obtain a patent for the invention, except for the following:

(i) inventions that were publicly known in Japan or a foreign country, prior to the filing of the patent application;

(ii) inventions that were publicly worked in Japan or a foreign country, prior to the filing of the patent application; or

---

[1] Refer to UNIT 2.
[2] Patent Law, Art. 49; Refer to Section 1, Part III of UNIT 5.
[3] Patent Law, Art. 123(1).
[4] Patent Law, Art. 125.
[5] Patent Law, Art. 104-3.

UNIT 3   Patent Law (2)

(ⅲ) inventions that were described in a distributed publication, or inventions that were made publicly available through an electronic telecommunication line in Japan or a foreign country, prior to the filing of the patent application.

(2)   Where, prior to the filing of the patent application, a person ordinarily skilled in the art of the invention would have been able to easily make the invention based on an invention prescribed in any of the items of the preceding paragraph, a patent shall not be granted for such an invention notwithstanding the preceding paragraph."

Article 29 can be understood to specify as patentability requirements: (1) being industrially applicable;[6] (2) having novelty;[7] and (3) having an inventive step.[8] In addition to these requirements, the first-to-file rule,[9] secret prior art,[10] and not being an unpatentable invention[11] requirements must be satisfied for an invention to be patented.

Apart from the above patentability requirements, a patent application must procedurally comply with the descriptive requirements for the specification and the scope of claims (also referred to as "claims").[12] In addition, an applicant must have a right to obtain a patent for the invention.[13]

Ⅱ   Industrial applicability

1   Definition of industrial applicability

The Patent Law sets forth in the main paragraph of Article 29 (1) that an industrially applicable invention can be patented. Thus, an invention must be industrially applicable to be patented, since the purpose of the Patent Law is "to contribute to the development of relevant industries."[14]

The industrial applicability is interpreted in a very broad sense, which includes not only engineering, but also agriculture, forestry, fishery, and mining industries. Also,

---

[6] Patent Law, Art. 29(1).
[7] Patent Law, items of Art. 29(1).
[8] Patent Law, Art. 29(2).
[9] Patent Law, Art. 39. This issue is also referred to as the "principle of prior applicant."
[10] Patent Law, Art. 29-2. This issue is also referred to as "Expanded scope of prior application" or "quasi-known."
[11] Patent Law, Art. 32.
[12] Patent Law, Art. 36; Refer to Part Ⅱ of UNIT 5.
[13] Refer to Part Ⅰ of UNIT 4.
[14] Patent Law, Art. 1.

30

Ⅱ   Industrial applicability

due to business model patents being recently accepted, the establishment of patents for financial businesses is not that rare any more.

The "industrially applicable invention" is not limited to a currently-used invention. Inventions which are expected to be used in the future can also be included even if they are not used immediately. Moreover, the requirement of industrial applicability can be satisfied regardless of its ability to be used commercially; and an invention with certain types of technical disadvantages is also acceptable. For example, with respect to an device of a bank note with a surface on which a punch hole is provided, a court held that since the device has achieved the technical objective of providing a bank note which can be easily and correctly distinguished by visually impaired people; the device, even if it has the disadvantage of reduced durability, is considered industrially applicable unless the disadvantage is so serious that the device cannot be implemented.[15]

With respect to a product invention or an invention of a process for manufacturing the product, even if the product is used for an "unproductive" game such as, for example, a bingo game device, the industrial applicability would not be rejected since the device itself can be manufactured and sold.[16] Thus, practically speaking, the industrial applicability is rarely disputed, but disputed only for medical inventions as mentioned below.

2   Medical invention

With respect to medical inventions, inventions of products and manufacturing processes relating to medicines and/or medical equipment can be patented. However, the method of the surgery, therapy, or diagnosis of a human; i.e., an invention of a medical act, is treated as an unpatentable invention under the patent examination practice in the JPO. This is (according to the JPO) because medical services are not included in the definition of an industry, and such related inventions would not be industrially applicable.

Of course, excluding medical services from the definition of an industry is not a logical interpretation of the term, but the substantial reason why a patent for a medical act invention is not granted is based on humanitarian reasons. In other words, if a patent for a medical act invention is granted, the implementation of the invention would be monopolized by the patentee, and the ability of doctors to appropriately and immediately

---

[15] Tokyo High Court decision of December 25, 1986, *Mutaisaishu*, Vol. 18, No. 3, p. 579.
[16] Tokyo High Court decision of December 15, 1956, *Gyoshu*, Vol. 7, No. 12, p. 3133.

UNIT 3   Patent Law (2)

perform the medical act could be hindered.

Although the patentability of a medicine or medical equipment is accepted, a doctor can perform medical acts by exercising his/her own ability and skills at a maximum level without using the patented medicine or medical equipment. Moreover, the Patent Law provides that even if a patent for a medicine or a process for manufacturing the medicine is granted, the patent right of the invention to mix the medicines will not be effective against the act of preparing the medicine as well as the medicine itself as is written in a prescription from a doctor.[17] In contrast, no similar provision is provided regarding medical acts. Considering these circumstances, a court held that if the patentability of a medical act was allowed, a doctor would perform the medical act under constant concern about whether the act would be the subject matter of a patent right and whether he/she would be liable for patent right infringement. The court specifically stated that "a system that puts doctors in such a situation should be considered to be significantly unreasonable in light of the nature of the medical acts."[18]

Recently, therapies such as gene and regenerative therapies have rapidly developed, and the research and development of medical technologies conventionally performed in university laboratories are also being performed in companies. Therefore, the issue of whether a patent for an invention relating to a medical act should also be granted to give companies incentive to develop new therapies has been vigorously discussed.

III   Novelty

1   Definition of novelty

(1)   Outline

According to the Patent Law, a patent right is granted as a benefit for publishing an invention so as to encourage the creation of inventions. If an invention for which an application was filed relates to some prior art which has already been published, there would be no reward in granting a patent right for the applicant. Thus, a patent right for such an invention does not need to be granted. Furthermore, if a patent right for a prior published art is granted, the art which has been freely accessed by the public will be

---

[17] Patent Law, Art. 69(3).

[18] Tokyo High Court decision of April 11, 2002, *Hanrei Jiho*, No. 1828, p. 99.

III   Novelty

monopolized and the development of relevant industries would be inhibited.

The Patent Law states in Article 29(1) that (1) "inventions that were publicly known;"[19] (2) "inventions that were publicly worked;"[20] and (3) "inventions that were described in a distributed publication or made available to the public through electronic telecommunication lines in Japan or a foreign country"[21] cannot be patented. As described above, an invention must relate to a new finding, not an art which has already been published. This is the novelty requirement. Inventions not satisfying the novelty requirement are abbreviated as (1) "publicly known" inventions (narrow definition); (2) "publicly worked" inventions (also referred to as "publicly used" inventions); and (3) inventions "described in publications, etc.," and are collectively referred to as "publicly known arts" or "publicly known inventions" (broad definition).

(2)   Time criterion for determination of novelty

The criterion for the determination of novelty is the time at which a patent application was filed (the time of filing), and is not the date of filing. For example, if an application for an invention of an art was filed in the afternoon, but the art had been published in the morning on the same date, the novelty requirement would not be satisfied and a patent for the invention would not be granted.

In contrast, an invention of an art which has not been published at the time of filing the application would satisfy the novelty requirement even if the art is published after the filing of the application. If the art has already been published before the filing of the application, the novelty requirement would not be satisfied in principle, even if the publication of the art was carried out by the applicant. However, there are exceptions to the lack of novelty in Article 30 of the Patent Law described in Section 7 below which may apply to the applicant.

(3)   Regional range of determination

The determination of the novelty requirement is made "in Japan or a foreign country" – i.e., on a global basis. Thus, the novelty requirement would not be satisfied if an invention for which an application was filed had already been published in a foreign country even if it had not been published in Japan, and a patent for such invention would not be granted.

---

[19] Patent Law, Art. 29(1)(ⅰ).
[20] Patent Law, Art. 29(1)(ⅱ).
[21] Patent Law, Art. 29(1)(ⅲ).

UNIT 3   Patent Law (2)

As of 1959 when the existing Patent Law was established, the subject matters of Article 29(1)(ⅰ) and (ⅱ) were limited to cases occurring in Japan, and only the subject matters of Article 29(1)(ⅲ) included cases occurring in foreign countries.[22] However, in response to the globalization of the world economy and the spread of the Internet, the Patent Law was revised in 1999 so that the cases occurring in foreign countries were also included as the subject matters of Article 29(1)(ⅰ) and (ⅱ), and the inventions disclosed on websites were added to the inventions defined in Article 29(1)(ⅲ).

2   The term "publicly"

The term "publicly" used in Article 29(1)(ⅰ) and (ⅱ) refers to the status of an invention that is no longer a secret. The number of people who know about the invention is irrelevant, and even if only one person knows the invention without being under any confidentiality obligations, the invention will be regarded as being in the public domain. In contrast, an invention will not be regarded as being in the public domain even if many people know about the invention as long as they must abide by certain confidentiality obligations. Confidentiality obligations are imposed on a person by a law or under an agreement, or are otherwise implicitly generated in some cases under common sense or business practice. When a person under a confidentiality obligation discloses the content of an invention to a person under no confidentiality obligations in violation of his/her confidentiality obligation, the invention will be in the public domain and naturally lose novelty.   However, there will remain the issue of whether the disclosing person will be liable for the violation of the confidentiality obligation.

Article 29(1)(ⅲ) does not include the term "publicly," but it implies that an invention as a subject matter of Article 29(1)(ⅲ) is in the public domain. With respect to the inventions described in publications which are described in Section 5, Part Ⅲ below, the Supreme Court construes "the 'distributed publication' in Article 29(1)(ⅲ) indicates 'documents or figures reproduced to be disclosed to the public by distribution, or other similar communication media which were distributed.'"[23] With respect to electronic telecommunication lines, Article 29(1)(ⅲ) provides "the inventions made available to the public." Thus, both inventions described in publications and inventions made available to the public through electronic telecommunication lines can be regarded as those in the

---

[22] Art. 29(1)(ⅲ) at that time provided only the inventions described in publications.
[23] Supreme Court decision of July 4, 1980, *Minshu*, Vol. 34, No. 4, p. 570.

34

public domain.

3   Publicly-known inventions

In interpreting Article 29(1)(i), case precedents and academic theories have not reached a consensus on whether an invention needs to be actually known to the public, or if it is sufficient for an invention to be accessible by the public. The former stance asserts that a person under no confidentiality obligation needs to actually know the contents of an invention, since if the latter stance is adopted, the inventions in Article 29(1)(ii) and (iii) will also become publicly known, and the provisions of the items (ii) and (iii) will lose their significance. In contrast, the latter stance asserts that it is sufficient for an invention to be available to a person under no confidentiality obligations. This stance argues it is unreasonable that, under the other stance, the novelty of an invention will still be acceptable even if the invention has become available to the public by a disclosure method not included in the provisions of Article 29(1)(ii) and (iii), such as an oral statement.

4   Publicly-worked invention

The "publicly worked" invention in Article 29(1)(ii) means the implementation of an invention through acts where the invention can be publicly known, including the production, use, and assignment provided in the items of Article 2(3) of the Patent Law. In other words, if an invention is implemented in a manner which makes it publicly known, the invention will be regarded as a publicly-worked invention, and the novelty of the invention will be denied. For example, if a person under no confidentiality obligations can observe the act of using a product which was manufactured by implementing an invention, such use would be considered an act which would make the invention "publicly-worked." Even the implementation in a factory can be regarded as being "publicly-worked" if no measures for confidentiality are taken. A court held that where a person visiting a factory for a reasonable purpose can freely enter the factory, observe a machine and its operational situation, or upon request, any unspecified people are allowed to do a tour of the factory without any measures being taken to prevent the observations of the machine, "the invention implemented into the machine can be sufficiently regarded as a publicly worked invention... regardless of whether the people who actually entered the factory were merely a few specific individuals or whether there were people who actually requested the factory tour."[24] However, where an invention relates to the internal

UNIT 3   Patent Law (2)

structure of a machine, in which the contents of the invention cannot be recognized even by observing the use of the machine, the invention is not regarded as a publicly-worked invention.

In addition, where a person under no confidentiality obligation obtains a product manufactured by implementing an invention, the invention can also be regarded as a publicly-worked invention. For example, if there is a product invention which has been sold in Japan and the creator of another product which has the same features as the sold product files a patent application, a court has held that "with respect to a product invention as in the present case, a purchaser could freely disassemble and analyze the product to understand the invention unless the seller prohibited the purchaser from performing such acts." The court added, "It should be therefore construed that the sale of the product made the invention available to be known by many unspecified people."[25] Therefore, the court has concluded that the sold product would be considered a publicly-worked invention (and the patent application of the similar product should be denied).

However, if the content of an invention cannot be recognized by disassembling and analyzing a product manufactured by implementing the invention, the invention will not be regarded as a publicly-worked invention. A court denied the publicly-worked status of a commercial drug that was produced by kneading a branched amino acid starting material and a kneading material, granulating the kneaded material, and further coating the obtained granules. Due to the nature of the drug, dividing each of the granules into individual particles of a certain diameter before the kneading was considered to be difficult. It was, therefore, extremely difficult to know, by analyzing the particle size of the branched amino acid particles from the commercial drug, that the drug had the feature of the invention for which an application was filed even by means of an analysis technique ordinarily accessible by a person skilled in the art.[26]

5   Description in publications

(1)   Publications

The "publication" in Article 29(1)(ⅲ) is construed to mean "documents or figures

---

[24] Tokyo High Court decision of April 10, 2003, (2001 (*Gyo-Ke*) No. 264).
[25] Tokyo High Court decision of March 24, 2004 (2002 (*Gyo-Ke*) No. 213); Intellectual Property High Court decision of January 14, 2016, (2015 (*Gyo-Ke*) No. 10069).
[26] Tokyo District Court decision of February 10, 2005, *Hanrei Jiho*, No. 1906, p. 144.

III　Novelty

reproduced to be disclosed to the public by distribution, or other communication media analogous thereto." This definition is not limited to documents or figures previously reproduced in a large number of copies which are broadly provided to the public. If an original itself is made public and is freely accessible to the public, and the copies of the original are issued without delay upon request by the public, the copies as such made and issued on demand will also be regarded as publications.[27]

The term "communication media" includes not only typographical printed matter, but also copies (hard copies), microfilms, negative films, and CD-ROMs. The term "distributed" indicates that the publication can be accessed by an unspecified person, and the fact whether anyone actually accessed the publication is not relevant. In contrast, in cases where documents describing an invention are distributed to many persons under confidentiality obligations, the documents will not be regarded as distributed publications.

(2)　Telecommunication lines

Due to the rapid proliferation of information disclosed on websites, the phrase "inventions made available to the public through electronic telecommunication lines" was added to Article 29(1)(iii) under the revision of the Patent Law in 1999. The description "made available to the public" means that an invention can be accessed by the public. If an invention is disclosed on a website, the invention will lose novelty even though nobody actually accessed the invention. Even if a password is required to access the website on which the invention is disclosed, or access to the website costs money, the invention will be regarded as being made available to the public if the presence of the information and the place where the information exists are known to the public, and simultaneously unspecified people can access the information.

In contrast, if an invention is disclosed on a company's intranet and is accessible exclusively by the company's employees, and if the information of the invention is also treated as confidential (i.e., not available to outside of the company), the invention will not lose novelty. This is because the invention is merely disclosed to specific employees under confidentiality obligations and cannot be regarded as being "made available to the public".

6　Determination method

To satisfy the novelty requirement, an invention for which an application was

---

[27] Supreme Court decision of July 4, 1980, *Minshu*, Vol. 34, No. 4, p. 570.

UNIT 3   Patent Law (2)

filed must not be identical with a publicly-known invention. Thus, the determination of novelty is made by a process comprising of: (1) specifying an invention for which an application was filed; (2) specifying a publicly-known invention (cited prior art); and (3) comparing both inventions.

The "invention for which an application was filed" in (1) above; i.e., the subject matter of novelty determination, is an invention described in the scope of claims attached to the patent application.[28] The determination of the technical content of the invention by recognizing the content is conventionally referred to as "the finding of the gist of an invention."

The publicly-known invention in (2) above is any one of the inventions referred to in the items of Article 29(1) of the Patent Law. The matters which can be derived by considering common technical knowledge at the time of filing the application can also be the bases for specifying a publicly-known invention.

Based on a comparison between (1) and (2), if both inventions are determined to be identical with each other, the applied-for invention's novelty will be denied; if both inventions are not identical, the applied-for invention's novelty requirement will be satisfied, but if the applied-for invention can be easily created from a publicly-known invention, the inventive step requirement[29] will not be satisfied and the invention cannot be patented.

7   Exceptions to the lack of novelty

(1)   Outline

As described above in Section 1(2), Part III, an invention will also lose novelty when the inventor discloses the invention. However, if the above principle is applied to every case, the development of technology may be negatively affected, which goes against the purpose of the Patent Law. For this reason, the Patent Law provides exceptions to the lack of novelty in Article 30. One exception is for an invention which was disclosed "against the will" of a person having the right to obtain a patent.[30] Another exception is an invention which was disclosed "due to an action" by the person having the right to obtain a patent.[31] These inventions will not be considered publicly known for the applications of

---

[28] Patent Law, Art. 36(5); Refer to Section 3, Part II of UNIT 5.
[29] Refer to Part IV of UNIT 3.
[30] Patent Law, Art. 30(1).

Ⅲ　Novelty

the inventions filed by the persons having the right to obtain a patent within six months from the day on which the inventions became publicly known "against the will" or "due to an action" of the person having the right to obtain a patent.

Accordingly, an invention which is identical with an invention which became publicly known under Article 30(1) or (2) will not lose novelty, and the inventive step[32] of an invention which can be easily conceived of based on the invention will not be denied.

However, the exceptions to the lack of novelty under Article 30 merely provides that an invention which became publicly known for the reasons stated in Article 30(1) and (2) shall not be regarded as a publicly-known invention, and will have no retroactivity to the filing date of the invention. For this reason, if another reason for the lack of novelty to which neither Article 30(1) nor Article 30(2) can be applied is found during the period from the point of time at which the invention became publicly known to the filing of the application for the invention, the invention cannot be patented.

(2) Invention which became publicly known "against the will" of the person having the right to obtain a patent

According to the provision of Article 30(1), cases where an invention which became publicly known "against the will" of the person having the right to obtain a patent shall be regarded as an exception to the lack of novelty. The purpose of this provision is to provide a remedy to the person having the right to obtain a patent where an invention was disclosed against the will of that person.

The description "against the will" means that an invention became publicly known while the person having the right to obtain a patent does not have the intent to disclose the invention. The above includes cases where an invention treated in confidence is disclosed by a person who obtained the invention by means such as theft and fraud, or cases where a person under confidentiality obligations discloses the invention in breach of his/her obligations.

(3) Invention which became publicly known "due to an action" by the person having the right to obtain a patent

According to the provision of Article 30(2), cases where an invention became publicly known "due to an action" by the person having the right to obtain a patent shall be regarded as an exception to the lack of novelty. Specific examples include:

---

[31] Patent Law, Art. 30(2).
[32] Refer to Part Ⅳ of UNIT 3.

UNIT 3   Patent Law (2)

(1) performing an experiment on an invention; (2) announcing an invention in publications or on a website; (3) presenting an invention at an academic conference, a workshop or a seminar; (4) displaying an invention at an exhibition; (5) disclosing an invention on TV or radio; and (6) disclosing an invention by selling a product relating to an invention. The purpose of this provision is to prevent the inventor from refraining to conduct the above actions based on the fear of losing novelty of the invention.

However, cases where an invention became publicly known by being disclosed in a patent publication are excluded.[33] The exceptions to the lack of novelty were inherently stipulated for the benefit of the inventors who disclosed their inventions "before the filing" of the applications for their inventions. A patent publication requires "the filing action" by the person having the right to obtain a patent. Therefore, in light of the purpose of the exceptions to the lack of novelty, such exceptions should not be applicable to an invention which became publicly known by being disclosed in a patent publication due to "the filing action" by the person having the right to obtain a patent. Moreover, if the above invention is subject to an exception to the lack of novelty, the person having the right to obtain a patent may use such an exception substantially to extend the protection period for such invention, which may result in abuse of the system.

(4)   Procedures to apply for an exception to the lack of novelty

A person having the right to obtain a patent who is seeking to apply for an exception to the lack of novelty must file an application for the invention within six months from the date on which the invention became publicly known. In addition, in order to apply the exception set forth under Article 30 (2), a person having the right to obtain a patent must submit a document explaining the situation at the same time when filing the application, and a document evidencing the reason for an exception within 30 days from the filing date.[34] In contrast, the person having the right to obtain a patent who is seeking to apply for an exception under Article 30(1) ("against the will" of the person having the right to obtain a patent) does not need to submit the aforementioned documents. This is because when an invention becomes publicly known "against the will" of a person having the right to obtain a patent, a majority of such persons are unaware of the fact that their inventions have become publicly known.

---

[33] Patent Law, Art. 30(2).
[34] Patent Law, Art. 30(3).

Ⅳ Inventive step

1 What is an inventive step?

When a person ordinarily skilled in the art of the invention (a "person skilled in the art") cannot create an invention based on a publicly known invention (in a broad sense) before the patent application, the invention is regarded as having an inventive step.

Even if an invention for which an application was filed is not identical with a publicly known invention, and thus novelty has not been denied, it may be easily created based on a publicly known invention. If that is the case, there is a lack of necessity or advantage of granting a patent for the invention in return for its first publication. This is the same as the case in which the invention can be regarded as being identical with a publicly known invention. Furthermore, such invention may be generally implemented by any business entity. Therefore, if a patent for the invention is granted for a particular party, other parties' business activities may be restricted, which may result in disturbing industrial development. Thus, Article 29(2) of the Patent Law stipulates that a patent having no inventive step cannot be patented.

2 Technological level by which the existence of an inventive step is determined – Person skilled in the art

The existence of an inventive step is determined by the technological level of a person skilled in the art. A person skilled in the art is one who is of an average level among technical experts in the technical field of an invention for which an application was filed. A person skilled in the art is specifically a hypothetical person who has common general knowledge including prior arts in the technical field of the invention at the time of the filing, who can use ordinary technical means for research and development, and who can exercise ordinary creativity in selecting materials and modifying designs.

According to the Patent Law, the concept of "a person skilled in the art" is also referred to in Article 36(4)(ⅰ) regarding the requirements for the specification of a patent application.[35] The law does not specifically define if the persons skilled in the art referred to in Articles 36(4)(ⅰ) and 29(2) are identical or not. However, at least, the abilities contemplated in both provisions are not necessarily identical; the inventive step

---

[35] Refer to Section 2, Part Ⅱ of UNIT 5; Patent Law, Art. 29(2).

UNIT 3   Patent Law (2)

requirement in Article 36(4)(ⅰ) focuses on a person's creativity, and the descriptive requirement in Article 29 (2) focuses on a person's ability to comprehend documents or to implement an experiment.

3   Determination method

The determination of an inventive step is performed by a process comprising of: (1) specifying an invention for which an application was filed; (2) specifying a publicly known invention (prior art); and (3) comparing both inventions in the same manner as performed in the process of determining novelty. Among the above, requirements (1) and (2) are identical with those required in the determination of novelty. Regarding (3), the differences in respect of the features of the inventions are emphasized, but the differences in respect of objects and effects also affect the determination of "whether the invention could have been easily achieved."

According to the examination practice in the JPO, whether an invention has an inventive step is determined by considering whether it can be logically determined that the invention could have been easily conceived of by a person skilled in the art based on a cited prior art. When such logical determination is possible, the inventive step will be denied. When such logical determination is impossible, the inventive step will not be denied.

This "logical" determination can be made from various viewpoints. For example, when an invention for which an application was filed can be created by selecting optimum materials from cited prior arts, optimally or preferably modifying numerical ranges, replacing materials with equivalents, performing design variation associated with an application of specific techniques, or merely juxtaposing prior arts, the inventive step of the invention will likely be denied since the invention as such can be created by a person skilled in the art with his/her ordinary creativity. In addition, if any factor which gives motivation to create an invention for which an application was filed is involved in the prior art, it will be regarded as supporting a lack of an inventive step. The examples of the factor are the relationship of technical fields, similarity of problems to be solved, similarity of operations or functions, and suggestions shown in the content of the cited prior arts. On the other hand, if the invention has effects which are superior to those achieved by the prior art, this will be taken into consideration as a fact which is useful in affirmatively assuming the existence of an inventive step.

IV　Inventive step

4　Inventive step of a use invention

With respect to a use invention,[36] novelty will be accepted if the use invention can provide a new application of a product which is different from the application of publicly known inventions, even if the product itself is publicly known. However, if a person skilled in the art can easily conceive of the application based on the known properties of the product, the inventive step will be denied.

5　Selection invention

In a technical field where an effect is difficult to predict based on the structure of a product, an invention expressed by selecting a more specific concept included in the general concept of a prior invention is a selection invention. For example, an invention of an insecticide in which a specific compound is selected as the active ingredient from compounds represented by a given general formula which are known to have insecticidal properties is a selection invention.

A selection invention is conceptually included in prior inventions. However, when the following requirements are satisfied, the novelty and inventive step of the selection invention will be accepted:

(1)　the invention is not specifically disclosed in a prior art document describing a prior invention; and

(2)　the invention has effects being different from or identical but prominently superior to those achieved by a prior invention described in a prior art document, and the effects as such cannot be predicted by a person skilled in the art.

With respect to the above example of an insecticide, the novelty and inventive step of the selection invention will be accepted if (1) the specific compound is not disclosed and (2) the specific compound is remarkably less poisonous to human beings than the other compounds represented by the general formula, and the effects achieved by the compound cannot be predicted.[37]

6　Numerically limited invention

A numerically limited invention is broadly defined as an invention in which a feature specifying the invention is quantitatively expressed by a numerical range, and is

---

[36] Refer to Section 2, Part IV of UNIT 2.
[37] Tokyo High Court, October 31 decision of 1963, *Gyoshu*, Vol. 14, No. 10, p. 1844.

UNIT 3   Patent Law (2)

narrowly defined as an invention in which a part of the features specifying a prior invention is numerically limited, which is a type of a selection invention. For example, with respect to a prior invention in which substances A and B are mixed in a given ratio and react with each other at a temperature between 300 °C and 700 °C to create a product C, an invention having features constituting the above prior invention except for the reaction temperature numerically limited to a range between 350 °C and 500 °C would be a numerically limited invention.

Since optimally or preferably determining a numerical range can be regarded as the exercise of ordinary creative activity of a person skilled in the art, neither novelty nor an inventive step can be recognized ordinarily. However, the novelty and inventive step of an invention will be accepted if the invention has, within a limited range of numerical values, (1) an advantageous effect which is not specifically disclosed in a prior art document describing a prior invention, (2) an effect being different in nature from an effect achieved by a prior invention, or being remarkably superior although it is the same as the effect achieved by the prior invention, and the above effects are unpredictable by a person skilled in the art based on common technical knowledge.

The existence of a remarkable quantitative difference in advantageous effects between the inside and outside of the boundary of a numerical limitation is referred to as the "critical significance." If a difference between a numerically limited invention and a prior invention lies only in the presence/absence of a numerical limitation and a common object exists, the numerical limitation must have critical significance. However, if both inventions have different objectives to be achieved and produce effects different in nature, the numerical limitation is not required to have critical significance.

With reference to the above example of substances A and B, if the yield of the obtained product C significantly increases compared with the yield achieved by a prior invention when the reaction is carried out at a temperature within the numerically limited range between 350 °C and 500 °C, the novelty and inventive step of the numerically limited invention will not be denied.

V   First-to-file system

1   Outline

In cases where multiple applicants completed the same invention independently

V   First-to-file system

of one another and filed applications for the invention, and if multiple patent rights for the same invention were redundantly granted, legal relationships would become complicated, and the significance of stipulating the duration of patent rights[38] would be lost. Thus, Article 39 provides that only the earliest applicant shall be granted a patent when multiple applications are filed for the same invention to avoid "double patenting." This is the first-to-file system (i.e., "principle of prior application"). Of course, an earlier filed application is not always patented, and the other patent requirements must naturally be satisfied. On this point, it is more appropriate to state that an earlier application has the effect of excluding a later-filed application (i.e., the "later application-excluding effect").

When several applications were filed for the same invention, there is another system for handling these applications in addition to the first-to-file system. In this system, the issue of who completed an invention earliest is addressed, and a patent for an invention is granted to the one who completed the invention the earliest. The system is called the "first-to-invent system," and was solely adopted in the U.S. However, the U.S. shifted from the first-to-invent system to the first-to-file system in 2011.

According to the first-to-file system, it is easy to determine which application was filed earlier/later. Thus, the first-to-file system has an advantage over the first-to-invent system, because it does not require any complicated procedures as those required for determining who completed an invention the earliest.

Moreover, an applicant who should be protected under the first-to file system is one whose invention will be published earlier by filing an application for the invention earlier than another applicant. This complies with the purpose of the Patent Law, which is to encourage inventions by publishing them.

2   Determination method

(1)   Date criterion for determination

Under the first-to-file system, the criteria for determining which application was filed earlier is not the <u>time</u> of filing, but the <u>date</u> of filing, unlike the determination of novelty. When several applications are filed on different dates, the applicant who filed the application earliest can obtain a patent.[39] In contrast, when several applications are filed on the same date, the applicant who can obtain a patent is determined by consultations

---

[38] Patent Law, Art. 67(1).
[39] Patent Law, Art. 39(1).

45

UNIT 3 Patent Law (2)

between the applicants. If no agreement is reached by such consultations or consultations cannot be held, none of the applicants can obtain a patent.[40]

(2) Determination of the identity of inventions

The purpose of Article 39 is to avoid double patenting for "the same invention." Therefore, this article is applied to cases in which an invention of an earlier application is identical to an invention of a later application (i.e., "the identity of inventions").

The identity of inventions is determined based on the inventions described in the scope of claims. This is the same as described in the determination of novelty.[41] Inventions according to the claims in the earlier application and in the later application are specified, compared with each other, and the identity of the inventions is determined.

(3) Earlier application having later application-excluding effect

An earlier application does not always exclude a later application. For example, (1) a waived application, (2) a withdrawn application, (3) a dismissed application, and (4) an application for which the examiner's decision or trial decision to the effect that the application is to be refused has become final and binding, do not have the effect of excluding a later application.[42] An application having the effect of excluding a later application is an application filed for an invention which was ultimately patented. In addition, regarding applications filed on the same date, the Patent Law provides that applications for which the examiner's decision or trial decision to the effect that the patent application is to be refused has become final and binding (since no agreement was reached by consultation or no consultation was held) shall also have the effect of excluding a later application.[43] If the above is not provided in the Patent Law, there would be an unfair result in which an applicant of a later application can obtain a patent right.

---

[40] Patent Law, Art. 39(2).
[41] Refer to Section 6, Part Ⅲ of UNIT 3.
[42] Patent Law, Art. 39(5), main text.
[43] Patent Law, Art. 39(5), proviso.

VI Secret prior art

1 Outline

Application A 	Application B 	Publication of Application A

(Inventions described in the description, 	(1.5 years after the filing of the application)
figures and drawings of Application A)

As described above, Article 39 of the Patent Law sets forth the first-to-file system which is applied to cases where an earlier application invention is identical with a later application invention. The identity of the inventions are determined based on the inventions described in the scope of claims.

Accordingly, as shown in the above figure, when the inventions described in the scope of claims in a later application B are not described in the scope of claims in a former application A and are identical only with the inventions described in the specification, figures and drawings of the former application A, the identity of the inventions cannot be found under Article 39 of the Patent Law, and the later application B will not be excluded by the former application A. If application B is filed after the publication of application A,[44] the novelty requirement will not be satisfied and the invention of application B cannot be patented. However, if application B is filed before the publication of application A, a novelty problem will not occur.

In response to the above situation, the Patent Law provides in Article 29-2 that a later application should also be excluded when the invention of the later application is identical with the invention described in the specification, figures and drawings of an earlier application. This is called "Expanded scope of a prior application" or "secret prior art" (or quasi-known "*Jun-Kochi*" (a later application invention regarded as a publicly known invention)).

---

[44] A patent application will be published 1.5 years after the filing of the application; Patent Law, Art. 64; Refer to Section 3, Part Ⅲ of UNIT 5.

UNIT 3   Patent Law (2)

2   Gist - why a secret prior art has exclusivity?

A secret prior art (i.e., an earlier filed patent application that has not yet been published at the time of filing of a later application may exclude the later application) was newly added at the time of the introduction of the publication before examination system under the Patent Law revision in 1970.

A secret prior art was provided for in the reasons mentioned below.

In the above figure, the inventions described in the specification, figures and drawings of application A will be published under the publication before examination system 1.5 years (at the latest) from the filing of the application, and application B will not be regarded as providing the society with a new art. Thus, a patent for the invention of application B does not need to be granted. In addition, an earlier applicant sometimes files an application for an invention (even though the applicant does not intend to obtain a patent for the invention) in order to prevent a third party from obtaining a patent for the invention and monopolizing the right, which is called a defensive application. If the earlier applicant can prevent a third party who is a later applicant from obtaining a patent by describing the invention in the specification, figures and drawings, the earlier applicant can be released from the burden of filing the defensive application. For these reasons, Article 29-2 was provided.

3   Determination method

(1)   Date criterion for determination

According to a secret prior art, whether an application was filed earlier or later is determined based on the filing date of the application. Unlike the provision of Article 39 relating to the first-to-file system, Article 29-2 is not applied to applications filed on the same date.

(2)   Determination of identity of inventions

The identity of inventions under a secret prior art is determined nearly in the same manner as determined under Article 39 of the Patent Law. The difference is that a later application invention is compared not only with the invention described in the scope of claims of the earlier application invention, but also with the invention described in the original specification, figures and drawings of the earlier application invention.

(3)   Prior application having later application-excluding effect

In order for a later application to be excluded under Article 29-2 of the Patent

Law, the following requirements must be satisfied: (1) an earlier application is published under Article 64 ; or (2) the invention is published in a patent publication under Article 66(3) after the establishment of a patent right for the earlier application invention has been registered. Once the above requirements are satisfied, the later application will be excluded even if the earlier application is waived, withdrawn, or dismissed, or a decision or an appeal decision to the effect that the application shall be denied becomes final and binding.

Ⅶ Unpatentable inventions

Article 32 states, "Notwithstanding Article 29, any invention that is likely to harm public order, morality, or public health shall not be patented." The above are also referred to as "the category of unpatentable inventions."

Inventions being unpatentable under Article 32 can be generally understood to mean inventions which could inevitably harm public order, morality, and public health when being implemented. These type of inventions cannot be patented because industrial development would not be achieved by encouraging these types of inventions. The term "public order and morality" refers to the basic order in societies and general morality. For example, "a method to transplant a human somatic cell nuclear transfer embryo into a human uterus" could fall under the category of unpatentable inventions. However, an invention shall not be regarded as harming the public order only for the reason that the implementation of the invention is prohibited by law.

UNIT 4 Patent Law (3)

- Inventors,
Misappropriated applications (*Bounin-shutsugan*) and
Employee inventions

I Right to obtain a patent

1 What is the right to obtain a patent?

The right to obtain a patent is the status of being able to file a patent application and request the grant of a patent. A patent application would be refused if "the applicant for the patent is not entitled to obtain a patent for the invention."[1] Therefore, a patent will not be granted for an invention filed by a person who has no right to obtain a patent. However, it is difficult for an examiner to determine whether or not the applicant has the right to obtain a patent, and therefore, a patent could be erroneously granted for an application filed by a person who has no right to obtain a patent. In such cases, since there is a reason for invalidation of the patent, such patent will be invalidated through a trial for invalidation.[2] Thus, under the Patent Law, not everyone who filed a patent application can obtain a patent, and whether the applicant is entitled to obtain a patent will become an issue.

After an invention is completed, who has the right to obtain a patent for the invention? The Patent Law states that "an inventor of an invention that is industrially applicable may be entitled to obtain a patent for the said invention."[3] Thus, a person who made an invention first acquires the right to obtain a patent. If a person who is not an inventor knew the invention by analyzing a product manufactured by working the invention and filed a patent application for the invention (even if the patent application was filed earlier than the application filed by the inventor), since the person is not an inventor, he/she has no right to obtain a patent for the invention.

---

[1] Patent Law, Art. 49(vii).
[2] Patent Law, Art. 123(1)(vi); Refer to Part II of present UNIT.
[3] Patent Law, Art. 29(1).

UNIT 4   Patent Law (3)

2   Who is an inventor?

(1)   Importance of identification of the inventor

As mentioned in the section "1 What is the right to obtain a patent?," to obtain a patent right, an application must be filed by a person who is entitled to obtain a patent. Since an inventor acquires a right to obtain a patent (except for the case of an employee invention which will be explained later), the issue of who is the inventor of an invention is very important as it directly connects to who can acquire a patent right.

If an invention was completed by a person who was confined to a home laboratory and did all of the research, this person is obviously an inventor of the invention. However, in the real world, many inventions are made through a project that involves a lot of people in a company, a university or a research institution, etc. Therefore, in order to identify who is entitled to obtain a patent, it must be determined who is the inventor of the invention among those involved in the project.

(2)   Specific criteria

There are many individuals involved in creating an invention who perform various tasks, including, for example, a researcher who is the main individual that performs research and development from the beginning to the end, a supervisor who instructs the research and development, and a person who engages in making a copy of documents according to the researcher's instructions, purchasing a reagent, and others.

An inventor is generally known as "a person who made a creative contribution to the invention"[4] or "a person who was involved in the creative activity of structuring the technical ideas concretely and objectively enough to enable a person ordinarily skilled in the art to work it."[5] However, it is difficult to identify the inventor in actual situations. Although, in general, a person who only supported the research, gave abstract instructions or orders, gave general advice or guidance, or provided funding or equipment is not considered to be an inventor, and the inventor is to be determined case-by-case based on each specific situation. Therefore, in the case of joint research, parties often clarify the attribution of a patent right in advance by an agreement.

3   Joint inventions

Many inventions are made through a joint invention arrangement. A joint

---

[4] Tokyo District Court decision of August 27, 2002, *Hanrei Jiho*, No. 1810, p. 102.
[5] Intellectual Property High Court decision of May 29, 2008, *Hanrei Jiho*, No. 2018, p.146.

Ⅱ   Misappropriated application

invention is an invention achieved by the creative contributions of two or more persons. The right to obtain a patent is, in principle, jointly owned by all of the joint inventors and a patent application must be filed by all the joint owners.[6] If a patent application is allowed to be filed by each respective joint owner, there may be an inappropriate situation where a patent right is granted to one person but not the other person for the same invention.

Additionally, the joint owner is not allowed to assign his/her respective share without the consent of all the other joint owners.[7]

4   Content of a right to obtain a patent

"A right to obtain a patent" is not identical to a patent right. It is merely a right to acquire a patent right by filing a patent application. Therefore, unlike the patent right, a right to obtain a patent does not provide a person with the ability to obtain an injunction against another person's working of the invention without permission from an inventor (e.g., producing a product) or claim damages.

A right to obtain a patent can be assigned.[8] For example, when a venture company created an invention, the venture company may assign the right to obtain a patent of the invention to a large company so that the venture company can raise funds and the large company can acquire a patent of the invention by filing a patent application. Thus, an inventor can make a profit from his/her own invention even before the invention is patented.

Ⅱ   Misappropriated application

1   What is a misappropriated application?

As mentioned in the previous Part Ⅰ "Right to obtain a patent," a patent is granted only for an application filed by a person who is entitled to obtain a patent. On the other hand, an application filed by a person who is not entitled to obtain a patent will be denied. Such application is called a misappropriated application. In general, a person who is entitled to obtain a patent is called a legitimately entitled person and a person who is not entitled to obtain a patent but applied for a patent falsely is called a fraudulent

---

[6] Patent Law, Art. 38.
[7] Patent Law, Art. 33(3).
[8] Patent Law, Art. 33(1).

UNIT 4   Patent Law (3)

applicant.

A misappropriated application is found where a fraudulent applicant intentionally stole an invention from a legitimately entitled owner and filed an application. Such application also applies to the case where a "fraudulent applicant" files an application in a joint development situation, in which there is a conflict in the identification of an inventor. For example, a person who considered that the invention was his/her own invention although it was jointly made by another party might file an application independently. In this case, the applicant is not a person who has absolutely no right to obtain a patent, but the examiner would likely determine that the applicant inappropriately filed an application in spite of the other party's share of the patent. The misappropriated application further includes not only the case where a person who is not entitled to obtain a patent files an application by himself/herself, but also the case where, after a legitimately entitled person filed an application, a fraudulent applicant makes a counterfeit of a document stating that the right to obtain a patent has been assigned to the fraudulent applicant so that the name of the patent applicant is transferred to the fraudulent applicant.

If an examiner can determine properly whether or not the applicant has a right to obtain a patent (i.e., the applicant is an inventor, or an assignee of a right to obtain a patent), a misappropriated application could be refused. In such case, the refused misappropriated application does not constitute a prior application.[9] Therefore, it is likely that a legitimately entitled person who notices a misappropriated application can obtain a patent by filing a patent application. However, due to the examiner's limited inspection capability and documentation, such misappropriated applications can be overlooked in some cases. When a misappropriated application is acknowledged as a prior application, a legitimate application would be refused due to the prior misappropriated application. Also, even if a decision of refusal was issued against a misappropriated application, an application filed by a legitimately entitled person may lack novelty if the misappropriated application was already published.[10]

Accordingly, a legitimately entitled person who intends to acquire a patent right would face a difficult situation if there is a relevant misappropriated application.

---

[9] Patent Law, Art. 39(5).
[10] Patent Law, Art. 64.

Ⅱ　Misappropriated application

2　Countermeasures to be taken by an entitled person

(1)　What should a legitimately entitled person do?

A legitimately entitled person may file a request for a trial for invalidation of a misappropriated application after such application was registered.[11] As already discussed, if a patent was granted to a person who had no right to obtain a patent, such patent has a reason for invalidation. Therefore, the misappropriated application could be invalidated by filing a request for a trial for invalidation. This countermeasure will work if the entitled person only wishes to work the invention but does not wish to obtain a patent right. As a result, any person can work the invention concerned.

However, if the entitled person wishes to obtain a patent right; i.e., the person wishes not only to work the invention but also to monopolize the invention and to prohibit another person from working the invention, filing a trial for invalidation does not provide a sufficient remedy to the entitled person because invalidation of the misappropriated application would not grant a patent right to the entitled person.

Also, as already suggested, even if an entitled person files a patent application, the application could be refused for the reasons of prior application or lack of novelty.

Therefore, it is necessary that the patent right is restored to a legitimately entitled person while the application and patent right of a fraudulent applicant are maintained.

(2)　Prior to the grant of a patent

Prior to the grant of a patent, a legitimately entitled person is allowed to claim a declaratory judgement on its right to obtain a patent against a fraudulent applicant and to claim a change of the name of the applicant based on the declaratory judgement. In other words, an entitled person can prove through a court action that he/she is legitimately entitled to acquire a patent and submit the court decision awarding his claim to the JPO so as to change the name of the applicant to the entitled person. Through this process, the entitled person can take over the application filed by a fraudulent applicant. In this case, since the above procedures are carried out during the examination process before a patent right is generated, changing the name of an applicant, when it is verified, would not cause any issues.

---

[11] Refer to Section 3, Part Ⅳ of UNIT 5.

UNIT 4   Patent Law (3)

(3) After the grant of a patent

Meanwhile, where a patent was already granted to a fraudulent applicant, the countermeasure discussed in the previous paragraph cannot be taken because the examination process has already been completed.

Since a legitimately entitled person has the right to obtain a patent, it seems that the entitled person should be entitled to restore a patent right from the fraudulent applicant. However, strictly speaking, the entitled person only has the right to obtain a patent but does not have a patent right *per se*. Therefore, it is uncertain whether the entitled person has the right to restore a patent right registered under a fraudulent applicant only because the entitled person has the right to obtain a patent. Particularly, where the entitled person has not filed an application, granting a patent right to the entitled person results in an extremely exceptional situation in which "a patent is granted to a person who has not filed an application."

Based on the above discussion, this issue was finally settled by a revision of the law. Specifically, the Patent Law states that "the person who is entitled to obtain a patent of the patented invention may request the patentee to transfer the patent right;" i.e., an entitled person has the right to restore a patent right from a fraudulent applicant (or from a patentee in the case where the patent right has been assigned).[12] Under this provision, a person who is entitled to obtain a patent (even if the person has not filed an application) is entitled to restore a patent right granted for a fraudulent applicant.

Upon approval of a request for transfer, the patent right is deemed to be originally owned by the legitimately entitled person.[13] On the other hand, a fraudulent applicant is deemed to have had no right from the beginning, and thus, the working of the invention by the fraudulent applicant is retroactively deemed as an infringement of the patent right. Also, when the patent right was transferred to an entitled person, an acquirer of the patent right from the fraudulent applicant and a licensee who has obtained a license from the fraudulent applicant are deemed to have acquired a patent right or a license from a person who had no right from the beginning. In other words, the above individuals are also deemed to have no rights of a patent or license.

However, such result would be too disadvantageous for a *bona fide* acquirer/licensee who did not know that the relevant patent right was granted for a

---

[12] Patent Law, Art. 74(1).
[13] Patent Law, Art. 74(2).

56

III Employee inventions

misappropriated application. Therefore, under the Patent Law, a statutory non-exclusive license is granted to the person to a certain extent.[14] Thus, such a *bona fide* acquirer/licensee is accordingly allowed to continue the working of the invention as long as certain requirements are met (in this case, reasonable consideration must be paid to a patentee = a legitimately entitled person).

III Employee inventions
1 Outline
(1) Significance of an employee invention system

As mentioned above, many inventions these days are made in a company by its employees. Companies make huge investments in research and development and many employees are involved in such R&D that innovative inventions are created and commercialized.

What happens if such invention is treated in the same manner as an invention created by an independent inventor? As a matter of principle, an employee, who is an inventor, would acquire a right to obtain a patent, and accordingly, could obtain a patent right. However, the invention was created by using equipment and resources of the employer (i.e., the company). Also, in order to commercialize the invention, the employer took an investment risk. If the employer receives nothing in return irrespective of its contribution to the invention, the employer would reduce its investment in inventions made by employees. As a result, it would be difficult for companies to create inventions which require a large investment.

On the other hand, if all rights of an invention made by an employee are given exclusively to an employer, the incentives for an inventor (i.e., the employee), could be impaired. Since it is the employee who made the invention, he/she should be rewarded in some way.

Given the relationship between an employer and an employee, it is important to give proper incentives of an invention to both the employer and employee. Therefore, the Patent Law provides an employee invention system to solve conflict of interests between the employer and the employee.

---

[14] Patent Law, Art. 79-2, Refer to Part III of UNIT 6.

UNIT 4   Patent Law (3)

(2)   Outline of the employee invention system

The outline of the employee invention system is described below.

When an invention constitutes an employee invention, (1) an employer is entitled to work the invention without consideration (i.e., a royalty-free statutory license is granted to the employer) and (2) an employer can establish in advance an agreement and other instruments, by stating that the employer acquires a right to obtain a patent, etc. Here, the "agreement and other instruments" would include employment regulations (or work rules) as well as a contract made by mutual consent. Further, (3) where an employer acquires a right involving an employee invention, an employee is entitled to claim a "reasonable benefit;" i.e., the employee who gives up his/her right regarding the invention so that the employer can enjoy such right can receive benefits in return. In this way, the profits made from an employee invention are distributed between the employer and the employee under the Patent Law.

2   Requirements for an employee invention

(1)   What invention would constitute an employee invention?

Whether a particular invention constitute an employee invention is an important issue because it determines whether the employee invention system will be applied. Generally speaking, an invention made by an employee (e.g., an engineer) in a company is regarded as an employee invention. However, there are various types of relationships between an employer and an employee. It is therefore necessary at the beginning to review what inventions are treated as an employee invention.

The Patent Law stipulates the following three requirements for an employee invention.[15] The employee invention must be (1) an invention made by an employee, (2) an invention of which nature falls within the scope of the business of the employee, and (3) an invention achieved by the employee's act(s) as part of the present or past duty of the employee owed to the employer.

(a)   Requirement (1): An invention made by an employee

In some cases, the court is required to find if there is, indeed, an employment relationship between an alleged employer and an alleged employee. In the case of a direct employment, the relationship of an employer and an employee would be met. However,

---

[15] Patent Law, Art. 35(1).

58

Ⅲ Employee inventions

since recently the form of employment has become more diversified, there is a complicated relationship between an employer and an employee. For example, where an employee works as a dispatched worker, the employee concludes an employment contract with a dispatching business operator and is dispatched to a company where he/she actually conducts R&D under the instruction of the company. If the dispatched worker made an invention in the above case, there would be an issue regarding whether the invention was an employee invention between the dispatched worker and the dispatching business operator or between the dispatched worker and the company where he/she was dispatched.[16]

(b) Requirement (2): the scope of the business of the employer

If an invention has no relationship with the business of the employer, the invention would not be regarded as an employee invention. The scope of business, however, should be broadly interpreted. For example, a future business that is, even if it is not performed at present, concretely predictable should be within the scope of the business because the business would change continuously according to economy and market conditions.

(c) Requirement (3): present or past duty of the employee

To constitute an employee invention, the invention must be made as a part of the employee's duty. The duty of an employee is not limited to a duty which is specifically ordered by an employer. According to a court precedent, if objectively observing the employee's duty, the invention was expected based on the relationship with the employer and if the employer contributed to the completion of the invention, the invention would be deemed as an employee invention.[17] Also, even if the employee was ordered by his/her supervisor to stop making the invention, the invention could be deemed as an employee invention under certain conditions.[18]

The term "present or past duty" means that if an employee's duty has been changed by, for example, being transferred to another section within the same company, an invention that was made as a part of an employee's past duty could be treated as an employee invention. To the contrary, an invention that was completed after the employee

---

[16] *See* Nobuhiro Nakayama, "*Tokkyo Hou* (Patent Law)," 3rd edition, 2016, pp. 58-59 (a scholarly opinion that the company for which a dispatched worker is working should be deemed as an "employer" for the purpose of an employee invention made by the dispatched worker).

[17] Osaka District Court decision of April 28, 1994, *Hanrei Jiho*, No. 1542, p. 115.

[18] Tokyo District Court interim decision of September 19, 2002, *Hanrei Jiho*, No. 1802, p. 30.

UNIT 4   Patent Law (3)

moved to another company, or an invention that was completed by continuing the former employee's study after his/her retirement would not be considered an employee invention of the former company. Otherwise, there would be confusion regarding whether the invention is an employee invention of the former employer or of the new employer. Also, if the invention was perpetually considered to be an employee invention of the former employer, it would be practically difficult for an employee to move to a new job in the related industry.

(2)   Employee invention and free invention

An invention which satisfies the above three requirements constitutes an employee invention and is subject to specific treatment between an employer and an employee.

On the other hand, an invention which does not meet the above requirements does not constitute an employee invention even if the invention was made by an employee in a company. Such invention may be called a "free invention," and the employee invention system does not apply to free inventions.

3   Effect of employee invention: statutory license of an employer

As discussed above, when an employee acquires a patent of an employee invention or when an employee assigns his/her right to obtain a patent to another person and that person acquires a patent by filing a patent application, an employer would be unable to work the invention (i.e., the act of working the invention by the employer would result in infringement of a patent right). However, under the Patent Law, the employer is granted a license to work the invention without having to pay any license fees even after the patent right was granted for the invention to an employee (or the employee's successor) because a minimal right of the employer on the invention should be secured.

This is a statutory license that is automatically granted by law without permission from the employee, and an employer is entitled to use the invention as he/she wishes at no cost. Since the employer does not have a patent right, the employer is not entitled to claim an injunction against a third party's working of the invention. The employer is only entitled to work the invention.

Ⅲ Employee inventions

4 Effect of employee invention: acquisition by an employer of a right to obtain a patent for an employee invention

As discussed in the section "3 Effect of employee invention: statutory license of an employer," even if an employee acquires a patent right, an employer is entitled to work the invention by a statutory license. However, this does not mean that the employer acquires a patent right. Most employers usually desire to acquire a right to obtain a patent or a patent right *per se* in order to prevent another person's working of the invention or to monopolize the merits of the invention.

For this purpose, an employer is allowed to set forth in an agreement or in the employment regulations or work rules (prior to the completion of an employee invention) that the right to obtain a patent shall be vested in the employer, etc.[19] The employer can not only work the invention as he/her wishes, but can also acquire a right to obtain a patent. It is a unique feature that the provision concerning the acquisition of a patent right by an employer may be provided in employment regulations or work rules made by the employer as well as in an agreement entered into by both parties. Practically speaking, in most cases, such provision is provided in employment regulations or work rules, or in the regulations concerning an employee invention. Thus, the employer can acquire a right to obtain a patent by stipulating the above provision in employment regulations, etc., in advance. This is an important for an employer who considers the royalty-free statutory license to be insufficient.

On the other hand, where an invention is a free invention which does not constitute an employee invention, the employer is not allowed to stipulate the acquisition for such free invention by the employee. Such provision, if any, shall be null and void.[20] This legislation is provided to protect an employee by prohibiting an employer (who has, in many cases, a position stronger than that of an employee) from stipulating that the employer acquires a right involving a patent for a free invention. If this is not the case, it would be unfair for an employee to lose his/her right for a free invention at an early stage when the content of an invention is unknown. On the contrary, an employer can acquire a right for a free invention from the employee by mutual agreement after completion of invention.

It must be particularly noted that where the provision provides that the right to

---

[19] Patent Law, Art. 35(2).
[20] Id.

UNIT 4   Patent Law (3)

obtain a patent shall be vested in the employer, such right belongs to the employer when the right becomes effective.[21] Prior to the revision of the Patent Law in 2015, a right to obtain a patent primarily belonged to an inventor, i.e. an employee, and then the right could be transferred to an employer. After the revision in 2015, however, an employer can acquire such right inherently when the right becomes effective, which prevents the employee from assigning such right to other competing companies.

5   Effect of employee invention: reasonable benefit

(1)   Outline

Under the Patent Law, an employee can receive a reasonable benefit from an employer who acquires a right to obtain a patent, etc.[22] This provision assures that an employee, who loses such right, can receive a certain amount of remuneration.

Where the method of determining the benefit is set forth in an agreement or in the employment regulations or work rules, and the provision of giving a benefit that is determined through the above method is not unreasonable, there would not be any issues.[23] However, if there is no provision concerning a reasonable benefit, or if giving a benefit in accordance with the method to determine the benefit is unreasonable, a court could determine the reasonable benefit and order the employer to provide it to the employee.[24] When the employer paid a certain amount to the employee, but the court decides that this amount is insufficient as a reasonable benefit, the employer must pay the deficient amount to the employee.

(2)   What is a reasonable benefit?

The term "reasonable benefit" is not clearly defined. The value and its calculation method are generally set forth in the regulations concerning an employee invention under the sections for compensation for application, compensation for registration or compensation for implementation. However, since there is no specific criteria for the calculation of the amount of a reasonable benefit, in some cases, a court has ordered an employer to pay a large amount to the employee.[25] Therefore, there had been a problem that the employer could not foresee the amount to be paid as a

---

[21] Patent Law, Art. 35(3), "inherently belongs to an employee."
[22] Patent Law, Art. 35(4).
[23] Patent Law, Art. 35(5).
[24] Patent Law, Art. 35(7).

62

reasonable benefit (which used to be "reasonable value" prior to the revision in 2015).

In order to resolve the above problem, under the Patent Law amended in 2004, whether the payable "benefit" is reasonable is determined based on the procedural elements between the parties. Specifically, the following are taken into account: (1) "the circumstances where negotiation between the employer and employee took place to set standards for the determination of the reasonable benefit;" (2) "the circumstances where the agreed standards were disclosed;" and (3) "the circumstances where the employee's opinions on the determination of reasonable benefit were received.[26] For example, if a company stipulates the standards for the calculation or determination of a reasonable benefit in consultation with an employee, discloses the standards within the company, receives the employees' opinion and consults with the employee, it is likely that giving a benefit determined through the above procedures would be regarded as being proper and reasonable. It is contemplated that, an appropriate reasonable benefit which is acceptable by both an employer and an employee could be determined through such process.

Of course, substantive elements such as the specific amount, as well as the procedural elements, can be taken into consideration to determine the reasonable benefits.

Where giving a "benefit" based on an agreement or employment regulations is not considered unreasonable in light of the above elements, it would be deemed as the giving of a reasonable benefit. It has been contemplated that the Minister of Economy, Trade and Industry will provide guidelines on the above procedures.[27]

A reasonable benefit means "reasonable monetary or other economic benefits."[28] Therefore, the reasonable benefit includes stock options or an opportunity to study abroad as well as a monetary benefit. However, uneconomical awards such as only honoring an employee for his/her achievements is not considered a reasonable benefit.

---

[25] Tokyo District Court decision of January 30, 2004, *Hanrei Jiho*, No. 1852, p. 36. It was decided that the reasonable consideration was approximately JPY20 billion Yen. According to the court decision, the original consideration was JPY60 billion and JPY20 billion was the claim amount, which is only a part of the original consideration. After the district court judgement, however, both parties agreed to settle the matter at the Tokyo High Court with the payment of about JPY800 million (including default interest of JPY200 million) (*see* Tokyo High Court settlement advisory report, January 11, 2005, *Hanrei Jiho*, No. 1879, p. 141).

[26] Patent Law, Art. 35(5)

[27] Patent Law, Art. 35(6)

[28] Patent Law, Art. 35(4)

UNIT 4   Patent Law (3)

(3)   Decisions made by courts

A court will decide a reasonable benefit where no provision for giving a reasonable benefit is stipulated or if there is a provision, giving a benefit based on the provision is considered unreasonable in light of the elements mentioned in the paragraph (2) "What is a reasonable benefit?" Court decisions are actually made where an employee files a claim for reasonable benefits against an employer.

The Patent Law stipulates that the content of the reasonable benefit should be determined "by taking into consideration the amount of profit to be received by the employer from the invention, the employer's relevant burden or cost, contribution and treatment of the employee and any other circumstances relating to the invention."[29] A court shall determine a reasonable benefit by taking into account the amount of profit received from an acquired right for an invention, and the amount of investment in the R&D made for the invention and the post-invention contribution such as commercialization of the invention or relevant marketing efforts (as stated the "burden/cost relating to the invention" is not only an investment for the invention *per se* but also an investment made after completion of the invention which can be taken into consideration).

---

[29] Patent Law, Art. 35(7)

UNIT 5 Patent Law (4)

• Filing of applications and
Examination・Trial

I Overview

The Patent Law is a law for protecting inventions by generating patent rights. An inventor who merely makes an invention cannot obtain a patent right. In order to obtain the patent right, a patent application must be filed with the Commissioner of the JPO. If Inventor A makes an invention but does not file a patent application and If Inventor B makes the same invention, files a patent application and obtains a patent right, Inventor A's working of this invention results in the infringement of Inventor B's patent right. The same also applies if Inventor A files the patent application after Inventor B.[1]

When a patent application is filed, it is examined by the JPO. If no reason for refusal listed in Article 49 is found, an examiner renders a decision to grant a patent right.[2] However, if the examiner determines that there is a reason for refusal in the patent application, the examiner will render a decision of refusal. If the applicant objects to the decision of refusal, the applicant can file a request for a trial against a decision of refusal.[3]

II Filing of patent applications

1 Overview

The filing of a patent application is an act of submitting an application to the Commissioner of the JPO and seeking a decision by the JPO to grant a patent right.[4] In the patent application, the name and domicile or residence of the patent applicant and the name and domicile or residence of the inventor (s)[5] must be stated, and the (1)

---

[1] Refer to Part V of UNIT 3, the first-to-file principle; Patent Law, Art. 39.
[2] Patent Law, Art. 51.
[3] Patent Law, Art. 121.
[4] 318,381 patent applications were filed in 2016.
[5] Patent Law, Art. 36(1).

UNIT 5   Patent Law (4)

specification (*meisaisho*), (2) claims (*seikyu-no-hani*), (3) drawings (where required) and (4) abstract must be attached.[6] The matters stated in the specification, claims, drawings and abstract are published as publication of application (*shutsugan-kokai*) in a patent gazette,[7] and when the establishment of the patent right is registered, the above matters are also published in a patent gazette.[8]

When a right to obtain a patent is jointly owned, the patent application must be filed by all joint owners.[9]

2   Specification

(1)   Overview

The specification must state (1) the title of the invention, (2) a brief explanation of the drawing(s) and (3) a detailed explanation of the invention.[10] By laying open the matters stated in the specification, the technical contents of the invention which are disclosed become technical knowledge generally available to the public and contribute to technical development. From this aspect, the specification plays the role of a technical document, and this role is mainly fulfilled by the detailed explanation of the invention.

(2)   Enablement requirement

The detailed explanation of the invention explains in detail the invention for which protection is sought. The statements of it must be clear and sufficient so as to enable any person skilled in the art to work the invention.[11] This is the "enablement requirement." The person skilled in the art is "a person ordinarily skilled in the art to which the invention relates to" and indicates an average engineer in the technical field of the invention for which protection is sought. If the person skilled in the art cannot work the invention by reading the specification, laying open such specification does not bring any benefit to the society in general. Thus, this requirement is needed.

(3)   Requirements for disclosure of information on prior art documents

If there are inventions known to the public through publication which are related to the applicant's own invention (i.e., the inventions provided in Article 29(1)(iii)), the

---

[6] Patent Law, Art. 36(2).
[7] Patent Law, Art. 64(2); Refer to Section 3, Part Ⅲ of UNIT 5.
[8] Patent Law, Art. 66(3).
[9] Joint application requirement; Patent Law, Art. 38.
[10] Patent Law, Art. 36(3).
[11] Patent Law, Art. 36(4)(i).

66

II Filing of patent applications

applicant must state in the detailed explanation of the invention the source of information regarding the published invention that he/she knows at the time of filing (such as the title of the published material stating the published invention).[12] Since the applicant normally searches for prior art documents at the time of filing, this system is intended to conduct an examination promptly and properly through the use of the information obtained in the search by the applicant.

3 Claims

(1) Overview

The claims "shall state all matters necessary to specify the invention for which the applicant requests the grant of a patent."[13] All the matters that specify the invention for which protection of a patent right is sought are stated in the claims. Upon granting the patent right, the statements of the claims serve as a basis for determining the technical scope of the patented invention, which is an objective scope where the patent right can be extended[14] and explicitly show the scope of protection of the patent right to the society. From this aspect, it is said that the claims play the role of a document which specifies the patentee's rights. The applicant determines the content of the claims and all the matters that specify the invention for which a patent is sought. Therefore, after the patent is granted, the applicant cannot argue that the invention is specified by matters not stated in the claims or that a part of the matters stated in the claims is redundant.

(2) Multiple claims system

In the past, claims were limited to a single claim corresponding to a single invention (single claim system), but currently, multiple claims can be separately stated. This is the "multiple claims system." It is not uncommon in technical development that not only a single invention, but multiple related inventions are created. The applicant can state in one application multiple inventions in multiple claims.

This does not mean that any multiple inventions can be included in one application. These inventions are required to be in a group of inventions fulfilling the requirements for "unity of invention" by possessing the technical relationship defined in the ordinance of the Ministry of Economy, Trade and Industry.[15]

---

[12] Patent Law, Art. 36(4)(ii).
[13] Patent Law, Art. 36(5).
[14] Patent Law, Art. 70(1); Refer to Section 1, Part II of UNIT 7.

UNIT 5   Patent Law (4)

In examination of the patent requirements such as novelty and inventive step,[16] the invention according to each claim is examined. In an application, if any of the inventions according to the claims does not satisfy the requirements for patentability, a decision to refuse the entire application will be rendered.[17] In this case, the applicant is required to, for example, delete or amend a problematic claim in order to avoid the decision of refusal.

(3)   Requirements for the statements of the claims

The statements of the claims must satisfy the following requirements:

(1)   "The invention for which a patent is sought is stated in a detailed explanation of the invention."[18] This is the "support requirement," and the inventions according to the claims need to be fully supported by a detailed explanation of the invention. Otherwise, the result could be a patent right for an unpublished invention.[19]

(2)   "The invention for which a patent is sought shall be clear."[20] If the invention for which a patent is sought cannot be clearly understood from the claims, the scope of protection of the patent right becomes unclear.[21]

(3)   "The statements for each claim shall be concise" in order for third parties to easily understand the inventions according to the claims.[22]

(4)   "The statements of the claims are composed in accordance with the ordinances of the Ministry of Economy, Trade and Industry." [23]

---

[15] Patent Law, Art. 37; Article 25-8 of the Enforcement Ordinance of the Patent Law specifically provides:
"1. The technical relationship designated in the ordinance of the Ministry of Economy, Trade and Industry under Article 37 of the Patent Law means a technical relationship in which two or more inventions are linked so as to form a single general inventive concept by having the same or corresponding special technical features.
2. The special technical feature provided in the former paragraph means a technical feature which defines a contribution made by an invention over the prior art.
3. The technical relationship provided in the first paragraph shall be examined, irrespective of whether two or more inventions are described in separate claims or in a single claim written in an alternative form."

[16] Refer to UNIT 3.

[17] For example Tokyo High Court decision of January 31, 2002, *Hanrei Jiho*, No. 1804, p. 108.

[18] Patent Law, Art. 36(6)(ⅰ).

[19] Intellectual Property High Court decision of November 11, 2005, *Hanrei Jiho*, No. 1911, p. 48.

4 Drawings and abstract

(1) Drawings

It is not always necessary to attach drawings to a patent application, but if the applicant considers certain drawings necessary, they will be attached to the application.[24] Article 36 also provides that the "brief explanation of the drawing(s)" should be stated in the specification,[25] but this explanation is, of course, stated only when drawings are attached to the patent application.

(2) Abstract

The summary of the invention stated in the specification, claims or drawings are stated in the abstract.[26] The main purpose of the abstract is to facilitate information retrieval of patent applications.

Ⅲ Examinations

1 Overview

When a patent application is filed, the Commissioner of the JPO first conducts a formality examination to examine whether the application has a formality error, etc. Subsequently, if a request for examination is filed, the examiner will conduct a substantive examination to examine whether there are any reasons for refusal (as listed in Article 49 of the Patent Law) in the application, such as whether the requirements for patentability are satisfied.

The Patent Law adopts the substantive examination principle where the requirements for protection are examined before a patent right is granted. In contrast, the Utility Model Act adopts the non-substantive examination principle where a utility model right is granted without substantive examination of (or a portion of) the requirements for protection. As compared with the non-substantive examination principle, the substantive examination principle is advantageous in that the granted right after substantive

---

[20] Clarity requirement; Patent Law, Art. 36(6)(ii).

[21] Supreme Court decision of June 5, 2015, *Minshu*, Vol. 69, No.4, p. 700 held that when a claim concerning a product invention states its manufacturing process, i.e., in the case of a product-by-process claim, the clarity requirement is satisfied "only when there were circumstances that it was impossible or utterly impractical to directly define the product by its structure or properties at the time of filing the application."

[22] Patent Law, Art. 36(6)(iii).

UNIT 5   Patent Law (4)

examination is less likely to be invalidated in the future, but is disadvantageous in that it takes more time to conduct an examination, which delays the grant of the right. Although the patent right is less challengeable in the substantive examination principle, because mistakes can arise in the examination process, the patent right granted in the substantive examination is not absolute. In the Patent Law, a system of a trial for invalidation[27] is established in order to extinguish an improperly granted patent right.

The substantive examination is not initiated automatically, but initiated after a request for examination is filed.[28] This is because for some applications, the applicant does not need to obtain a patent right, and thus, an examination would be unnecessary. Examples of such applications include: 1) an application filed in order to block third party's application for the same innovation (i.e., a defensive application); and 2) an application that the applicant filed in order to obtain a patent right at the time of filing, but later decided not to obtain the patent right. Any person can file a request for examination within three years from the filing date.[29] If a request for examination is not filed within this period, the patent application is deemed to have been withdrawn.[30]

If no reasons for refusal are found in the patent application, the examiner must render a decision to grant a patent.[31] In this case, upon payment of patent fees,[32] the establishment of the patent right is registered,[33] and the patent right is obtained.[34] In contrast, if any reason for refusal is found, the examiner sends to the applicant a notification (notification of reasons for refusal) which states the reasons for refusal and gives the applicant an opportunity to provide a response.[35] In the response to this notification, the applicant can submit a written opinion or amend the specification, etc. If

---

[23] Patent Law, Art. 36(6)(iv); Article 24-3 of the Enforcement Ordinance of the Patent Law specifies: "The statement of claims designated in the ordinance of the Ministry of Economy, Trade and Industry under Article 36(6)(iv) of the Patent Law shall satisfy the following items:
(i) for each claim, the statement shall start on a new line with one number being assigned thereto;
(ii) claims shall be numbered consecutively;
(iii) in the statement in a claim, reference to other claims shall be made by the numbers assigned thereto; and
(iv) when a claim refers to another claim, the claim shall not precede another claim to which it refers."
[24] Patent Law, Art. 36(2).
[25] Patent Law, Art. 36(3)(ii).
[26] Patent Law, Art. 36(7).
[27] Refer to Section 3, Part IV of UNIT 5.
[28] Patent Law, Art. 48-2.
[29] Patent Law, Art. 48-3(1).

Ⅲ　Examinations

the examiner determines that the application does not have a reason for refusal based on the applicant's response, the examiner will render a decision to grant a patent. On the other hand, if the applicant files no response or the examiner determines that the applicant's response cannot overcome the reason for refusal, the examiner renders a decision of refusal. If the applicant is dissatisfied with the decision of refusal, he/she can file a trial against a decision of refusal.[36]

Moreover, regardless of the state of examination or whether a request for examination is filed, a patent application is published as a publication of application in principle after a lapse of one year and six months from the filing date.[37]

2　Amendments

(1)　Overview

Amendments are supplements or corrections of procedures or documents of patent applications or other procedures which are legally incorrect or have deficiencies, errors or ambiguous descriptions in procedural documents. Amendments can be made "only while the case is pending in the Patent Office."[38] The effect of an amendment is considered to be retroactive to the time of filing the application, although there is no clear stipulation regarding when the amendment becomes effective. Accordingly, if the claims are amended, the application is treated as if the application had been filed with the claims after the amendments.

(2)　Restrictions on amendments to the specification, claims, or drawings

The amendments to the specification, claims or drawings specified in Article 17-2 are particularly important. Because an applicant needs to file an application quickly under the first-to-file principle, it is often difficult to state and submit the complete specification, claims or drawings at the time of filing the application. For this reason, if

---

[30] Patent Law, Art. 48-3(4).
[31] Patent Law, Art. 51.
[32] Patent Law, Art. 107.
[33] Patent Law, Art. 66(2).
[34] Patent Law, Art. 66(1); note that 203,087 patents were registered in 2016.
[35] Patent Law, Art. 50; in 2016, the average period (first action period) from when a request for examination is filed to when a first notification regarding the examination results (i.e., a decision to grant a patent or a notification of reasons for refusal) issued by an examiner is 9.5 months.
[36] Patent Law, Art. 121.
[37] Patent Law, Art. 64.
[38] Patent Law, Art. 17(1).

UNIT 5   Patent Law (4)

amendments to the specification, claims or drawings were not allowed at all, the invention would not be appropriately protected. On the contrary, if amendments were allowed without limitation, a third party who files applications later or relies on the contents of the specification, claims or drawings before the amendments would be treated unreasonably and unfavorably. This also goes against the first-to-file principle and would make it difficult for the JPO to conduct an examination promptly and efficiently. Thus, amendments to the specification, claims or drawing are only allowed under certain chronological and substantive restrictions.

(a)   Chronological restrictions on amendments

The specification, claims or drawings can be amended before a certified copy of the decision to grant a patent is provided to the applicant. However, after a notification of reasons for refusal is received, amendments can only be allowed in the following four cases:

(1)   Within the period designated in the first notification of reasons for refusal.[39]

(2)   If a notification under Article 48-7 concerning the statements of information about inventions known to the public through publication[40] is received after receipt of a first notification of reasons for refusal, within the period designated in such notification under Article 48-7.[41]

(3)   Within the period designated in a final notification of reasons for refusal if two or more notifications of reasons for refusal are issued.[42]

(4)   At the same time when a trial against a decision of refusal is filed.[43]

In principle, the "first notification of reasons for refusal" is to notify the applicant of reasons for refusal for the first time, while the "final notification of reasons for refusal" is to notify only the reasons for refusal which correspond to the applicant's amendments in response to the first notification of reasons for refusal. The significance of distinguishing between these notifications is that the substantive restrictions on amendments differ between them. An examination is delayed if amendments are made extensively each time a notification of reasons for refusal is received. Therefore, the amendments in response to the "final notification of reasons for refusal" are limited so that they do not cause

---

[39] Patent Law, Art. 17-2(1)(i).
[40] Patent Law, Art. 36(4)(ii); Refer to Section 2(3), Part II of UNIT 5.
[41] Patent Law, Art. 17-2(1)(ii).
[42] Patent Law, Art. 17-2(1)(iii).
[43] Patent Law, Art. 17-2(1)(iv).

Ⅲ　Examinations

repetition of the examination procedure. On the other hand, amendments can be made relatively freely in response to the "first notification of reasons for refusal."

(b)　Substantive restrictions on amendments

The substantive restrictions on amendments are: (ⅰ) prohibition on adding new matters; (ⅱ) prohibition of shift amendments; (ⅲ) limitation on purposes; and (ⅳ) requirements for patentability (independent patentability requirement).

(ⅰ)　Prohibition on adding new matters

Amendments to the specification, claims or drawings "shall be made within the scope of the matters described in the specification, claims or drawings originally attached to the application form."[44] Since the effect of amendments is retroactive to the time of filing the application, if amendments are made beyond the scope of the matters stated in the specification, claims or drawings originally attached to the application form, subsequent applications would be treated unfairly and third parties who rely on the matters stated in the application would suffer from unexpected disadvantages.[45]

(ⅱ)　Prohibition of shift amendments

If amendments to the claims after receipt of a notification of reasons for refusal largely change the invention stated therein (i.e., shift amendments), such amendments would prevent a prompt examination from being conducted. Thus, "the invention for which determination of its patentability is stated in the notification of reasons for refusal received prior to making the amendment" and "the invention specified by the matters described in the amended claims" must be of a group of inventions fulfilling the requirements for "unity of invention."[46] Therefore, after receipt of the notification of reasons for refusal, an applicant is prohibited from amending the invention stated in the claims to another invention which has different technical features.

(ⅲ)　Limitations on purposes

Amendments to the claims made after receipt of a final notification of reasons for refusal and when a trial against a decision of refusal is filed are limited to those made for the following purposes so that the examination that has been already conducted is used to the fullest extent.[47]

---

[44] Patent Law, Art. 17-2(3).
[45] Intellectual Property High Court decision of May 30, 2008, *Hanrei Jiho*, No. 2009, p. 47.
[46] Patent Law, Arts. 37 and 17-2(4).
[47] Patent Law, Art. 17-2(5).

73

UNIT 5   Patent Law (4)

(1)   Deletion of claims;

(2)   Restriction of claims;

(3)   Correction of errors; and

(4)   Clarification of ambiguous statements.

For example, assuming the claims specifies Constituent Elements A, B, and C, the restriction of claims could mean replacement of Constituent Element C with its subordinate concept c1. On the other hand, before receipt of a notification of reasons for refusal or within the period designated in the first notification of reasons for refusal or the period designated in the notification under Article 48-7, it is possible to add claims or enlarge claims provided that they do not add any new matters and are not shift amendments.

(iv)   Requirements for independent patentability

If the purpose of the amendment is the restriction of claims, the invention stated in the amended claims is required to be independently patentable.[48] This requirement is established because the restriction of claims makes it necessary to conduct an examination again regarding whether the requirements for patentability are fulfilled or not.

By the way, after the granting of a patent right, an application is no longer pending in the JPO, and thus, the specification, claims or drawings cannot be corrected as amendments under Article 17. For such a correction, a request for a trial for correction (or a request for correction in a trial for invalidation) described below must be filed. The substantive restrictions in this case are the same as the substantive restrictions made within the period designated in a final notification of reasons for refusal.

3   Publication of application

Intrinsically, the patent system is intended to grant patent rights in return for the laying open of applications. However, the growing number of patent applications have lengthened the period of examinations and caused a delay in the laying open of inventions. Also, the period in which filed applications are undisclosed to the public has increased and that has worsened a detrimental effect, such as the duplication of investment in research and development of the inventions. Furthermore, the introduction of the request for examination system enables applicants to delay the laying open of their applications based

---

[48] Patent Law, Art. 17-2(6).

III   Examinations

on their sole discretion. Thus, with the revision of the Patent Law in 1970, as well as the request for examination system and the expanded scope of prior applications,[49] the system of publication of application was introduced.

The publication of application means that an application is laid open in a patent gazette after the lapse of one year and six months from the filing date, regardless of the state of examination or whether a request for examination has been filed.[50] However, applications to be laid open are limited to those pending in the JPO at the time they are to be laid open. If an application has been withdrawn, waived or dismissed, or if a decision of refusal or a trial decision of refusal has become final and binding, such application is not laid open. Moreover, the applicant can request that the application be laid open before the lapse of one year and six months from the filing date.[51]

4   Patent oppositions

When the establishment of a patent right is registered and the patent right is obtained, the matters stated in the application form and the matters stated in the specification and claims attached to the application form are published in a patent gazette issued by the JPO.[52] Within six months from the publication date of the patent gazette, any person can file a patent opposition to the Commissioner of the JPO on the ground that the patent falls under the reasons for opposition listed in Article 113. The reasons for opposition are almost the same as the reasons for invalidation.[53]

A patent opposition is examined and decided by a panel consisting of three or five trial examiners.[54] If the trial examiners determine that there is a reason for opposition in a patent, the trial examiners will render a decision to the effect that the patent is to be cancelled (decision of cancellation) and, if not, render a decision to the effect that the patent is to be maintained (decision of maintenance).[55] When the decision of cancellation becomes final and binding, the patent right is deemed to have never existed.[56]

---

[49] Patent Law, Art. 29-2; Refer to Part VI of UNIT 3.
[50] Patent Law, Art. 64(1); however, if a patent gazette is issued upon registration of the establishment of a patent right, such an application does not need to be laid open again and is excluded.
[51] Patent Law, Art. 64-2.
[52] Patent Law, Art. 66(3).
[53] However, misappropriated applications and violations of the joint application requirement are not the reasons for opposition; Refer to Section 3, Part IV of UNIT 5.
[54] Patent Law, Art. 114(1).
[55] Patent Law, Art. 114(2) and (4).

75

UNIT 5   Patent Law (4)

This patent opposition system was established by the revision of the Patent Law in 2014 in order to correct defective patent rights and to obtain strong and stable patent rights at an early stage.

Ⅳ   Trials

1   Overview

A trial generally indicates a system in which an administrative agency makes certain decisions in accordance with quasi-judicial procedures, which are similar to litigation procedures. Under the Patent Law, there are primarily four types of trials:

(1)   Trials against a decision of refusal (for lodging an appeal against an examiner's decision of refusal);[57]

(2)   Trials for invalidating a patent (Trial for invalidation) (for retroactively extinguishing a patent right);[58]

(3)   Trials for correction (for making corrections to the specification, claims or drawings attached to an application form);[59] and

(4)   Trials for invalidating a registration of extension (for invalidating the registration of extension of the term of a patent right).[60]

A trial is conducted by a panel consisting of three or five trial examiners of the JPO.[61] The Commissioner of the JPO designates the trial examiners who will constitute the panel and designates one of them as the chief trial examiner.[62] The chief trial examiner presides over the matters relating to the trial.[63]

A trial against a decision of refusal is requested by an applicant who received a decision of refusal, and a trial for correction is requested by a patentee. In either case, no opposing party exists, and this type of trial is called an ex-parte trial. In contrast, in the case of a trial for invalidation and a trial for invalidating the registration of extension, an adversarial system is adopted in which a party who asserts invalidation files a request for a

---

[56] Patent Law, Art. 114(3).
[57] Patent Law, Art. 121.
[58] Patent Law, Art. 123.
[59] Patent Law, Art. 126.
[60] Patent Law, Art. 125-2.
[61] Patent Law, Art. 136(1).
[62] Patent Law, Arts. 137(1) and 138(1).
[63] Patent Law, Art. 138(2).

trial (petitioner) and the patentee is the opposing party (respondent). This type of trial is called an inter-partes trial.

A trial procedure is initiated with a written request for a trial submitted by the petitioner, and in principle, is concluded with a trial decision.

A party who is not satisfied with a trial decision may file an action against such a trial decision. The exclusive jurisdiction for an action against a trial decision is with the Tokyo High Court, where a motion must be filed with the Intellectual Property High Court (IP High Court) which is a special branch of the Tokyo High Court.[64]

2   Trials against a decision of refusal

If a person who receives a decision of refusal is dissatisfied with the decision, he/she can request a trial against a decision of refusal within three months from the date on which a certified copy of the decision is served.[65] That is, the petitioner of the trial is the applicant who received the decision. When a right to obtain a patent is jointly owned, a request for a trial must be filed by all joint owners.[66]

The trial examiners can determine that the reason for refusal on which the decision of refusal is based is a legitimate reason for refusal, and can also find a new reason for refusal which is different from the initial reason for refusal. Based on the new reason for refusal, they can render a trial decision to dismiss the request for a trial. However, if a new reason for refusal is found, a notification of the reason for refusal must be delivered to give the applicant an opportunity to submit a written argument or an amendment.[67] On the other hand, if the trial examiners determine that there is no reason for refusal, they will render a trial decision to the effect that the patent is to be granted.[68]

---

[64] Patent Law, Art. 178(1) and Law for Establishment of the Intellectual Property High Court, Art. 2(2).
[65] Patent Law, Art. 121(1).
[66] Patent Law, Art. 132(3).
[67] Patent Law, Art. 159(2) referring to Patent Law, Art. 50.
[68] Patent Law, Art. 159(3); a trial decision can also be made which cancels a decision of refusal and orders an examiner to carry out a further examination (i.e., a trial decision for remand, Article 160 (1) of the Patent Law), but such a trial decision is usually not made. The ruling made in the trial decision for remand binds upon the examiner with respect to the case (Patent Law, Article 160(2)). Thus, the examiner who is ordered to carry out a further examination cannot contradict the ruling in the trial decision.

UNIT 5   Patent Law (4)

3   Trials for invalidating a patent (Trial for invalidation)

If a patent that has been once granted is defective, third parties are unreasonably prevented from working the invention, which inhibits the development of the relevant industries. In the Patent Law, a trial for invalidation was established as a system for extinguishing defective patents.

The reasons for invalidation are listed in the items of Article 123(1). These reasons for invalidation are nearly identical to the reasons for refusal.[69] Unlike the trial against a decision of refusal, an adversarial system is adopted in a trial for invalidation, and the petitioner files a request for a trial with the patentee as the opposing party. Since the patentee is directly interested in the existence of the patent right, the trial examination is conducted with the patentee as the opposing party, and not with the JPO as the opposing party.

Only an interested person can request a trial for invalidation.[70] Further, when misappropriated applications[71] or violations of the joint application requirement are reasons for invalidation, only a person who has the right to obtain a patent can file a request.[72] In contrast, the respondent of a trial for invalidation is the patentee. When a patent right is jointly owned, the trial must be jointly requested with all joint owners of the patent right as the respondents.[73]

If the trial examiners determine that there is no reason for invalidation, they will render a trial decision to dismiss the request for a trial. On the other hand, if the trial examiners determine that there is a reason for invalidation, the trial examiners will render a trial decision to approve the request for a trial (a trial decision of invalidation). When the trial decision of invalidation becomes final and binding, the patent right is deemed to have never existed.[74]

4   Trials for correction

If the specification, claims or drawings attached to an application form are corrected after obtainment of a patent right, there is the possibility that such corrections

---

[69] Patent Law, Art. 49.
[70] Patent Law, Art. 123(2).
[71] Refer to Part II of UNIT 4.
[72] Patent Law, Art. 123(2).
[73] Patent Law, Art. 132(2).
[74] Patent Law, Art. 125.

would change the contents of the patent right and impair legal stability. However, there is also the possibility that minor deficiencies will cause meaningless disputes. Moreover, it will be a harsh result for a patentee if his/her patent which partially falls under a reason for invalidation is entirely invalidated. For this reason, the Patent Law allows the patentee to correct the specification, claims or drawings within a certain scope by requesting a trial for correction.

The petitioner of the trial for correction is the patentee. When a patent right is jointly owned, the trial must be jointly requested by all joint owners of the patent right.[75]

Corrections are approved mainly when the following requirements for correction are satisfied:

(1) Corrections must be for the purpose of: (a) restriction of claims; (b) correction of errors or incorrect translations; (c) clarification of ambiguous statements; and (d) resolution of the dependency between claims.[76]

(2) Corrections must be made within the scope of the matters stated in the specification, claims or drawings, and any addition of new matters is not allowed.[77]

(3) Corrections must not substantially enlarge or alter claims.[78]

(4) When corrections are made for the purpose of the above items (1)(a) or (b), the corrected invention must be independently patentable.[79]

A request for a trial for correction cannot be filed during the period from when a trial for invalidation has become pending with the JPO and until the trial decision has become final and binding.[80] However, in the procedure of the trial for invalidation, the respondent of the trial for invalidation can file a request for correction.[81] The requirements for approving the request for correction in the trial for invalidation are almost the same as those in the case of the trial for correction.

If the trial examiners do not approve of the correction, they will render a trial decision to the effect that the request for a trial is to be dismissed. On the other hand, if they approve of the correction, the trial examiners render a trial decision to approve the

---

[75] Patent Law, Art. 132(3).
[76] Patent Law, Art. 126(1).
[77] Patent Law, Art. 126(5).
[78] Patent Law, Art. 126(6).
[79] Patent Law, Art. 126(7).
[80] Patent Law, Art. 126(2).
[81] Patent Law, Art. 134-2(1).

UNIT 5   Patent Law (4)

request for a trial (a trial decision of correction). If the trial decision of correction has become final and binding, the effect is retroactive to the filing date, and "the filing of the patent application, the laying open of the patent application, the examiner's decision or the trial decision to the effect that the patent is to be granted, or the registration of the establishment of the patent right, shall be deemed to have been made based on the corrected specification, claims or drawings."[82]

5   Trials for invalidating the registration of extension

The term of a patent right ends 20 years from the application filing date.[83] However, in the case of pharmaceutical inventions, etc., a considerable time period is often necessary for dealing with matters such as obtaining approvals in accordance with relevant laws (e.g., in the case of pharmaceutical drugs, these matters involve laws relating to the quality, effectiveness, and safety of drugs, medical devices, etc.), and a patented invention cannot be worked during that period. In such a case, the term of a patent right can be extended for up to 5 years.[84]

The trial for invalidating the registration of extension is a procedure for invalidating the registration of extension of the term of such a patent right.[85]

If a trial decision to invalidate a registration of extension becomes final and binding, the extension of the term through such registration of extension will be deemed as not to have been made from the outset.[86]

---

[82] Patent Law, Art. 128.
[83] Patent Law, Art. 67(1).
[84] Patent Law, Art. 67(2).
[85] Patent Law, Art. 125-2(1).
[86] Patent Law, Art. 125-2(4).

Patent Law (5)

● Utilization of rights

I Overview

Upon acquisition of a patent right, a patentee is able to eliminate another party's working of the patented invention. The patentee is able to benefit from working his/her patented invention by, for example, manufacturing or selling the products which result from working the patented invention.

Also, instead of working the patented invention by himself/herself, a patentee is able to obtain compensation by transferring the patent right to a third party or by granting a license to a third party. A patentee can also raise money by establishing a pledge on the patent right.

In addition, there are cases where a third party may acquire a license irrespective of the patentee's intent to protect his/her patented invention. Statutory licenses (*hotei jisshiken*) and awards granting a non-exclusive license (*saitei jisshiken*) are examples of such cases. Although these licenses are considered to be limitations on a patent right for a patentee rather than utilization of a patent right, since these types of licenses are also included in the category of licenses, these licenses will also be explained in this unit.

II Utilization of patent right

1 Working of patented invention

A patentee is able to eliminate a third party's working of the patentee's patented invention and exclusively benefit from working the patented invention. A patentee can freely work the patented invention without any limitations when there is only one patentee, but will there be any limitations on the working of the patented invention when the patent right is jointly owned by more than one patentee?

Article 73(2) of the Patent Law provides for the working of a patented invention where the patent right is jointly owned by more than one patentee. Article 73(2) provides

81

UNIT 6   Patent Law (5)

that each of the joint owners of a patent right may work the jointly-owned patented invention without the consent of the other joint owner(s) unless otherwise agreed in an agreement. Unlike the usage of real estate, the working of an invention does not involve possession. The working of a jointly-owned patented invention by one joint owner therefore does not interfere with the other joint owners' working of the jointly-owned patented invention, and there is no need to negotiate the scope of each owner's working of the invention. This is why freedom to work a jointly-owned patented invention is allowed. However, where allowing freedom to work the jointly- owned patented invention is undesirable for the joint owners, the joint owners may agree otherwise in an agreement, and whether or not each joint owner may work a jointly-owned patented invention is subject to the provisions in the agreement.

2   Transfer of patent right

(1)   Requirements for transfer of patent right

A patent right may be transferred since it is a property right. A patentee can therefore profit from transferring a patent right. Transfer of a patent right can be considered to be an effective way of utilizing a patent right when a patentee does not have the ability to work a patented invention or when a patentee has the ability but does not plan to work a patented invention.

A patent right may be freely transferred in principle, but registration of the transfer is required for the transfer to take effect.[1] In other words, a transfer of a patent right will not take effect even when the parties concerned have agreed to the transfer, unless the transfer is registered. A registration is required for the purpose of clarifying who is the patentee (i.e., the patent holder). However, a transfer will take effect without a registration in the case of general succession such as inheritance, merger or the like in order to avoid a situation where there is no owner of a patent right during the period from the cause of the general succession (such as inheritance) and until the registration of the transfer.[2] Nonetheless, the general succession must be notified to the Commissioner of the JPO without delay so as to clarify who is the patentee.[3]

---

[1] Patent Law, Art. 98(1)(ⅰ).
[2] Patent Law, Art. 98(1)(ⅰ).
[3] Patent Law, Art. 98(2).

(2) Transfer of share of patent right when a patent right is jointly owned

In the case where a patent right is jointly owned, a joint owner is not allowed to transfer his share of the patent right to a third party without the consent of the other joint owners(s).[4] Since a joint owner of a patent right is allowed to freely work the jointly-owned patented invention as mentioned above, a joint owner may become a competitor to the other joint owner(s) and may greatly affect the other joint owner(s) financially, economically, etc. The identity of the other joint owner(s) is therefore an important concern for a joint owner. For example, the business activity of other joint owner(s) would be greatly affected when a small- to medium-sized company who jointly owned a patent right transfers its share to a large company. The Patent Law gives consideration to the effect of a joint owner of a patent right on the other joint owner(s) by requiring the consent of the other joint owner(s) when a joint owner intends to transfer his share. This system avoids the situation where a third party becomes a joint patent right owner in a joint ownership without the knowledge of the other joint owner(s).

Also, consent is not required for transfers of one's share of a patent where such share is transferred by general succession such as inheritance, merger or the like.

3 License by agreement

In general, a right to work a patented invention is called a license (*jisshiken*), and a party to whom a license is granted is called a licensee. A license that takes effect upon patentee's grant of the license can be divided into an exclusive license (*senyo jisshiken*) and a non-exclusive license (*tsujo jisshiken*).

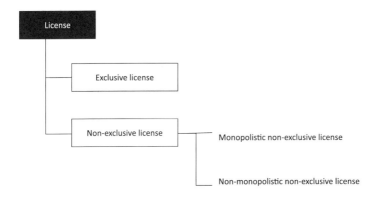

---

[4] Patent Law, Art. 73(1).

UNIT 6   Patent Law (5)

(1)   Exclusive license (*senyo jisshiken*)

(a)   Effect of exclusive license

An exclusive license is a right to solely work a patented invention to the extent provided in a license agreement, and even the patentee is not allowed to work the patented invention within the scope of the license agreement. [5] An exclusive licensee has the right to seek an injunction[6] and damages[7] in his own name on account of an infringement of the exclusive license when an unauthorized third party works the patented invention within the scope provided in the license agreement.

(b)   Establishment of exclusive license

An exclusive license occurs upon permission of the patentee, but it does not take effect until it is registered in the patent registry.[8] A public notice is required for an exclusive license since it is an exclusive and monopolistic right as mentioned above.

When a patent right is jointly owned, an exclusive license cannot be established without the consent of the other joint owner(s).[9] As with the transfer of a share of the jointly-owned patent right, this requirement is provided because the working of a jointly-owned patented invention by a third party without the consent of the other joint owner(s) could negatively impact the interests of the other joint owner(s).

(c)   Scope of exclusive license

The scope of an exclusive license may be unlimited or may be limited in terms of place, time or contents, and such limitations to the scope of an exclusive license must also be registered.[10] Since an exclusive license is a monopolistic right, only a single exclusive license can be established for a single scope of a patent right.

Also, as an exclusive license is solely effective within the agreed scope of a license agreement, an exclusive licensee's working of the patented invention outside the agreed scope would constitute a patent infringement.

(d)   Transfer of exclusive license, grant of non-exclusive license

An exclusive licensee is allowed to transfer the exclusive license only: 1) when the business involving the working of the relevant invention is also transferred; 2) when

---

[5] Patent Law, Art. 77(2).

[6] Patent Law, Art. 100.

[7] Civil Code, Art. 709.

[8] Patent Law, Art. 98(1)(ii).

[9] Patent Law, Art. 73(3).

[10] Patent Registration Order, Art. 43(1).

84

II   Utilization of patent right

the consent of the patentee is obtained; 3) or when the transfer occurs as a result of general succession such as inheritance.[11] It is readily apparent that an exclusive license should be transferred when the consent of the patentee is obtained or in the case of general succession. A transfer of an exclusive license is also allowed when done with the transfer of the business which works the relevant invention, since without such license transfer, the transferee of the business would be unable to work the invention and utilize the facilities used for working the invention when the business is transferred. Indeed, unused and wasted facilities would be against public policy and the economic interests of Japan.

As registration of an exclusive license is required for the exclusive license to take effect, a registration is also required for a transfer of an exclusive license to take effect (excluding a transfer arising from general succession such as inheritance).[12]

Grant of a non-exclusive license by an exclusive licensee is allowed only when the consent of the patentee is obtained.[13]

(e)   Extinguishment of exclusive license

An exclusive license extinguishes in the following situations: 1) lapse of the patent right; 2) expiration of the term set in the exclusive license agreement; 3) termination of the exclusive license agreement; 4) waiver of the exclusive license; or 5) merger of rights (a case where a single party becomes both the exclusive licensee and the patentee as a result of a transfer of the patent right from the patentee to the exclusive licensee or the like).[14]

(2)   Non-exclusive license (*tsujo jisshiken*)

(a)   Effect of non-exclusive license

A non-exclusive license is a right to work a patented invention within the scope provided in a license agreement.[15] Unlike an exclusive license, a non-exclusive license merely provides a contractual status where the patentee cannot demand an injunction or claim damages against the licensee, and the patentee is therefore able to work the patented invention even after granting a non-exclusive license. Also, in general, a non-exclusive licensee cannot demand an injunction or claim damages against a third party's

---

[11] Patent Law, Art. 77(3).
[12] Patent Law, Art. 98(1)(ii).
[13] Patent Law, Art. 77(4).
[14] Civil Code, Art. 179(2).
[15] Patent Law, Art. 78(2).

UNIT 6   Patent Law (5)

unauthorized working of the patented invention (however, see the explanation below with respect to the case with a monopolistic non-exclusive licensee).

(b)   Grant of non-exclusive license

A non-exclusive license occurs upon a grant of a non-exclusive license from the patentee (or from the exclusive licensee with the consent of the patentee). Unlike an exclusive license, registration is not required for a non-exclusive license to take effect.

In the case where the patent right is jointly owned, the consent of the joint owners is required for the grant of a non-exclusive license as with the case of an exclusive license.[16]

(c)   Scope of non-exclusive license

The scope of a non-exclusive license is equivalent to that of an exclusive license, although a patentee can grant non-exclusive licenses with the same contents to multiple parties since a non-exclusive license is not exclusive. However, in actual practice, there are cases in which a special provision is added to a license agreement which stipulates that a license cannot be granted to a third party. This type of non-exclusive license is called a monopolistic non-exclusive license.

A monopolistic non-exclusive licensee substantially has a "monopoly" with respect to the working of the patented invention. This monopoly is a benefit that deserves legal protection, and a monopolistic non-exclusive licensee is allowed to claim damages against a third party's unauthorized working of the patented invention.[17] However, a monopolistic non-exclusive licensee does not have the right to demand an injunction against a third party because the monopoly of the monopolistic non-exclusive licensee is merely based on an agreement.

(d)   Transfer, re-grant of non-exclusive license

A non-exclusive licensee is allowed to transfer the non-exclusive license only when the business which works the relevant invention is also transferred, when the consent of the patentee (or the patentee and the exclusive licensee in the case of a non-exclusive license granted by an exclusive licensee) is obtained, or when the transfer occurs as a result of general succession such as inheritance,[18] as with the case of the transfer of an exclusive license.

---

[16] Patent Law, Art. 73(3).
[17] Osaka District Court decision of December 20, 1984, *Mutaisaishu*, Vol. 16, No. 3, p. 803.
[18] Patent Law, Art. 94(1).

II   Utilization of patent right

Unlike the case with an exclusive license, there is no provision in the Patent Law with respect to a non-exclusive licensee's re-grant of the license (non-exclusive licensee's grant of the license to a third party within the granted scope). However, re-grant of the license is considered to be possible when the consent of the patentee is obtained.

(e)   Duty asserting by operation of law

As explained earlier, a non-exclusive license is established upon grant of such license and registration is not required for the establishment of the right. However, prior to an amendment of the Patent Law in 2011 which removed the registration requirement, non-exclusive licensees could not assert their license rights against a transferee of the patent right or a third party who was granted an exclusive license from the patentee unless the non-exclusive licensee registered their non-exclusive license. Therefore, non-exclusive licensees were subject to potential infringement claims for damages if they did not register their non-exclusive license. The 2011 Patent Law amendment to remove such requirement was done to make a non-exclusive license more straightforward and made a non-exclusive license effective against the parties who acquired the patent right after the grant of the non-exclusive license.[19] Therefore, a non-exclusive licensee is able to assert his/her non-exclusive license against a third party without registration (registration system of a non-exclusive license was abolished by the 2011 amendment).

(f)   Extinguishment of non-exclusive license

An exclusive license is extinguished in the case of lapse of the patent right (termination of the exclusive license is also included in the case of a non-exclusive license granted by an exclusive licensee), a non-exclusive license terminates due to expiration of the term set in the exclusive license agreement, termination of the agreement, waiver of the non-exclusive license or confusion of rights.[20]

(3)   Comparison between exclusive license and non-exclusive license

The following table shows a comparison between an exclusive license and a non-exclusive license.[21]

---

[19] Patent Law, Art. 99.
[20] Civil Code, Art. 179(2).

UNIT 6   Patent Law (5)

	Exclusive license	Non-exclusive license
Party having the right to grant license	Patentee	Patentee or exclusive licensee
Registration in the patent register	Required	Not required
Nature of license	Exclusive and monopolistic effect (effect *in rem*) · Right to exclusively work a patented invention within the scope provided in a license agreement · Right to demand an injunction and to claim damages upon a third party's unauthorized working of the patented invention	Non-exclusive and non-monopolistic effect (effect *in personam*) · Right to work a patented invention within the scope provided in a license agreement · No right to demand an injunction or to claim damages upon a third party's unauthorized working of the patented invention *A monopolistic non-exclusive licensee is considered to have an inherent right to claim damages, but not to have the right to demand an injunction.
Working by the patentee	Even the patentee is not allowed to work the patented invention within the scope for which the exclusive license is established.	The patentee may work the patented invention also within the scope for which the non-exclusive license is granted.
Grant of multiple licenses by the patentee	No other license can be granted within the scope for which the exclusive license is established.	Exclusive/non-exclusive license can be granted to a third party also within the scope for which the non-exclusive license is granted.

---

[21] "Exclusive License" is specifically provided for in the Patent Law in Japan. An exclusive license provides very strong rights to a licensee and requires registration. Thus, an exclusive license is not often used in patent license practice. On the other hand, there are many license agreements in the market which provide an "exclusive license" and that the governing law is Japanese law. Under these license agreements, typically, licensors intend to give a licensee "exclusivity" to work the patented invention for a specific region (e.g., Japan, Eastern Asia, etc.). Such exclusive license agreement may not constitute an "exclusive license" under the Patent Law in Japan, but, in many cases, may constitute a monopolistic non-exclusive license with specific restriction/covenants.

III Statutory license (hotei jisshiken)

4 Establishment of right of pledge

Since a patent right is a property right, it can be the subject of a pledge. A pledge may also be established on an exclusive license or a non-exclusive license with the consent of the patentee (with the consent of the patentee and the exclusive licensee in the case of a non-exclusive license on an exclusive license).[22] Since the exclusive license or the non-exclusive license will be transferred to a third party when the pledge is exercised, the consent of the patentee is required so as to avoid unexpected disadvantages for the patentee.

III Statutory license (*hotei jisshiken*)

A license, which is a right to work a patented invention, includes, besides the aforementioned licenses by agreement, those that are provided under the law irrespective of the intent of the patentee and based on the perspective of the necessity of the public interest or the fairness of the parties. This type of license is called a statutory license. A statutory license has no exclusivity and constitutes a non-exclusive license. The Patent Law provides the following types of statutory licenses: (1) non-exclusive license of an employer on an employee's invention;[23] (2) non-exclusive license based on prior use;[24] (3) non-exclusive license due to working of the invention prior to registration of transfer of the patent right;[25] (4) non-exclusive license due to working of the invention prior to registration of request for an invalidation trial;[26] (5) non-exclusive license after expiration of a design right;[27] and (6) non-exclusive license due to working of a patent prior to registration of a request for retrial.[28]

Statutory licenses can be divided into licenses which require no fees and licenses which require consideration; i. e., the licensee is obligated to pay a reasonable consideration to the patentee or to the exclusive licensee. Licenses (1) and (2) above are gratuitous, (3), (4) and (6) requires consideration, and (5) is gratuitous for a former

---

[22] Patent Law, Art. 77(4).
[23] Patent Law, Art. 35; Refer to Section 3, Part III of UNIT 4.
[24] Patent Law, Art. 79; Refer to Section 3, Part III of UNIT 7.
[25] Patent Law, Art. 79-2; Refer to Section 2(3), Part II of UNIT 4.
[26] Patent Law, Art. 80.
[27] Patent Law, Arts. 81 and 82.
[28] Patent Law, Art. 176.

UNIT 6   Patent Law (5)

patentee and requires consideration for a former licensee.

IV   Award granting non-exclusive license (*saitei jis-shiken*)

1   What is an award granting non-exclusive license?

"Award granting non-exclusive license" is a type of compulsory license in Japan. Besides the aforementioned statutory license, there is another license that is granted irrespective of the patentee's intent, which is an award granting a non-exclusive license. An award granting a non-exclusive license is established by an award, which is an administrative disposition by the relevant authorities for the necessity of the public interest. As with a statutory license, an award granting a non-exclusive license constitutes a non-exclusive license. The Patent Law provides the following three types of awards granting non-exclusive licenses: (1) award granting a non-exclusive license where the patented invention is not being worked;[29] (2) award granting a non-exclusive license where the working of a party's own patented invention involves using another party's patented invention;[30] and (3) award granting a non-exclusive license for the public interest.[31]

In all cases of awards granting a non-exclusive license, the parties are required to have failed to reach agreement through the voluntary consultation process (the "consultation first principle") before requesting an award granting a non-exclusive license.

2   Award granting non-exclusive license where patented invention is not worked

In the case where a patented invention has not been worked in Japan for a consecutive three years or longer, a request for an award granting a non-exclusive license can be filed with the Commissioner of the JPO. However, such request cannot be filed unless four years have lapsed from the filing date of the application of the patented invention even when the patented invention has not been worked for a consecutive three years.[32] Also, the request cannot be filed if the patented invention is currently worked

---

[29] Patent Law, Art. 83.
[30] Patent Law, Art. 92.
[31] Patent Law, Art. 93.

IV Award granting non-exclusive license (saitei jisshiken)

even when the invention had not been worked for a consecutive three years in the past. Since an award granting a non-exclusive license where a patented invention is not worked is part of a system to promote the working of inventions, it is not applied to currently worked patented inventions.

However, the Commissioner of the JPO cannot render an award of a non-exclusive license when there are reasonable grounds for the patentee to fail in properly working the patented invention.[33]

3 Award granting non-exclusive license where the working of one's patented invention involves using another party's patented invention

A request for an award granting a non-exclusive license may be filed with the Commissioner of the JPO where the working of one's patented invention involves using another party's patented invention that is based on an application filed prior to the application date of one's patented invention.[34] However, the Commissioner of the JPO cannot render an award granting a non-exclusive license when granting of such license would unreasonably damage the interests of the patentee.[35]

4 Award granting non-exclusive license for public interest

A request for an award granting a non-exclusive license may be filed with the Minister of Economy, Trade and Industry when the working of the patented invention is "particularly necessary for the public interest."[36] This award granting a non-exclusive license is different from where the patented invention has not been worked or where the working of one's patented invention involves using another party's patented invention as the request is made to the Minister of Economy, Trade and Industry for such award.

An example of where the working of the patented invention is "particularly necessary for the public interest" is when there is an outbreak of a new type of flu virus and there is a patented invention for a specific remedy for the new type of flu virus, and the death rate from such flu virus can be notably reduced by working the patented

---

[32] Patent Law, Art. 83.
[33] Patent Law, Art. 85(2).
[34] Patent Law, Art. 92(3).
[35] Patent Law, Art. 5.
[36] Patent Law, Art. 93(2).

UNIT 6　Patent Law (5)

invention.

UNIT 7
Patent Law (6)

• **Patent disputes**

I   Overview

A patentee has an exclusive right to work a patented invention in the course of business.[1] The objective scope of a patent right is called the technical scope of a patented invention. When a third party makes, uses, assigns, etc., a product or process in the course of business and such product or process falls within the technical scope of a patented invention, the result is a patent right infringement.

A unique attribute of patent infringement is that there can be patent infringement even when a third party independently creates and works an invention which is same as a patented invention. "In the course of business" in the above paragraph means that the private working of an invention and the domestic use of an invention at one's residence would be excluded. Irrespective of whether an act is for commercial or non-commercial purposes, any acts which are not the private working of an invention or the use at home would potentially fall under working an invention "in the course of business."

Patent right infringement includes literal infringement and infringement under the doctrine of equivalents (equivalent infringement).

In addition, Article 101 of the Patent Law specifies that a certain act is assumed to be an infringement even though the act may not fall within the technical scope of the patented invention – i.e., an indirect infringement. Preliminary acts that are highly likely to cause a literal infringement or an equivalent infringement (which are direct infringements as opposed to indirect infringements) are deemed an infringement, which intends to secure the effectiveness of patent protection.

A patentee may seek an injunction,[2] damages[3] and other remedies with respect to a patent right infringement. An injunction may not require the infringer's intent or

---

[1] Patent Law, Art. 68; the "working" of an invention is defined in Patent Law Art. 2(3).
[2] Patent Law, Art. 100.
[3] Civil Code, Art. 709.

UNIT 7   Patent Law (6)

negligence to obtain, but compensation for damages would require the infringer's intent or negligence (note, however, that Article 103 presumes an infringers' negligence). Therefore, alleged infringers must prove their absence of negligence to be exempt from liability for damages.

An alleged infringer can provide the following defenses against a claim of infringement by the patentee: (1) limitations on the effect of a patent right,[4] (2) prior use right,[5] (3) invalidiy defense,[6] and (4) exhaustion of a patent right, etc. If any of these defenses is accepted by the court, the alleged infringer will be exempt from any liability for the infringement.

Ⅱ   Patent right infringement

1   Literal infringement

Article 70(1) specifies that the technical scope of a patented invention "shall be determined based upon the statements of the claims attached to the application form". The claims shall state "all matters necessary to specify the invention for which the applicant requests the grant of a patent,"[7] which set out to make the scope of the patent right known to the public. Therefore, it is natural that the technical scope of a patented invention is determined on the basis of the statements of the claims. However, a claim expresses an invention (i.e., a creation of a technical idea) in words and letters, and the language stated in claims is often open to interpretation. Therefore, the interpretation of the language stated in the claims (claim interpretation) is important to determine the technical scope of the patented invention.

A patent right infringement is established when an alleged infringer's product or process ("Alleged Infringing Product") falls within the technical scope of the patented invention, which is determined based upon the statement of the claims. The infringement, in this case, is called literal infringement.

The establishment of a literal infringement is determined by the following processes: (1) the claim is divided into technical elements (constituent features of the

---

[4] Patent Law, Art. 69.
[5] Patent Law, Art. 79.
[6] Patent Law, Art. 104-3.
[7] Patent Law, Art. 36(5); Refer to Section 3, Part Ⅱ of UNIT 5.

Ⅱ Patent right infringement

patented invention), (2) the features of the Alleged Infringing Product are also separated, and (3) the constituent features of the patented invention are compared with the corresponding features of the Alleged Infringing Product. The Alleged Infringing Product is construed to fall within the technical scope of the patented invention when it fulfills all of the constituent features of the patented invention, upon which a literal infringement will be found.

2 Doctrine of equivalents

As previously mentioned, the claims are to clarify the scope of the patent right to the public. Therefore, if the protection of a patent right is acknowledged beyond the claims, a third party would suffer unexpected disadvantages. However, undue attention to the language of the claims can impair the protection of the patent right in a practical sense. Therefore, there is a notion that a third party's product, which has partially different features but is overall identical or equivalent to the feature of the claims, would conflict with the patent right. This notion is referred to as the doctrine of equivalents. The Supreme Court noted the following five requirements for application of the doctrine of equivalents in the Ball Spline case.[8]

(1) The different feature is not an essential feature of the patented invention,

(2) The objective of the patented invention can be achieved and the same beneficial effect can be obtained even if the different feature is replaced by the Alleged Infringing Product,

(3) A person skilled in the art could have easily imagined the convertibility of the different feature of the Alleged Infringing Product at the time of their manufacturing, etc., of the Alleged Infringing Product,

(4) The Alleged Infringing Product is not identical to the publicly known art or is not easily conceivable from said publicly known art by the person skilled in the art at the time of their filing, and

(5) There are no particular circumstances, for example, that the Alleged Infringing Product is intentionally excluded from the claims in the filing procedure of the patented invention.

The "essential feature" of the patented invention in requirement (1) is the

---

[8] Supreme Court decision of February 24, 1998, *Minshu*, Vol. 52, No. 1, p. 113.

UNIT 7　Patent Law (6)

characterizing portion of the claims of the patented invention that constitutes a unique technical idea not present in conventional art. Whether this requirement is met is determined based on whether the Alleged Infringing Product also possesses the essential feature of the patented invention. If the Alleged Infringing Product possesses the essential feature, the different feature should not be regarded as an essential feature.[9] Requirement (2) requires the Alleged Infringing Products to share the same effect with the patented invention. Requirement (3) refers to easiness of convertibility of the different feature. For requirement (3), the determination is made on the basis of the timing of manufacturing, etc., of the Alleged Infringing Product while for requirement (4), the determination is made on the basis of the timing of filing of the application of the patented invention. Requirement (4) is based on the idea that a technique, which was publicly known at the time of filing of the patented invention or could have easily been conceived of from publicly known art, is a technique for which not anyone could be granted a patent and such technique cannot fall within the technical scope of the patented invention.[10] Requirement (5) is based on the notion that it is unjust under the doctrine of estoppel that the patentee seeks protection from inventions which were already intentionally excluded from the scope of the claims in the filing procedure, e.g., an invention removed from the claims by decreasing the scope of the invention through the application procedure.

According to the above court decision, when the above five requirements are satisfied, the Alleged Infringing Product is regarded as equivalent to the feature stated in the claim and falls within the technical scope of the patented invention.

3　Indirect infringement

(1)　Overview

The working of only a part of a constituent feature of the patented invention does not constitute a direct infringement in the strict sense. However, when an infringement arises by the working of such portion, the effectiveness of patent protection can be impaired unless a proper action is taken against such partial working. An example is the act of manufacturing and selling a component that is used only for making of a product where the patented invention is a product invention. Thus, preliminary acts that are highly likely to cause a certain infringement are regarded as infringement acts in accordance with

---

[9] Intellectual Property High Court decision of March 25, 2016, *Hanrei Jiho*, No. 2306, p. 87.
[10] *See* Patent Law, Arts. 29(1), (2); Refer to Parts Ⅲ and Ⅳ of UNIT 3.

II Patent right infringement

Article 101. This is indirect infringement.

Indirect infringement specified in each item of Article 101 is classified into the following three types: (1) indirect infringement related to exclusive goods ((ⅰ) and (ⅳ)), (2) indirect infringement related to multi-functional goods ((ⅱ) and (ⅴ)), and (3) indirect infringement to promote proliferating counterfeit products ((ⅲ) and (ⅵ)).

(2) Indirect infringement related to exclusive goods

Indirect infringement related to exclusive goods occurs by an act of making or assigning, in the course of business, an exclusive good that is "a product used only for making of the product" where a patent has been granted for an invention of a product or is "a product used only for use of a process" where a patent has been granted for an invention of a process.[11] For the purpose of this type of infringement, a patent infringement is found if the Alleged Infringing Product has no other commercial or economical use other than implementing the patented product/process

(3) Indirect infringement related to multi-functional goods

Indirect infringement related to multi-functional goods requires the following: (1)a product is indispensable to resolve a certain issue that is solved by the patented invention, (2) which product is not a general-purpose good (those widely distributed within Japan), and (3) the subjective requirement of knowing that the invention is a patented invention and that the product is used for the working of the invention.

A general-purpose good is typically a general product which is widely distributed in Japan, such as screws, nails, bulbs, and transistors. Specifically, general-purpose goods are understood to indicate standard goods or popular goods that are not custom-made goods but can be used for other usages and are generally available in market.[12]

Indirect infringement related to multi-functional goods was newly introduced by the revision of the Patent Law in 2002. The revision was to respond to the situation where a great number of multi-functional (i.e., multi-purpose) products had emerged in the market and the indirect infringement related to exclusive goods did not properly control the situation. Given that such multi-functional products can be used to infringe on existing patented inventions, the new revision provides that the making or assignment of

---

[11] The word "only" used herein does not have the strict meaning that there are no permissible uses except for the working of the patented invention, but indicates that there are no other commercially and economically practical uses.

[12] Intellectual Property High Court decision of September 30, 2005, *Hanrei Jiho*, No. 1904, p. 47.

UNIT 7   Patent Law (6)

multifunctional products which are "indispensable (rather than "only for" as in the case of exclusive goods) to resolve a certain issue to be solved by the patented invention" would constitute infringement of such patented invention. This revision, however, requires subjective requirements mentioned above (i.e., knowledge of the patented invention and usage of the products in issue).

(4)   Indirect infringement to promote proliferation of counterfeit products

Indirect infringement to promote proliferation of counterfeit products was created to prevent the international proliferation of counterfeit products. This type of indirect infringement occurs by the act of possessing the product (where a patent has been granted for a product invention) or the product produced by the process (where a patent has been granted for an invention of a process to produce the product) for the purpose of selling or exporting the product in the course of business. The actual act of selling or exporting "the product" or "the product produced by the process" in the course of business would constitute a direct infringement.[13] Indirect infringement to promote proliferation of counterfeit products regards the possession, which is a preliminary stage, as an infringement.

Ⅲ   Defense against a claim of infringement

1   Overview

If a defense against the patentee's infringement claim is accepted by the court, the alleged infringer will be exempt from liability for infringement and will not be required to discontinue manufacturing and selling a product or pay any damages. There are various types of defenses, such as (1) limitations on the effect of a patent right, (2) prior use right, (3) invalidity defense, and (4) exhaustion of a patent right.

2   Limitations on the effect of a patent right

(1)   Overview

In the Patent Law, an invention is protected by a patent. However, in some cases, industrial/economic development, which is the ultimate objective of the Patent law, can be impaired unless the effect of a patent right is limited. Thus, Article 69 provides

---

[13] *See* Patent Law, Arts. 2(3)(ⅰ) and (ⅲ).

Ⅲ   Defense against a claim of infringement

limitations on the effect of a patent right with respect to particular products or acts. Article 69 specifies that a patent right is not effective against (1) the working of the patented invention for experimental or research purposes,[14] (2) transportation related inventions which merely pass through Japan,[15] (3) products existing in Japan prior to the filing of the application,[16] and (4) the act of preparing a medicine as is written in a prescription from a physician or a dentist.[17]

(2)   Working for experimental or research purposes

A patent right is not effective against the working of the patented invention for experimental or research purposes.[18] Generally, working for experimental or research purposes has no considerable effect on the interests of a patentee. On the other hand, it would be difficult to create any new inventions if a patent right is effective against experiments or research for improvement and development of another person's patented invention.

For limitations on the effect of a patent right, the experiments or research must be directed to the patented invention itself. The effect of a patent right is not limited with respect to the working of a patented invention for experimental or research purposes that are directed to a technique other than the patented invention. If otherwise, a patent right would not be effective against the working of an invention of an experimental apparatus or equipment, and granting a patent right for such an invention would be meaningless.[19]

(3)   Transportation related inventions which merely passes through Japan

A patent right is not effective against transportation related inventions such as vessels or aircraft which merely pass through Japan, or machines, apparatuses, equipment or other products used for such transportation.[20] Such transportation leaves Japan in a short time. Therefore, the working of a patented invention that constitutes an infringement would provide little disadvantage to the patentee. On the contrary, if the patent right is effective against such transportation and the use of such transportation is prohibited, international traffic would be negatively impacted, and therefore, this limitation of a patent right exists to curb such effect.

---

[14] Patent Law, Art. 69(1).
[15] Patent Law, Art. 69(2)(ⅰ).
[16] Patent Law, Art. 69(2)(ⅱ).
[17] Patent Law, Art. 69(3).
[18] Patent Law, Art. 69(1).

99

UNIT 7   Patent Law (6)

(4)   Products existing in Japan prior to the filing of the application

A patent right is not effective against products existing in Japan prior to the filing of the application.[21] Clearly, it is unjustifiable that a patent right would be effective against products which already existed at the time of the filing of the application. Those products which existed after the filing of the application are subject to a patent right. If the product is destroyed but later reproduced, the reproduced product is subject to the effect of a patent right.

(5)   Act of preparing medicine as is written in a prescription from a physician or a dentist

A patent right for an invention of a pharmaceutical product to be manufactured by mixing two or more medicines or for an invention of a process of manufacturing a medicine by mixing two or more medicines is not effective against the act of preparing medicine as is written in a prescription from a physician or a dentist and the medicine itself as prepared pursuant to a prescription from a physician or a dentist.[22] This limitation of a patent right is intended to prevent medicine-related patent rights from interfering with medical treatment.

3   Prior use right

The act of working another person's patented invention could be deemed an infringement even if the worked invention is not an imitation of the patented invention and is created independently. However, when such working of an invention inevitably constitutes an infringement and the working is prohibited, it can be inequitable for the party that works the invention because of the waste of money spent and equipment used

---

[19] Supreme Court decision of April 16, 1999, *Minshu* Vol. 53, No. 4, p. 627 involved a case where a person had a patent right for a chemical substance and a drug containing such chemical substance as an active constituent. The court determined that a third party's act, for the purpose of manufacturing and selling a drug (generic drug) where the active constituent is the same as that of the drug according to the patented invention after the term of the patent right, which produced a chemical substance or drug that fell within the technical scope of the patented invention and carried out an experiment to acquire information to be attached to an application form using said chemical substance or the drug during the term of the patent right (in order to file an application for approval required for manufacturing under pharmaceutical regulations required for its manufacturing) would fall under the "working of the patented invention for experimental or research purposes" as set forth in Article 69(1).

[20] Patent Law, Art. 69(2)(i).

[21] Patent Law, Art. 69(2)(ii).

[22] Patent Law, Art. 69(3).

Ⅲ   Defense against a claim of infringement

to work the invention.

Therefore, Article 79 specifies a prior use-based non-exclusive license (i.e., a prior use right). A prior use right is obtained if the following requirements are met:

(1)   The invention is made by a person whose invention is identical to the patented invention without knowledge of the contents of the claims in the application of the patented invention, or the person learns about the invention from a person who made an invention identical to the patented invention without knowledge of the contents of claims in the application of the patented invention; and

(2)   There is a business or preparation for a business involving the invention which is conducted in Japan at the time of the filing of the patent application for the patented invention.

When the above requirements are met, a prior use right is obtained to the extent of the invention that is worked and the purpose of the business that such invention is used.

4   Invalidity defense

(1)   What is an invalidity defense?

When a trial decision for invalidation becomes final,[23] the patent right shall be deemed to have never existed from the outset.[24] Previously, when a patent right involved a reason for invalidation, the effect of the patent right would not be invalidated until a trial decision for invalidation became final. A court examining a lawsuit for patent right infringement used to be deemed not entitled to determine whether the patent right involved a reason for invalidation.

This situation was drastically changed by the Supreme Court decision in the Kilby Case of 2000.[25] The Supreme Court ruled as follows: "It should be construed that, even before a trial decision for patent invalidation becomes final, a court examining a lawsuit for patent right infringement is entitled to determine whether it is clear that there is a reason for invalidation of the patent, and when it is clear that the patent involves a reason for invalidation as a result of the court examination, any claims for an injunction, damages, or the like based on [enforcement] of the patent right would constitute an abuse of rights and

---

[23] Patent Law, Art. 123; Refer to Section 3, Part Ⅳ of UNIT 5.
[24] Patent Law, Art. 125.
[25] Supreme Court decision of April 11, 2000, *Minshu*, Vol. 54, No. 4, p. 1368.

UNIT 7   Patent Law (6)

would not be accepted unless there are special circumstances."

The aforementioned Supreme Court decision was constructively transformed into law, and Article 104-3 was newly established by the revision of the Patent Law in 2004. Article 104-3 (1) stipulates, "Where, in lawsuits concerning the infringement of a patent right or an exclusive license, a patent is recognized as one that should be invalidated by a trial for invalidating a patent or the registration of an extension of duration is recognized as one that should be invalidated by a trial for invalidating a registration of extension, the rights of the patentee or exclusive licensee may not be exercised against the adverse party." The defense set forth by this Article is called the "invalidity defense."

Even a person who makes or uses the Alleged Infringing Product that falls within the technical scope of the patented invention of another person is exempted from liability for infringement by asserting and proving the invalidity defense when the patent right is recognized as involving a reason for invalidation. Even when an invalidity defense is accepted on the ground that the patent right involves a reason for invalidation in an infringement litigation, the decision of invalidation is only effective between the parties or in the case in question. Thus, a court examining a different infringement litigation at trial does not have to follow such precedent and is entitled to rule otherwise (although in reality this would hardly be the case).

(2) Counterargument by correction

Even when a patent right involves a reason for invalidation, the patentee may eliminate the reason for invalidation in a trial for correction[26] or by filing a request for correction in a trial for invalidation.[27] Similarly, when an invalidity defense is claimed in an infringement action, the patentee may deny or overturn the invalidity defense, e.g., by arguing that the reason for invalidation will be eliminated by correction. Such an argument is called a "counterargument by correction."

The requirements for a counterargument by correction are as follows: (1) the request for trial for correction or the request for correction in a trial for invalidation has commenced legitimately; (2) the reason for invalidation that the alleged infringer argues can be eliminated by such a correction; and (3) the Alleged Infringing Product falls within the technical scope of the corrected patented invention. The issue here is, when a request

---

[26] Patent Law, Art. 126; Refer to Section 4, Part Ⅳ of UNIT 5.

[27] Patent Law, Art. 134-2.

Ⅲ　Defense against a claim of infringement

for trial for correction or a request for correction in a trial for invalidation is filed, whether the reason for invalidation can be eliminated in the future by a requested correction. However, even when the reason for invalidation is determined to be eliminated, a counterargument by correction is not affirmed when the Alleged Infringing Product does not fall within the technical scope of the patented invention after the correction.

5　Exhaustion of patent right

(1)　Doctrine of exhaustion

A patentee has the exclusive right to work the patented invention. Therefore, when the Patent Law is applied formally, the act of using or selling, without consent of the patentee, the product according to the patented invention sold by the patentee constitutes an infringement.[28] However, adopting such a conclusion leads to the unjust result that the efficient distribution of the relevant product may be impaired because a bona fide purchaser could be an "infringer," and the patentee may enjoy undue profits. Thus, to prevent such result, the doctrine of exhaustion was established.

The Supreme Court adopted the doctrine of exhaustion stating as follows: "It should be understood that, when a patentee or a licensee who has been granted a license from the patentee sells the patented product in Japan, the patent right of the patented product is exhausted as its objective is deemed to have been achieved, the patent right is no longer effective against use, sale, etc., of the patented product, and the patentee is not allowed to exercise the patent right over the patented product."[29]

The "working of an invention" of a product means the act of making, using, selling, etc., exporting or importing, or offering for selling, etc., of the product.[30] All of these acts, except for making, are subject to exhaustion.

The effect of exhaustion arises when the patentee/licensee sells the patented product, and this effect cannot be prohibited by an agreement between parties. For example, if an agreement between the patentee/licensee and the customer states that resale is prohibited, but the customer resells the patented product in violation of the agreement, there will be a breach of contract by the customer. However, the customer's

---

[28] Patent Law, Arts. 2(3) and 68.
[29] Supreme Court decision of November 8, 2007, *Minshu*, Vol. 61, No. 8, p. 2989; Supreme Court decision of July 1, 1997, *Minshu*, Vol. 51, No. 6, p. 2299.
[30] Patent Law, Art. 2(3)(ⅰ).

UNIT 7   Patent Law (6)

act of resale and the subsequent use, resale, etc., by the subsequent purchaser would not infringe the patent right because such right had been exhausted.

(2)   When a patented product is assigned in a foreign country

The aforementioned section applies where a patented product is distributed in Japan. When a patentee sells a patented product in a foreign country, is it a patent infringement to import and resell the patented product in Japan? The issue is whether the doctrine of exhaustion is applied to international distribution; i.e., whether the patent right of a product in Japan is exhausted when the patentee distributes the patented product in a foreign market.

The Supreme Court has dismissed the doctrine of international exhaustion, because the patentee in Japan does not necessarily have a patent right (equivalent patent right) for the same invention in a country where the patented product was sold, and even if the patentee has an equivalent patent right in the other country, the Japanese patent right and foreign equivalent patent right are different, and thus such patentee is entitled to claim against the infringement of both patent rights.[31]

However, since international economic transactions have increased and developed in today's modern economy, the Supreme Court has decided that when a patentee in Japan or its equivalent party has sold a patented product in a foreign country, the patentee is not entitled to exercise its patent right in Japan over the product against its purchasers unless there is an agreement with them that Japan is excluded from the areas of selling and using of the product, or against its repurchasers unless there is an aforementioned agreement and clear indication of this exclusion for products subsequently resold to other purchasers. Therefore, the patentee can exercise the patent right against the importing and selling of the patented product in Japan based on the aforementioned agreement and indication, but cannot exercise it without such agreement and indication.

---

[31] Supreme Court decision of July 1, 1997, *Minshu*, Vol. 51, No. 6, p. 2299.

UNIT 8 Copyright Law (1)

● Copyrightability

I Copyrightability
1 What is copyrightable?
(1) Overview

The act of using other person's literary works and/or photographic works without permission would be considered a typical copyright infringement. This concept appears to be broadly recognized.

In fact, however, the unauthorized use of another person's literary works or photographic works cannot be immediately determined to be a copyright infringement, since several requirements must be satisfied in order for the act to be recognized as a copyright infringement. This unit will review what is "copyrightable," which is one of the requirements for copyright infringement.

(2) Original works as subject matters for protection by Copyright Law

The purpose of the Copyright Law is to ensure protection for the rights of authors, and to contribute to the development of culture.[1] The subject matter for the rights under the Copyright Law is an original work. A person who creates an original work is an "author,"[2] and the rights provided to the author are the copyright and a moral right of an author.[3]

Being an original work is primarily required to receive protection under the Copyright Law, and whether a work should be protected by the Copyright Law is determined by examining whether the work is an original work. A work determined not to be an original work is not protected under the Copyright Law, and a copyright infringement will not occur regarding such work.

The Copyright Law defines an original work as "a work in which thoughts or

---
[1] Copyright Law, Art. 1.
[2] Copyright Law, Art. 2(1)(ii).
[3] Copyright Law, Art. 17(1).

UNIT 8   Copyright Law (1)

sentiments are originally expressed and which falls within the literary, academic, artistic or musical domain."[4] According to the definition, the following four requirements must be satisfied in order for a work to be regarded as an original work:

(1)   be related to thoughts or sentiments;

(2)   be expressed;

(3)   be original (having "creativity"); and

(4)   fall within the literary, academic, artistic or musical domain.

In the following section, the above requirements are reviewed separately.

2   Thoughts or sentiments

(1)   Elements

In order for a work to be regarded as an original work, "thoughts or sentiments" must be expressed. Although the description "thoughts or sentiments" may infer that an original work must be sophisticated, an original work does not need to be understood in such a restrictive way since the copyrightability is determined based on all of the above four requirements including this requirement and a purpose of this requirement is to distinguish a work from a natural object or (historical) facts. Further, as creativity can be evaluated in the requirements of "expression" or "originality" it is sufficient if any thoughts or sentiments of an author are just expressed in a work; i.e., if a work can be regarded as a result of the creative activities of individuals.

(2)   Examples of not being copyrightable

Since an original work must be a work in which "thoughts or sentiments" are expressed, a work not involving the originality of individuals is not regarded as an original work. For example, objects such as beautiful stones and giant trees, which can be aesthetically appreciated, are not regarded as original works since they are natural objects and are not works in which thoughts or sentiments of individuals are expressed.

In addition, facts such as historical facts and experimental data do not involve the thoughts or sentiments of individuals, and cannot be regarded as original works. Even if a party expended great costs and efforts to find the facts, the facts themselves would not be treated as original works. Thus, literary works made to merely convey the facts cannot be treated as original works. The copyrightability of facts should also be denied since facts

---

[4] Copyright Law, Art. 2(1)(i).

I   Copyrightability

should be freely accessible by everyone.

However, if an individual expresses/conveys a fact by performing creative activities, the resulting text, for example, could be regarded as an original work. For example, an ordinary newspaper article is not intended to merely convey a fact as it is; a newspaper article is composed of information such as the background and progress of the facts, which can be regarded as being made by performing creative activities to intelligibly convey the fact to readers. Thus, the newspaper article can be evaluated as a work in which "thoughts or sentiments" are expressed.

3   Expression

The second requirement for copyrightability is that a thought or sentiment is "expressed." An expression is a state in which other people can recognize a thought or sentiment. No matter how remarkable a thought or sentiment may be, if it is not expressed, it is not being conveyed to other people, and will therefore, not contribute to cultural development. The present requirement is provided for this reason. However, the thoughts or sentiments are not required to be fixed into a material object. When improvised music is played, for example, and where ad-lib melodies are simply played without being recorded, the audience can listen to the melodies. Thus, the improvised music would be regarded as a work in which thoughts or sentiments are expressed. Of course, if a work in which thoughts or sentiments are expressed is not fixed into a material object, it will sometimes be difficult for the author to prove that the work is his/her own original work if there is a subsequent dispute over his/her work. However, this would only be a matter of proof, and the work as such would still be deemed to be a work in which thoughts or sentiments are "expressed," which would satisfy the requirement for copyrightability.

With the expression requirement, it is clear that the Copyright Law does not provide copyright protection for an idea itself. For example, in a mystery novel there is a locked-room trick which by itself is merely an idea. However, the expression of the idea is the text which describes the situation in which a character of the novel commits a crime using the trick. Therefore, even if another novelist used the same locked-room trick, but expressed the act in completely different writing, such expression would not be considered to cause any Copyright Law issues. This is because the act of the novelist is merely the "stealing" of the idea of the locked-room trick.

107

UNIT 8   Copyright Law (1)

4   Originality

(1)   Elements

The third requirement for copyrightability is having "originality." In order for a work to be an original work, thoughts or sentiments must be "originally" expressed. Many theories and precedents state that a work in which any individuality of an author is expressed can be regarded as having originality, and originality is often loosely interpreted. This is because strictly interpreting originality is of minimal significance since the existence of various and diverse expressed works is important in promoting cultural development which is one of the goals of the Copyright Law; and it is not exceptional that the value and evaluation of an expressed work will greatly change with the times. In addition, originality should be reasonably accepted if any individuality of an author is expressed, and when rights are exercised, the scope of rights to be protected should be appropriately restricted.

(2)   Examples of not being copyrightable

Although the requirement for originality is loosely interpreted, there are situations where originality will be denied and the work will not be copyrightable.

First, it is clear that a simple imitation of a pre-existing work (i.e., a slavish imitation) does not have originality since the individuality of the imitator is not expressed. The same applies to a precisely-made replica.[5] In addition, a photograph of a two-dimensional work such as a painting or a photograph (i.e., a photograph of a photograph) cannot be regarded as a work in which the individuality of the photographer is expressed, and the originality of the photograph will also be denied.

Second, originality of a work expressed by "common expressions" is also denied. "Common expressions" mean expressions which are unambiguous or are limited in the manner in which the expressions are made due to the purpose or nature of the expressions, where anyone could make the same or similar expressions. For example, a court held that, where a magazine is suspended or discontinued, it is natural for the message to the readers to contain an announcement that the magazine will be suspended or discontinued, a statement of thanks and apologies to the readers, an expression of sentiments that the suspension or discontinuation of the magazine is regrettable, etc. Therefore, a message merely describing the above contents in common expressions

---

[5] If it is not a slavish imitation but an imitation to which an original expression of the imitator has been added, the imitation can be accepted as a derivative original work of the imitator in some cases (Refer to Section 1, Part Ⅲ of UNIT 8).

II   Types of works

cannot be determined to have originality as an original work.[6]

5   Falling within the literary, academic, artistic or musical domain

The fourth requirement for copyrightability is that a work in which thoughts or sentiments are expressed falls within "the literary, academic, artistic or musical domain." The above requirement is not intended to clarify that a work belongs to a particular literary, academic, artistic or musical domain, but that the work must be the one obtained by intellectual and cultural mental activities.

The Copyright Law has the purpose of protecting cultural activities among the creative activities of individuals. The fourth requirement has significance in excluding practical and industrial activities from subject matters for protection by the Copyright Law, and in distinguishing the Copyright Law from the Patent Law, the Utility Model Law, and the Design Law. For example, the design of a single-lens reflex camera is very original in that the camera is easy to grip, the shutter button is easy to press, and an excellent balance is achieved when a lens is attached. However, since the above are regarded as constituting a practical or industrial creation, the design itself is construed not to be a subject matter for protection by the Copyright Law.

II   Types of works

1   Overview

In the above sections, an original work as a subject matter for protection by the Copyright Law has been explained mainly based on the requirements for copyrightability. However, the specific meaning of "an original work" still remains abstract. Since being an original work is a primary requirement for receiving protection under the Copyright Law as described above, the description of an original work should be explained more specifically. The Copyright Law does not only define an original work under Article 2(1)(i), but also illustrates specific examples (types) of the original works in the items of Article 10(1).[7]

The specific examples of original works are: novels, scenarios, articles, lectures,

---

[6] Tokyo District Court decision of December 18, 1995, *Chitekisaishu*, Vol. 27, No. 4, p. 787.
[7] Works illustrated in Art. 10(1) of the Copyright Law are clear examples of original works, and copyrightability can also be accepted for works which are not described therein.

and other literary works;[8] musical works;[9] choreographic and pantomimic works;[10] paintings, woodblock prints, sculptures, and other artistic works;[11] architectural works;[12] maps and other diagrammatic works of an academic nature, such as plans, charts, and models;[13] cinematographic works;[14] photographic works;[15] and computer programs.[16]

The following section describes the original works in the items of Article 10(1) of the Copyright Law. The literary and photographic works will be reviewed first, and the other original works will be subsequently explained briefly. Derivative works, compilations, and database works which are based on pre-existing works will be reviewed in chapter Ⅲ.

2 Literary works

Literary works mean works expressed by a linguistic system, such as novels, scenarios, articles, and lectures.[17] A work, which is expressed by a linguistic system, is not required to be written in a document, etc.

The scope of literary works is very broad and also includes those works expressed in short sentences such as a *tanka* (thirty-one syllabled verse) and a *haiku* (seventeen-syllabled verse), and copyrightability is frequently denied in cases of book titles, catchphrases, mottos, and slogans. However, the copyrightability of titles and mottos is denied not because they are titles or mottos. Instead, the requirement for originality is frequently denied since titles or mottos ordinarily use simple facts or common expressions; for example, "Patent Law" and "Midnight express" (in book titles), and "Don't drive if you drink, and don't drink if you drive" (in mottos).

3 Photographic works

Photographic works mean works in which an object such as a person or a

---

[8] Copyright Law, Art. 10(1)(i)
[9] Copyright Law, Art. 10(1)(ii)
[10] Copyright Law, Art. 10(1)(iii)
[11] Copyright Law, Art. 10(1)(iv)
[12] Copyright Law, Art. 10(1)(v)
[13] Copyright Law, Art. 10(1)(vi)
[14] Copyright Law, Art. 10(1)(vii)
[15] Copyright Law, Art. 10(1)(viii)
[16] Copyright Law, Art. 10(1)(ix)
[17] Programs expressed by a programming language are not included in the definition of literary works since the Copyright Law separately stipulates "original works of computer programs" in Art. 10(1)(ix).

II Types of works

landscape is expressed as an image on a film or similar medium with a camera. Digital images taken with a digital camera are also to be included in photographic works.

The creation of photographs greatly depends on equipment such as cameras and lenses. During photography, however, the individuality of a photographer is exhibited in a variety of factors such as the selection of the: object; time of taking the photo; lens; photographic composition; exposure settings; lighting; photo opportunity; etc., and based on these factors, the originality is expressed in the photographs. Thus, copyrightability of photographs is broadly accepted. However, with respect to photographs such as ID photos taken by a completely-automated photography process, the copyrightability of the photographs will be denied since the photographs cannot be regarded as expressing the individuality of a photographer. Copyrightability of a photograph in which a painting, etc., was authentically photographed is also denied as described above. A photograph of a painting is not copyrightable because the requirement for originality is not satisfied since the individuality of the photographer is not expressed on the photograph. Even if a sophisticated technique is required to take an authentic photograph of an object, such a technique would not be considered a subject matter for protection by the Copyright Law.

4 Musical works

Musical works mean works expressed by using sounds. Since the expression is not required to be recorded, improvised music is also included in musical works. Music with lyrics is also regarded as a musical work. Even if the lyrics are made in accordance with the music, the lyrics would also be independent literary works, and even if the music is composed in accordance with the lyrics, the music itself would also be an independent musical work.

5 Choreographic and pantomimic works

Choreographic and pantomimic works mean works expressed by gestures and actions. Examples are dances and pantomimes. A distinguishing fact is that the subject matter for protection is not the acting which corresponds to the performance of dances or pantomimes, but is the form on which the acting is based. The acting itself is regarded as a "performance"[18] and is protected by the neighboring rights.[19]

---

[18] Copyright Law, Art. 2(1)(ⅲ).
[19] Copyright Law, Chapter Ⅳ.

UNIT 8   Copyright Law (1)

The basic steps of waltzes, the basic motions such as the running man and waves of hip-hop dances, or such combinations, contain no originality and are regarded as common expressions, and therefore, such motions would not be considered original works.

6   Artistic works

Artistic works mean works expressed by shapes or colors such as paintings, engravings, and sculptures. For artistic works, exhibition rights[20] as derivative rights[21] which are not applied to the other works are established. A comic book (*manga*) is an artistic work in terms of shapes and colors, but since it is composed of words in addition to shapes and colors, it also has the aspect of a literary work.

Among the arts, those solely for aesthetic appreciation are referred to as "fine arts," and it is evident that works of fine arts are protected as artistic works. The Copyright Law defines artistic works to also include works of artistic craftsmanship.[22] A work of artistic craftsmanship is a work such as a jar or a ceramic tea cup being used for practical applications, and is only one example of handcraft arts which can be an object of aesthetic appreciation.

In contrast, arts which are applied to mass-produced utility articles are referred to as "applied arts," which can be protected by the Design Law,[23] and have not been protected by the Copyright Law in principle. However, certain works of applied arts which have an aesthetic appreciation feature similar to that of works of fine arts can be considered an exception and included in the category of artistic works.[24]

Recently, there have been many objections raised against the determination of copyrightability of a work of applied arts being made on the basis of criteria different from those applied to other original works, such as whether the aesthetic appreciation feature of the work is strong or weak, etc. It has been strongly asserted that a work of applied arts, which satisfies the requirements for copyrightability set forth under Article 2(1)(i) of the Copyright Law, should be interpreted to receive protection as "an artistic work" under the Copyright Law; and the originality of applied arts should also be determined by specifically

---

[20] Copyright Law, Art. 25.

[21] Refer to Part I of UNIT 10.

[22] Copyright Law, Art. 2(2).

[23] Refer to UNIT 13.

[24] Osaka High Court decision of July 28, 2005, *Hanrei Jiho*, No. 1928, p. 116.

II   Types of works

examining each work in respect of whether the individuality of the creator is exhibited.[25]

7   Architectural works

Architectural works mean works expressed as an architectural work, exemplified by a palace and a triumphal arch.

Since the Copyright Law does not define what the "architecture" means, whether gardens etc., are also included has been disputed. A precedent determined that a building, a garden adjacent to the building, and sculptures in the garden as a whole constitute an architectural work.[26]

8   Diagrammatical works

Diagrammatical works mean maps or works expressed by plans, charts, models, etc., of an academic nature. The maps are those in which topography is graphically expressed and simultaneously symbols are described therein. The plans, charts, and models are exemplified by design drawings, graphs, schemes, terrestrial globes, and manikins.

The copyright of a design drawing extends to the act of reproducing or adapting the design drawing as a plan, but does not extend to the act of producing an object based on the design drawing. With respect to a design drawing of an architecture, however, the architecture which was built in accordance with the design drawing is regarded as a reproduction of "an architectural work."[27]

9   Cinematographic works

The Copyright Law does not define what a cinematographic work means, but a cinematographic work is interpreted to be a work originally expressed by a sequence of images which are fixed into a physical object. The fixation into a physical object means a state in which an original work exists while maintaining its identity by combining with a physical object by a given method, and simultaneously can be reproduced.

The Copyright Law also stipulates that a cinematographic work includes a work

---

[25] Intellectual Property High Court decision of April 14, 2015, *Hanrei Jiho,* No. 2267, p. 91.

[26] Tokyo District Court decision of June 11, 2003, *Hanrei Jiho,* No. 1840, p. 106, and Osaka District Court decision of September 6, 2013, *Hanrei Jiho,* No. 2222, p. 93.

[27] Copyright Law, Art. 2(1)(XV)(b).

UNIT 8   Copyright Law (1)

rendered in the manner which produces a visual or audio-visual effect analogous to that of cinematography and which is fixed into a physical object.[28] Thus, cinematographic works include not only theatrical films but also video game software.[29]

With respect to cinematographic works, special provisions are stipulated regarding the range of the authorship,[30] distribution rights,[31] the ownership of a copyright,[32] and the term of protection,[33] etc.

10   Computer programs

A computer program is "something expressed as a set of instructions written for a computer, which makes the computer function so that a specific result can be obtained."[34] Among the computer programs, those having originality are regarded as original works of computer programs. However, protection for an original work of a computer program does not extend to the programming language, coding conventions, or algorithms.[35]

An original work of a computer program can also be regarded as falling within literary works category since it uses a programming language. A computer program, however, is not intended to directly convey information to other people. Thus, original works of computer programs are illustrated distinctively from literary works to clarify its protection.

With respect to works of computer programs, special provisions are provided regarding jurisdiction,[36] the authorship of a work for hire,[37] and acts deemed to constitute infringement,[38] etc.

---

[28] Copyright Law, Art. 2(3).
[29] Supreme Court decision of April 25, 2002, *Minshu*, Vol. 56, No. 4, p. 808.
[30] Copyright Law, Art. 16.
[31] Copyright Law, Art. 26.
[32] Copyright Law, Art. 29.
[33] Copyright Law, Art. 54.
[34] Copyright Law, Art. 2(1)(X)-2.
[35] Copyright Law, Art. 10(3).
[36] Code of Civil Procedure, Art. 6.
[37] Copyright Law, Art. 15.
[38] Copyright Law, Art. 113(2).

Ⅲ Works based on pre-existing works, etc.

1 Derivative work

A derivative work is "a work created by translating, composing as a musical arrangement, reformulating, dramatizing, making into a cinematographic work, or otherwise adapting a pre-existing work."[39] A derivative work is a work created by adding a new original expression to a pre-existing work, which is exemplified by translations of novels or comics, dramas or films based on the novels or comics as original pieces, or a pop song arranged in a bossa nova style.

A work on which a derivative work is based is referred to as an original work. With respect to a relationship between the protection of a derivative work and the protection of the original work, the Copyright Law states in Article 11 that the protection of a derivative work does not affect the rights of the author of the original work. In other words, the original work remains protected, and the act of exploiting a derivative work also means the act of exploiting the original work. Thus, the author of the original work can also exercise his/her right in connection with the exploitation of the derivative work.[40] Accordingly, when exploiting a translated novel, not only authorization from the translator but also authorization from the novelist will be required.

2 Compilations

A compilation (except a compilation constituting a database) that has originality by reason of the selection or arrangement of its contents is regarded as an original work.[41] When the content of a compilation is an original work, the relationship between the protection of the compilation and the protection of the content of the original work will become an issue as with the cases of derivative works. On this point, the Copyright Law also sets forth that the protection of a compilation "does not affect the rights of the author of the work that forms a part of the compilation."[42]

The content of a compilation is not required to be an original work. Thus, a compilation such as a telephone directory in which facts as content have been compiled

---

[39] Copyright Law, Art. 2(1)(xi).
[40] Copyright Law, Art. 28.
[41] Copyright Law, Art. 12(1).
[42] Copyright Law, Art. 12(2).

UNIT 8   Copyright Law (1)

could be an original work.

Since a compilation of a work is a type of an original work, the expression of selecting or arranging content is a subject matter for protection, and planning, editorial policies, and editorial methods are not protected. Even though the collection of the content takes great effort and expense, if the selection and arrangement of the content are common, the requirement for originality will not be satisfied and the resulting compilation cannot be an original work.

3   Database works

The Copyright Law states in Article 12-2(1), "A database that, by reason of the selection or systematic construction of information contained therein, constitutes originality, is protected as an original work." Therefore, a database shall be protected as an original work under certain conditions. A database means an aggregate of data such as articles, numerical values, or diagrams, which are systematically constructed so that such data can be searched with a computer.[43]

With respect to a database, information constituting the database is not required to be a work. However, if the information is a work, the Copyright Law provides that the protection of the database does not affect the rights of the author of the work constituting the database.[44]

In order for a database to be protected as an original work, any one or both of the selection of information and the systematic construction contained in the database must be determined to have originality. The protection of a database only extends to the act of exploiting the originality of the selection or systematic construction of the information, and does not extend to the act of merely exploiting information extracted from information cumulated in the database.

---

[43] Copyright Law, Art. 2(1)(X)-3
[44] Copyright Law, Art. 12-2 (2).

Copyright Law (2)

- Authors works for hire

I Definition of authors

1 Overview

Article 17(1) of the Copyright Law provides that copyrights vest in authors in principle.

2 Creator doctrine

(1) Authors

The Copyright Law states that an author is "a person who creates an original work."[1] It also provides that the author's rights; i.e., copyrights and moral rights vest in the author.[2] This is a principle of the Copyright Law called the creator doctrine.

Since only natural persons can conduct creative activities, the principle of the creator doctrine means that only natural persons can become authors.

(2) Exception to the creator doctrine

The Copyright Law adopts the creator doctrine with the following two exceptions. One exception is set forth in the provision regarding works for hire[3] which is explained below in Part Ⅱ (Works for hire) of this UNIT 9 and the other exception is provided in the provision regarding the copyright ownership of cinematographic works[4] which will be discussed in this paragraph.

Under the creator doctrine, the copyright and the moral right of an author vest initially in the author who created a work. The term "vest initially in" means that these rights vest in the author at the same time when the rights are created.

However, in the case of a cinematographic work, Article 29 of the Copyright Law

---

[1] Copyright Law, Art. 2(1)(ⅱ).
[2] Copyright Law, Art. 17(1).
[3] Copyright Law, Art. 15.
[4] Copyright Law, Art. 29.

UNIT 9   Copyright Law (2)

defines that, under certain conditions, the copyright vests in its producer. The maker of the cinematographic work is defined as a person who takes the initiative and has the responsibility for the cinematographic work.[5] The maker of the cinematographic work does not need to be its creator.

Therefore, in the case of a cinematographic work, a person who does not create an original work; i.e., a person who is not the author, can be approved as its copyright holder. This is an exception to the creator doctrine.

3   Determination of authors

(1)   Overview

Under the creator doctrine, the copyrights and moral rights of authors vest initially in the authors. For this reason, the determination of an author is important because the determination of whom a copyright vests in starts from who the author is.

Referring again to Article 2(1)(ⅱ) of the Copyright Law, which defines the author, it states that the author is "a person who creates an original work." Therefore, a person who does not create an original work is not the author. Further, the person who created an original work does not need to be a single person for a single work. Since a creation is to express an author's individuality as explained in Section 4, Part Ⅰ of UNIT 8, multiple people can express their individualities to create a single work. A single work created by multiple people is also contemplated in the Copyright Law, and several special provisions are established for such original work as a joint work.[6]

(2)   Method of determining authors

The author is a person who created an original work. The original work means a production in which thoughts or sentiments are originality expressed.[7] Thus, a person who makes an original expression is considered to be the author.

Accordingly, because an original expression is a key element, a person who cannot be regarded as making an expression cannot be the author. For example, a person who merely offers an idea or a plan or a person who merely asks someone to create an original work is not the author. These people are not involved in the expression. Moreover, if the act is not original, a person who is involved in the expression would not be

---

[5] Copyright Law, Art. 2(1)(ⅹ).
[6] Copyright Law, Art. 2(1)(ⅹⅱ).
[7] Copyright Law, Art. 2(1)(ⅰ).

118

I   Definition of authors

recognized as the author. For example, there would not be any originality for proofreading, such as checking typographical errors of a manuscript sent from a novelist, or for making a pose or facial expression by a model according to a cameraman's instruction.

(3)   Presumption of authors

Although the identity of the author is determined from circumstances relating to the creation of an original work, such circumstances often cannot be understood from the work itself. This may cause issues; for example, it is not clear to whom a user requests permission to use the work. Particularly, in the case of a work that multiple people are involved in creating, it is usually not clear who are the authors.

The Copyright Law defines that the person whose name or appellation (true name), or whose pseudonym used as a substitute for the person's true name by which that person is commonly known, is indicated as the name of the author in the customary manner on the work or at the time when the work is offered to or made available to the public is presumed to be the author of that work.[8]

The above term "customary manner" means that the author's name is written at a position based on the common practice in society. For example, "Author: ○○" is written on the cover or the colophon of a book or "Lyrics By ○○" and "Music By ○○" are written on the jacket or lyric sheet of a CD. In the case of a painting, the signature "○ ○" is written at the bottom right of the work.

This provision is a presumptive provision and can be overcome by providing evidence to the contrary. For example, in the case where "Lyrics By ○○" is written on the jacket or the lyrics sheet of a CD, but the lyrics are actually written by a ghostwriter and this fact is proven, the indicated person will not be considered the author.

4   Joint works

(1)   What are joint works?

A joint creation is the act of jointly creating an original work by multiple people. An original work created by this joint creation is called a joint work, and the people who created this joint work are called co-authors. The Copyright Law defines the joint work as "an original work jointly created by two or more people whose contributions to the original work cannot be separated so as to allow each portion of the original work to be

---

[8] Copyright Law, Art. 14.

UNIT 9   Copyright Law (2)

used independently."[9]

(2)   Requirements for joint works

According to the definitions of Article 2(1)(xii), the requirements for a joint work are as follows: (a) the work is created by two or more people; (b) the work is jointly created; and (c) the contribution of each person cannot be separated (impossibility of separate use).

(a)   Creative act by two or more persons

One of the requirements for a joint work is that two or more people make a creative activity. Because a joint work is also an original work, the same requirements are adopted. Thus, offering a plan or idea and conducting only a supplementary work are not included in the creative activity. As to a collaborative paper in which accomplishments of collaborative research, etc., are collected, even if a person participates in the collaborative research that serves as a basis of the collaborative paper and has an important role, it does not directly mean that such person is a co-author of the collaborative paper. Whether the person is a co-author or not is determined based on whether the person conducts a creative activity of the collaborative paper that is an original work.[10]

(b)   Joint creation

Joint creation means that a creative activity is jointly conducted. A typical example is that one painting is drawn and completed together by two people. To the contrary, if a creative activity is separately conducted, for example, if text written in Japanese by one person is translated into English by another person, this act would not be considered as being jointly created.

(c)   Impossibility of separate use

The impossibility of separate use means that the portion of the original work (e. g., a painting which is drawn by two people or a carving completed by three people), which is contributed by each person cannot be extracted and independently used as an original work.

In the case of a song, the music and lyrics are typically used together in an integral manner. However, as music and lyrics can also be separately used, they are not considered to be joint works.

---

[9] Copyright Law, Art. 2(1)(xii).
[10] *See* Osaka High Court decision of April 28, 2005 (2004 (*Ne*) No. 3684).

I   Definition of authors

(3) Legal effect of joint works

Joint works have the following legal effects.

(a)   Ownership of the moral rights of authors

All individuals who create a joint work become authors (co-authors).

Since all the creators are authors, all of them have the moral rights of an author. In this case, the moral rights of authors vest in the respective authors, and the moral right of one author is not jointly-owned with the other co-authors.

(b)   Limitations on the exercise of the moral rights of authors

In principle, the moral right of the co-authors of a joint work cannot be exercised without the unanimous agreement of all the co-authors.[11] The term "exercise" means an act of actively realizing a right; for example, deciding when to publicize an unpublished work. As to the unanimous agreement of all the co-authors, the Copyright Law states that "[a] co-author may not unreasonably prevent a [unanimous] agreement⋯from being reached."[12] For example, a co-author cannot refuse an agreement just to offend the other co-authors. To the contrary, the exercise of a right to demand an injunction against a third party who infringes on the moral right of authors is not the realization of a right, but the preservation of a right and thus can be made without the unanimous agreement of all the co-authors.[13]

(c)   Ownership of joint copyrights

Unlike the moral right of authors, the copyrights of joint works are jointly owned by co-authors (joint copyright).

(d)   Limitations on the exercise of joint copyrights

Except a transfer by general succession such as inheritance, each co-owner cannot transfer the share of the joint copyright without the agreement of the other co-owners. The joint copyright also cannot be exercised without the unanimous agreement of all the co-owners.[14] The term "exercise" also means an act of actively realizing a right and, for example, means authoring others to use the work. However, without justifiable grounds, each co-owner cannot refuse the above consent or prevent the agreement from being reached.[15] "Justifiable grounds" include where a party who is to be authorized to

---

[11] Copyright Law, Art. 64(1).
[12] Copyright Law, Art. 64(2).
[13] Copyright Law, Art. 117.
[14] Copyright Law, Art. 65(1) and (2).
[15] Copyright Law, Art. 65(3).

UNIT 9   Copyright Law (2)

use the work is in a bad financial condition and will possibly fail to make the timely payment of license fees or where a party who is to be authorized to use the work is a competitor. Similar to the moral right of authors, an injunction demand or a demand for damages against the infringement of the joint copyright by a third party can be made without the unanimous agreement of all the co-owners.[16]

(e)   Duration of protection of joint works

The duration of protection of a work lasts for fifty years after the death of the author.[17] The duration of protection of a joint work lasts for fifty years after the death of the last surviving author among the co-authors.[18] For this reason, the duration of the copyright of an author who passed away early among the co-authors is the same as the duration of the copyright of the author who passed away last.

II   Works for hire

1   Overview

A work for hire is an original work made by an employee during the course of his/her employment where the author of the original work is the employer. Works for hire is set forth in Article 15 of the Copyright Law. Since the employer is the author, the author's rights vest initially in the employer.

Therefore, in the case of a work for hire, no rights under the Copyright Law vest in the employee who physically conducts a creative act. In this respect, a work for hire is recognized as an exception to the principle of the creator doctrine.

2   Requirements for works for hire

(1)   Overview

Article 15(1) of the Copyright Law states that "[f] or an original work (except an original work of computer programming) that the employee of an employer (e.g., a corporation, individual employer, etc.) makes in the course of employment at the initiative of the employer, and which the employer makes public as an original work of its own authorship, the author is the employer as long as it is not stipulated otherwise in a

---

[16] Copyright Law, Art. 117.
[17] Refer to Part III of UNIT 10 for further details.
[18] Copyright Law, Art. 51(2).

Ⅱ　Works for hire

contract, employment rules, or elsewhere at the time the original work is made."

Based on Article 15(1), the requirements in which an original work for hire is established are as follows: (1) the original work is made at the initiative of the employer; (2) the original work is made by the employee of the employer; (3) the original work is made during the course of employment; (4) the publicized name is the employer; and (5) unless otherwise stipulated by a contract.

The following are the details of each requirement.

(2)　Requirement in which the original work is made at the initiative of the employer

This requirement means that the employer has the initiative in creating the original work. For example, in the case where an employee makes a brochure of a campaign, the employee follows the instructions from the supervisor. Also, it is generally understood that if a subordinate proposes to the supervisor to create a brochure for a campaign and creates it after obtaining the supervisor's approval the brochure would fall under a work for hire. That is, the initiative of the employer does not necessarily mean only proposing the idea or project of creating the original work, but is based on whether the employer or employee had the initiative during the entire course of creating the original work.

(3)　Requirement in which the original work is made by the employee of the employer

This requirement is a factual act that the creation of the original work was conducted by the employee of the employer.

The employee of the employer undoubtedly includes a person who has a regular employment relationship with the employer, but issues arise for dispatched workers and other non-regular workers.

To determine whether a person falls under "the employee of the employer," it is important to consider whether that person has an employment relationship with the employer as described above. When the existence of an employment relationship is in dispute, the Supreme Court, by comprehensively taking into account detailed facts, such as the business style, the presence or absence of direction and supervision, the amount of compensation, and the payment method etc., determines the following: (1) whether the services provided by the individual was under the direction and supervision of the employer and (2) whether compensation was paid by the employer to the individual as

UNIT 9   Copyright Law (2)

consideration of his/her labor.[19]

(4) Requirement in which the original work is made during the course of employment

The third requirement for the original work for hire is that the original work is made during the course of employment. The term "during the course of employment" means that the employee of the employer creates the original work as part of a job assigned to him/her. This requirement is satisfied only if the original work is created during the course of employment, even if it is made during off hours.

On the contrary, a work created with no direct relation to an employee work duty and a work indirectly created or derivatively from a duty in the course of employment would not fall under works for hire. For example, it is a work duty for a university teacher to give a lecture. However, it is not a work duty to prepare a draft, etc., for the lecture. Thus, the created draft for the lecture is considered not to be a work for hire.

(5) Requirement in which the publicized name is the employer

As the fourth requirement for the work for hire, it is necessary that the employer "makes (the original work) public as an original work of its own authorship."[20] Thus, if a work is created during the course of employment, but made public under the name of the creator, a work for hire is not established.

The term "as the original work of its own authorship" means indicating clearly that the employer itself is the author. Therefore, this requirement is not satisfied when the name of the employer is merely indicated as a publisher. In addition, in the case of a work of computer programming, the name of an author is not planned to be publicized in most cases. Therefore, for computer programs, the requirement of publicizing the name does not need to be satisfied to establish a work for hire.[21]

(6) Requirement "unless otherwise stipulated"

Even if the above four requirements regarding the work for hire are satisfied, a work for hire is not established if there is a specific stipulation to the contrary in a contract, work regulations, etc., between the employer and the employee.

However, the stipulation in the contract, work regulations, etc., must exist "at the time of creating" the original work. This is significant point in that the author of the

---

[19] *See* Supreme Court decision of April 11, 2003, *Hanrei Jiho* No. 1822, p. 133.
[20] Copyright Law, Art. 15(1).
[21] Copyright Law, Art. 15(2).

II   Works for hire

created work cannot be changed by an ex-post facto contract.

3   Legal effect of works for hire

Once a work for hire is established, the legal effect is that the employer becomes the author of the original work. Since the copyright and author's moral rights vest initially in the author,[22] the employer would own the copyright and author's moral rights of the original work.

---

[22] Copyright Law, Art. 17.

Copyright Law (3)

- Contents of a copyright

I What is a copyright?

1 Overview

By creating a work, the author obtains the rights of an author over the work. Unlike a patent right, the author is able to automatically enjoy the rights of an author upon creation of a work without any formalities.[1] This is the principle of no formalities.

The rights of an author consist of moral rights of an author and copyrights. Moral rights of an author protect moral interests of an author,[2] whereas copyrights protect the proprietary interests of an author. The duration of a copyright begins at the time a work is created, and, in principle, expires 50 years after the death of the author.[3]

Since a copyright is a property right, it can be transferred to a third party.[4] Therefore, although a copyright originally vests in the author,[5] it may be owned by a person other than the author as a result of a transfer of the copyright.

In the case of a patent right, a patent right for a patented invention provides protection against the working of an invention that is identical to the patented invention even if the worked invention is not an imitation of the patented invention and was independently developed. In contrast, a copyright only prohibits imitation, and the protection by a copyright does not extend to the exploitation of an independently created work. Therefore, even when a work that is objectively identical to a work is exploited, the copyright for the work is exercisable only in the case where the exploited work was created by imitating the original work. In other words, the copyright for the work does not

---

[1] Copyright Law, Art. 17(2).
[2] Refer to UNIT 12.
[3] Copyright Law, Art. 51. Refer to Part Ⅲ of this UNIT.
[4] Copyright Law, Art. 61(1).
[5] With respect to a cinematographic work, Refer to Article 29 of the Copyright Law. Refer to Section 2 (2), Part Ⅰ of UNIT 9.

UNIT 10   Copyright Law (3)

extend to a case where another work was independently created, and there would not be an infringement of a copyright in such a case.[6]

A copyright holder may demand an injunction against a party who is infringing on his/her copyright,[7] and may claim compensation for damages caused by the infringement.[8]

2   Sub-divided rights (*shibunken*)

Copyrights consist of rights intended for specific acts of exploiting a work. These rights are called sub-divided rights (*shibunken*), and copyrights are considered to be "a bundle of sub-divided rights." The sub-divided rights are provided under Articles 21 to 28 of the Copyright Law. The sub-divided rights will be explained later in details under Part II of this UNIT.

In short, copyrights enable a copyright holder to prohibit an unauthorized third party's acts that are subject to the sub-divided rights, and any act that is subject to a sub-divided right made by an unauthorized third party constitutes an infringement of the copyright.[9] Since copyrights do not cover acts other than those that are subject to the sub-divided rights, such acts do not constitute a copyright infringement. For example, an act of "reading" a novel is considered to be an act of exploiting the novel in daily life, but since the act of "reading" is not subject to any of the sub-divided rights, it does not constitute a copyright infringement.

It is therefore important to understand the contents of the sub-divided rights so as to understand the specific acts of exploiting a work that is protected by copyrights and that would constitute a copyright infringement if made by an unauthorized third party. However, an act that is subject to a sub-divided right made by an unauthorized third party would not constitute a copyright infringement when limitations of a copyright apply. The limitations of a copyright will be explained in UNIT 11.

---

[6] Supreme Court decision of September 7, 1978, *Minshu* Vol. 32, No. 6, p. 1145.
[7] Copyright Law, Art. 112.
[8] Civil Code, Art. 709.
[9] Article 113 of the Copyright Law further provides that certain acts other than the acts that are subject to Articles 21 to 28 also constitute an infringement of copyrights.
[10] Copyright Law, Art. 2(5).
[11] Copyright Law, Art. 21.
[12] Copyright Law, Art. 2(1)(XV).

128

II Contents of sub-divided rights

1 Overview

Sub-divided rights are provided under Articles 21 to 28 of the Copyright Law. Sub-divided rights fall into the following four categories: (1) right to produce a copy; (2) right to communicate a work directly or by using a copy; (3) right to provide a copy; and (4) right to create and exploit a derivative work.

The right in (1) above is related to the act of newly producing a tangible object from a work. The right in (2) above is related to the act of presenting a work "without transferring the possession" of the original or its copy. The right in (3) above is related to the act of providing an original work "by transferring the possession" of the original or reproduction of the original work, and the right in (4) above is related to the act of creating a derivative work and the act of exploiting the created derivative work.

The right of reproduction which corresponds to the right in (1) above applies to all types of reproductions. Since a reproduced work may be repeatedly exploited in the future, the right of reproduction applies to all types of reproductions to protect the author's interests from being damaged. In contrast, sub-divided rights that fall under the rights in (2) and (3) above only apply to cases in which the act is directed to the public. This is because the acts that fall under these sub-divided rights do not involve producing a reproduction, and nothing is left after the act is performed, particularly for the right in (2), and therefore, the author's interests would not be greatly affected unless the act is directed to the public. Also, if the protection of a copyright covered a case in which a work was exploited in a private area, this would greatly restrict each individual's activities, and, at the same time, it would be practically difficult to enforce a copyright against an individual's activities in his/her private domain. Under the Copyright Law, the term "public" includes, but not limited to, a large number of specified persons.[10]

2 Right to produce a copy

The right of reproduction is the author's right to reproduce a work.[11]

Reproduction means "reproduction in a tangible form by printing, photographing, photocopying, making sound or visual recordings or other methods."[12] "Reproduction in a tangible form" means having the work contained in a tangible object so that the work can be repeatedly used. Familiar examples of reproduction in daily life

UNIT 10   Copyright Law (3)

include producing copies with the use of a photocopier and downloading a music file onto the hard disk of a PC.

3   Right to communicate an original work directly or with the use of its copy

(1)   Right of performance

The right of performance is the author's "right to give a stage or musical performance for the purpose of making a work to be directly seen or heard by the public."[13]

A stage or musical performance means performing a work.[14] A musical performance corresponds to a performance where music is performed (including singing), and other performances correspond to a stage performance. Also, stage and musical performances include not only live performances, but also the replaying of a sound or visual recording on a CD or DVD, and the transmission of the performances by means of electronic telecommunications equipment (excluding those that fall under public transmission).[15]

(2)   Right of on-screen presentation

The right of on-screen presentation is the author's "right to make a work publicly available by a screen presentation."[16] A on-screen presentation means the projection of a work on a screen or other objects,[17] and "a screen or other objects" used for the projection include TVs and PC monitors. Also, a projection includes the projection of a still image such as a photograph or slide in addition to the projection of a cinematographic work recorded on a DVD. A projection further includes the replay of sounds that are fixed in a cinematographic work, such as a soundtrack, along with the projection of the cinematographic work.[18] Although a replay of sounds would be considered to fall under a musical performance, the replay of sounds that are fixed in a cinematographic work itself is treated in the same manner as the projection of a cinematographic work, given the close

---

[13] Copyright Law, Art. 22.
[14] Copyright Law, Art. 2(1)(xvi).
[15] Copyright Law, Art. 2(7).
[16] Copyright Law, Art. 22-2.
[17] Copyright Law, Art. 2(1)(xvii).
[18] Copyright Law, Art. 2(1)(xvii).

II Contents of sub-divided rights

relationship between them.

(3) Right of public transmission, etc.

Methods have been developed for transmitting works to a broad range and a large number of people by sending them via various communication means. "Broadcasting" is a typical example of such transmission, but the transmission by way of the Internet has been considerably developed recently, and the Internet has become an important tool for exploiting original works.

The Copyright Law defines transmission intended for direct reception by the public as "public transmission"[19] and provides that the author has an exclusive right to make a public transmission of his/her work (right of public transmission).[20] The Copyright Law also provides for the right of the author to publicly communicate and transmit his/her work by means of a transmission apparatus (right of public communication).[21] For example, public communication would include a case where a show broadcasted on TV is viewed by the public.

Since a public transmission is intended for direct reception by the public, an ordinary e-mail which is sent to a small number of specified persons, for example, would not be considered a public transmission. However, a bulk e-mail using a mailing list may be considered a public transmission. Therefore, among the cases where the Internet is used, some transmissions would be considered a public transmission.

Forms of a public transmission include broadcasting,[22] wire-broadcasting,[23] and an automatic public transmission.[24] Broadcasting and wire-broadcasting are intended for simultaneous transmission of identical information to the public, and broadcasting is a transmission by wireless communication while wire-broadcasting is a transmission by wire-telecommunication. An automatic public transmission is a form of public transmission that "occurs automatically in response to a request from the public". When a work is uploaded to a server connected to the Internet, it would be transmitted to the user upon access to the server. This type of transmission made automatically upon a user's access would be considered an automatic public transmission.

---

[19] Copyright Law, Art. 2(1)(vii)-2.

[20] Copyright Law, Art. 23(1).

[21] Copyright Law, Art. 23(2).

[22] Copyright Law, Art. 2(1)(viii).

[23] Copyright Law, Art. 2(1)(ix)-2.

[24] Copyright Law, Art. 2(1)(ix)-4.

UNIT 10   Copyright Law (3)

The right of public transmission covers not only the public transmission actually made, but also the act of making a work transmittable in the case of automatic public transmission.[25] Specifically, "the act of making a work transmittable" means the act of enabling a work that was not automatically publicly transmittable to be automatically publicly transmittable.[26] A typical example of such an act would be uploading a work to a server that is connected to the Internet; e.g., the unauthorized uploading of another person's work to a video-sharing service on the Internet will constitute an infringement of the right of public transmission. Since it is difficult for the copyright holder to find out whether a work has been automatically publicly transmitted, an infringement occurs at the moment where a work is uploaded to the server without authorization prior to the automatic public transmission.

A public transmission made on the same premises is excluded from the scope of a public transmission even when the transmission in its form appears to fall under the definition of public transmission.[27] For example, if a video of a concert being performed is transmitted to a separate room via LAN to be viewed by the audience who overflowed from the main concert hall to the separate room on the same premises, such video transmission would not be considered a public transmission. Since the performance in the main concert hall can be protected by other sub-divided rights such as the right of performance, there is no need to regard the transmission of the video in a separate room as constituting an infringement on the right of public transmission. However, a transmission of a work of a computer program is excluded from this exception.

(4)   Right of recitation

The right of recitation is the author's right to orally present his/her literary work in public.[28]

A recitation means orally communicating a literary work except for any oral communication that constitutes a performance.[29] A recitation also includes the replay of an audio or visual recording of a recitation of a work (except for those that fall under the definitions of a public transmission or screen presentation) and a transmission via electronic telecommunications equipment (except for those that fall under the definition

---

[25] Copyright Law, Art. 23(1).
[26] Copyright Law, Art. 2(1)(ix)-5.
[27] Copyright Law, Art. 2(1)(vii)-2.
[28] Copyright Law, Art. 24.
[29] Copyright Law, Art. 2(1)(xviii).

II Contents of sub-divided rights

of a public transmission).[30]

(5) Right of exhibition

The right of exhibition is the author's right to exhibit the original piece of an artistic work or an unpublished photographic work to the public.[31] This right is provided since, unlike a literary work, the tangible form of an artistic or photographic work is directly appreciated by people.

4 Rights to provide a copy

(1) Right of distribution

The right of distribution is the author's right to distribute his/her cinematographic work by distributing reproductions of the work.[32] The term "distribution" means a transfer or rental of reproductions of a work to the public with or without charge.[33] A transfer or rental of reproductions of a cinematographic work to a small number of specified persons would also fall under the term "distribution" if such transfer or rental is made for the purpose of presenting the work to the public as with a screen presentation.[34]

The object of the right of distribution is a cinematographic work. However, musical or artistic works that were reproduced in a cinematographic work are also regarded as the object of the right of distribution since they are distributed together with the reproduction of the cinematographic work.[35] In this connection, the author of a movie (e.g., a novelist) is able to assert the right of distribution as the right of an author in relation to the use of a derivative work.[36]

The purpose of the right of distribution of a cinematographic work is to protect the traditional distribution system whereby the distribution route of film production, film distribution and screening, theaters for screening, and timing for screening have been controlled. Therefore, unlike the right of transfer mentioned later, the Copyright Law does not provide that the right of distribution is exhausted once a reproduction is lawfully transferred.

---

[30] Copyright Law, Art. 2(7).
[31] Copyright Law, Art. 25.
[32] Copyright Law, Art. 26(1).
[33] Copyright Law, Art. 2(1)(ixx).
[34] Copyright Law, Art. 2(1)(ixx).
[35] Copyright Law, Art. 26(2).
[36] Copyright Law, Art. 28. Refer to Section 5, Part II of this UNIT.

UNIT 10   Copyright Law (3)

However, in the case of used home video game software (which would be categorized as a cinematographic work and of which purpose was not to be presented to the public) where its copyright holder claimed that reselling the software by a reseller infringed its right of distribution, the Supreme Court held that, the copyright of the gaming software would not prevent it from being resold by a reseller since the copyright holder's right to distribute copies of an original work to the public was exhausted once the software was sold by the copyright holder or its licensee, which accomplishes the purpose of the right of distribution [37]. It is understood that the decision above will apply not only to game software, but also to DVDs of movies that are widely distributed in the market.

(2)   Right of transfer of ownership

The right of transfer of ownership is the author's right to provide his/her work to the public by transferring the piece or its reproduction, except for cinematographic works and works reproduced in cinematographic works (these works are subject to the aforementioned right of distribution).[38]

However, the right of transfer of ownership does not apply to the re-transfer after the work has once been lawfully transferred,[39] which is called exhaustion of the right. Exhaustion of the right of transfer of ownership only applies to the cases provided under Article 26-2(2), including international exhaustion which provides that the right of transfer does not extend to the re-transfer inside Japan of a piece or a reproduction of a work that has been lawfully transferred outside Japan in accordance with the copyright law of the foreign country.[40]

(3)   Right of rental

The right of rental is the author's right to provide his/her work (except for cinematographic original works) to the public by renting out its reproduction.[41]

The term "renting out" includes any action that grants a person the authority to use the reproduction of the work, irrespective of the name given to such action, or the manner in which it is done.[42] Further, the renting out is irrespective of whether it is done with or without charge. A right of rental also covers a reproduction of the work of which

---

[37] Supreme Court decision of April 25, 2002, *Minshu*, Vol. 56, No. 4, p. 808.
[38] Copyright Law, Art. 26-2.
[39] Copyright Law, Art. 26-2(2).
[40] Copyright Law, Art. 26-2(2)(ⅳ).
[41] Copyright Law, Art. 26-3.
[42] Copyright Law, Art. 2(8).

II   Contents of sub-divided rights

the right of transfer has been exhausted as a result of the legitimate transfer of the reproduction by the copyright holder.

5   Rights to create and exploit a derivative work

(1)   Right of translation and adaptation etc.

The author has the right to translate, arrange musically, transform, dramatize cinematize, or make any other adaptation of his/her original work.[43]

This right is the right to adapt (in a broad sense) an original work, and since a derivative work[44] is produced as a result of the adaptation, this right may also be understood as the right to create a derivative work. The original author's copyright covers the exploitation of the derivative work created.[45]

With respect to adaptation, the Supreme Court held that "adaptation of a literary original work[46] means an act of creating another original work based on an existing one by maintaining the essential characteristics of its expressions; modifying, increasing, reducing, or altering its specific expressions; and newly expressing thoughts or feelings in a creative manner, where those who have access to the created original work are able to directly perceive the essential characteristics of the expressions of the existing original work."[47]

Thus, even when an original work is modified, increased, decreased, or altered, and no creativity is newly added, such work is not an adaptation but just a reproduction, and it would constitute an infringement of a right of reproduction if made by an unauthorized third party. In contrast, even when a work is produced based on an existing original work, if the essential characteristics of the expressions of the existing original work are no longer directly perceivable in the newly-created work as a result of dramatic changes that were made, an independent original work would have been newly created, and such a work would not constitute a copyright infringement.

(2)   Right of original author in relation to exploitation of a derivative work

The original author of a derivative work (i.e., the author of the original work which was used as a base for the derivative work) exclusively has the same types of rights

---

[43] Copyright Law, Art. 27.
[44] Copyright Law, Art, 2(1)(xi). Refer to Section 1, Part III of UNIT 8.
[45] Copyright Law, Art. 28. Refer to Section 5(2), Part II of this UNIT.
[46] Copyright Law, Art. 27.
[47] Supreme Court decision of June 28, 2001, *Minshu*, Vol. 55, No. 4, p. 837.

UNIT 10   Copyright Law (3)

as those possessed by the author of the derivative work in relation to the exploitation of the derivative work.[48] Therefore, when a third party intends to use a derivative work β originating from an original work α, he/she must obtain an authorization from the copyright holder of work α in addition to that from the copyright holder of work β.

Ⅲ Term of protection

1 General principle

Although a copyright occurs upon creation of a work, it will not exist forever. The term for the protection of a work is limited, and a copyright expires after a certain period of time. In principle, a copyright expires 50 years after the death of the author.[49] If an author lives 20 years after the creation of a work, the work will be protected for a total of 70 years (20 years ＋ 50 years) before and after the death of the author.

The term for the protection of a work is calculated according to the calendar year method starting from the first day of the year following the year in which the author died.[50] Specifically, the protection of a work starts on the day when it was created, and it will be protected during the life of the author plus 50 years after his/her death, which is calculated from the first day of the year following the year of the author's death until December 31 of the 50th year.

With respect to a work of joint authorship, it is necessary to decide whose date of death should be used as the starting point for calculating the date of copyright expiration since a single copyright must have a single expiration date even if there are multiple authors. The Copyright Law provides that the date of death of the last surviving co-author should be regarded as the starting point for calculating the expiration date of a copyright of a work of joint authorship.[51]

2 Exceptions to the term of protection

(1) Term of protection of an anonymous or pseudonymous work

A copyright of a work that was created anonymously or pseudonymously (using a

---

[48] Copyright Law, Art. 28.
[49] Copyright Law, Art. 51(2).
[50] Copyright Law, Art. 57.
[51] Copyright Law, Art. 51(2).

III   Term of protection

pen name, stage name, etc.) expires 50 years after the original work was made public.[52] The time when the work was made public is regarded as the starting point of the expiration of the term because it is difficult for the users of an anonymous or pseudonymous work to recognize who is the actual author and his/her date of death. However, in cases where the true name of the author of an anonymous or pseudonymous work is registered,[53] or where the actual author of an anonymous or pseudonymous work is well-known, or in similar cases, the term of protection is calculated according to the aforementioned principle.

(2)   Term of protection of an original work whose authorship is attributed to a corporate entity

Similarly, the time when the original work was made public is regarded as the starting point of the expiration of the term of protection of a work whose authorship is attributed to a corporate entity, and the copyright expires 50 years after its publication.[54] This is because the concept of the author's death does not apply to a corporate entity. However, if a work whose authorship is attributed to a corporate entity was not made public within 50 years from its creation, the protection of the original work expires 50 years after the creation.[55]

In the case of a computer program which was made by an employee of a corporate entity, since it is not required that the program be made public under the name of the corporate entity in order for the program to be categorized as a work made for hire,[56] there are cases in which a work of a corporate entity author will not be made public under the name of the corporate entity. However, even in such cases, the authorship of such a work is deemed to be attributed to the corporate entity, and the term of its protection commences when it is published.[57]

(3)   Term of protection of a cinematographic work

In considering the term of protection of a cinematographic work, the time when the work was made public is the starting point of the term.[58] This exception is provided

---

[52] Copyright Law, Art. 52(1).
[53] Copyright Law, Art. 75(1).
[54] Copyright Law, Art. 53(1).
[55] Copyright Law, Art. 53(1).
[56] Copyright Law, Art. 15(2). Refer to Section 3(5), Part II of UNIT 9.
[57] Copyright Law, Art. 53(3).
[58] Copyright Law, Art. 54(1).

UNIT 10   Copyright Law (3)

since a cinematographic work often involves multiple authors,[59] and it is therefore difficult to determine who is the author and when the author died.

However, it should be noted that the term of protection of a cinematographic work is 70 years after its publication, not 50 years.[60] Although the term of protection of a cinematographic work was previously 50 years from its publication, the term was extended to 70 years by considering the fact that the term of protection applied in major Western countries is 70 years.

A copyright of the original novel that was adapted in a cinematographic work also expires at the same time as the copyright of the cinematographic work so as to facilitate the use of cinematographic works.[61] However, this solely applies to the case of the exploitation of a cinematographic work, and does not, for example, apply to publishing of the original novel.

(4)   Time of publication of serial publications, etc.

As explained above, the time when a work was made public is regarded as the starting point for calculating the expiration of the term of protection with respect to an anonymous or pseudonymous work, a work under the name of a corporate entity, and a cinematographic work, and therefore, the time of the publication is of importance for these works. How do we determine the time of publication of a work for serial publications that are made public in successive volumes, issues or installments, or in the case of a work that is made public sequentially in different parts?

As for a serial publication, the Copyright Law provides that the time of its publication is the time when each volume, issue or installment was made public.[62] In other words, the term of protection is calculated for each publication.

In contrast, as for a work that is made public sequentially in parts (e.g., a serialized novel or comic series), the Copyright Law provides that the time when the last part was made public is the starting point of the term for the whole publication.[63]

---

[59] Copyright Law, Art. 16.
[60] Copyright Law, Art. 54(1).
[61] Copyright Law, Art. 54(2).
[62] Copyright Law, Art. 56(1).
[63] Copyright Law, Art. 56(1).

Copyright Law (4)

- Limitations of a copyright

I Overview

1 What are the issues?

We have already reviewed that general issues in relation to copyright infringement disputes are: (1) whether an alleged infringing work is classified as an original work; (2) whether a person claiming a copyright infringement is a legitimate copyright holder; and (3) whether a certain act constitutes copyright infringement.[1] However, even if the answer to these three issues indicate that there is a copyright infringement, there is still a fourth issue which needs to be resolved and that is: (4) whether the act falls under the exceptions or limitations of a copyright as provided under Articles 30 to 49 of the Copyright Law.

This fourth issue, the limitations of a copyright, will be explained in this UNIT.

2 Purpose of the limitations of a copyright

The Copyright Law provides certain limitations of a copyright where acts of utilizing a work do not constitute copyright infringement.[2]

Because a copyright allows a specific person to have exclusive control over a particular expression, the copyright imposes certain constraints on another person's freedom of expression. The justification for such constraints on the freedom of expression is that the protection of a copyright provides incentive for new creation, and a variety of expressive activities will take place which contributes to the development of culture. Therefore, if the exercise of the copyright by its holder would not work as an incentive for new creation, or if there is another interest which is more important than the promotion of new creation, then the exercise of the copyright should be limited as provided in the

---

[1] For issue (1), UNIT 8 explains issues regarding the copyrightability of an original work; for issue (2), UNIT 9 explains the determination of authorship; for issue (3), UNIT 10 explains sub-divided rights.
[2] Copyright Law, Arts. 30 to 49.

UNIT 11   Copyright Law (4)

limitations of copyright in the Copyright Law.

However, since the provisions on the limitations of copyright do not affect the moral right of an author,[3] there may be cases where acts which, although being covered by the provisions on the limitations of copyright and thus not constituting copyright infringement, would constitute infringement on the author's moral right.

II   Provisions on the limitations of a copyright

1   Overview

The provisions on the limitations of copyrights as set forth in the Copyright Law are as follows: (1) reproduction for private use;[4] (2) incidental use of a work;[5] (3) reproduction at libraries, etc.;[6] (4) use of quotation;[7] (5) use for education and examination questions;[8] (6) use for people with disabilities;[9] (7) non-profit performances, etc.;[10] (8) use for media reporting;[11] (9) use for governmental activities;[12] (10) temporary fixations [of ephemeral recordings] by broadcasters;[13] (11) provisions relating to artistic works;[14] (12) and provisions relating to programs, the Internet, etc.[15]

The following will explain the key provisions on the limitations of a copyright.

2   Key provisions on the limitations of a copyright

(1)   Reproduction for private use

Article 30(1) provides that an original work can be reproduced when its purpose of use is for private use, except for certain cases. The reasons for this provision are because: (1) the reproduction for private use would have only slightly impact to the copyright holder; (2) even if the copyright holder wished to exercise the copyright, it

---

[3] Copyright Law, Art. 50; Refer to UNIT 12.
[4] Copyright Law, Art. 30.
[5] Copyright Law, Art. 30-2.
[6] Copyright Law, Art. 31.
[7] Copyright Law, Art. 32.
[8] Copyright Law, Arts. 33 to 36.
[9] Copyright Law, Arts. 37 and 37-2.
[10] Copyright Law, Art. 38.
[11] Copyright Law, Arts. 39 to 41.
[12] Copyright Law, Arts. 42 to 42-3.
[13] Copyright Law, Art. 44.
[14] Copyright Law, Arts. 45 to 47-2.
[15] Copyright Law, Arts. 47-3 to 47-9.

Ⅱ   Provisions on the limitations of a copyright

would be practically impossible because the reproduction is being conducted privately; and (3) the freedom of personal activities which are done privately should not be restricted.

Private use means the "personal or family use or other equivalent uses within a limited scope."[16] This would include, for example, the act of a person recording a television program onto a hard disk recorder so that he/she can watch the program after returning home, or the act of dubbing one's own CD or a rental CD onto a portable music player.

The term "equivalent uses within a limited scope" can be regarded to be a group of a few people who may have strong personal relationships, where the group consists of about 10 people, such as a shared-interest group or club, who gather for the purpose of a certain hobby or activity. On the other hand, the reproduction by a company for its internal business use would not be considered the "equivalent use within a limited scope."[17]

There are no restrictions on the means of reproduction, and handwritten duplication, as well as scanned documents and photographs for personal browsing on a tablet PC, are also included in the scope of reproduction. However, since the Copyright Law provides that the user of a work may reproduce it, the reproduction must be carried out by the person who will use it privately. Note that it is permissible for a user to have somebody else perform the reproduction on behalf of the user.[18]

Even if the copies used during the reproduction were illegal, it is legally allowed to reproduce the copies for the purpose of private use. However, if a person, who had learned that a work was distributed illegally, conducted sound and/or video recordings in a digital format, such recordings would not be allowed by the limitations of a copyright even if the recordings were made for the purpose of private use.[19] This provision was introduced by the revision to the Copyright Law in 2009 in order to deal with the marked increase of the distribution of illegal copies of music, etc., over the Internet.

However, a person who makes a reproduction by a sound and/or video recording by a machine with a digital format sound and/or video recording function, onto a recording

---

[16] Copyright Law, Art. 30(1).
[17] Tokyo District Court decision of 22 July, 1977, *Mutaisaishu*, Vol. 9 No. 2, p. 534.
[18] In relation to this issue, Refer to: Intellectual Property High Court decision of 22 October, 2014, *Hanrei Jiho* No. 2246, p. 92.
[19] Copyright Law, Art. 30(1)(ⅲ).

UNIT 11   Copyright Law (4)

medium provided for such digital form sound and/or video recording, then the person must pay a reasonable amount of compensation to the copyright holder, even if the reproduction is made for the purpose of private use.[20] Since there is essentially no degradation in the quality of a reproduction in digital form, there would be a great economic adverse impact to the copyright holder even if the reproduction was made for the purpose of private use. Hence, the copyright holder who is not entitled to a request for injunction may claim compensation.

(2) Incidental use of a work

(a) Overview

Article 30-2 (1) provides that, in creating a work by a method such as photography, a photographer may, in association with the creation, reproduce or adapt another work which was incidentally taken in the picture due to the difficulty in separating the subject matter of the photograph.

This is a provision for the act of using a work that is incidental to the subject matter and is referred to as 'utsuri-komi (i.e., an "inclusion")'. When taking photographs or filming videos of street scenery or shop interiors visited during holiday travel, for example, there are cases where paintings depicted in signs and posters are filmed, and/or music played in the shop are recorded. This inclusion exists when another person's work such as a painting or music ends up being reproduced, in addition to the primary objective in a photographic work.

As mentioned in section 2(1) above, if the photograph which contains the inclusion is used for a private purpose such as personal enjoyment, then it would not constitute an infringement of a right of reproduction as private use.[21] However, if the photograph with the inclusion was used beyond the scope of private use (e.g., it was uploaded on a blog so that a lot of people may view it), then such use would constitute an infringement on the right of reproduction or public transmission. However, in most cases, the actual damages suffered by the copyright holder due to the inclusion is negligible. Further, if the copyright holder could exercise his/her right over the inclusion, then it would restrict the freedom of expression of the general public. Thus, the Copyright Law was revised in 2012 so that it limits, under specific requirements, the right to reproduce

---

[20] Copyright Law, Art. 30(2); the "machine" and "the recording medium" as specified by a cabinet ordinance.

[21] Refer to Section 2(1), Part II of this UNIT.

II   Provisions on the limitations of a copyright

and adapt a work which was reproduced and/or adapted by such inclusion.

(b)   Incidental inclusion of a work

A prerequisite for an Incidental inclusion of a work is that a work must be "difficult to separate off" when photographing a primary subject matter.

Whether it is difficult to separate the work from the subject matter is determined in light of common sense at the time of creating the photographic work. For example, if there is a painting on the wall which is behind the subject matter to be photographed, it would be difficult, from the perspective of common sense, to remove the painting and take the photograph.

Furthermore, an inclusion of a work must be a "negligible component" of a photographic work. Whether such inclusion would be a negligible component is specifically determined on a case-by-case basis by taking the type and nature of the work into account.

Moreover, Copyright Law 30-2(1) provides that the limitation of the copyright does not apply if the "interest of the copyright holder is unjustly harmed in light of the type and applications of the inclusion, and the embodiment of the reproduction or adaptation of the inclusion." This provision protects the copyright holder from being unjustly harmed.

(c)   Incidental use of a work in association with the use of a photographic work

Article 30-2(2) provides that an inclusion reproduced or adapted in accordance with Article 30-2(1) above can be used in association with the use of a photographic work. This provision allows acts such as uploading a photographic work to internet blogs and video-sharing sites.

However, it is not permissible if the interest of a copyright holder is unjustly harmed in light of the type and applications of the Incidental Inclusion of a work, and the embodiment of use of an Incidental Inclusion of a work,[22] the restriction of which is similar to Article 30-2(1) above.

(3)   Reproduction at libraries

The National Diet Library and other libraries and institutions (as non-profit entities)[23] whose purpose is to provide the public use of books, recordings and other materials, may reproduce works of the books, recordings and other materials held by

---

[22] Copyright Law, Art. 30-2(2).

UNIT 11   Copyright Law (4)

these libraries in specific cases.[24]

For example, there are cases where a library would provide someone with a copy of an excerpt of literature owned by the library which is required for the one's research and study.

Also, the National Diet Library may reproduce (digitalize) their own materials in order to provide a substitute of an original copy for public utilization to prevent the loss of the original copy, or in order to automatically and publicly transmit to a library the materials which are difficult to obtain due to being out-of-print.[25]

Furthermore, the National Diet Library may automatically and publicly transmit to a library any digitalized duplicate of the out-of-print materials prepared in accordance with Article 31(2) of the Copyright Law if the purpose is to make the contents of the out-of-print materials available to the public through the library.[26] Because of this provision, a user may browse the out-of-print materials transmitted from the National Diet Library at his/her nearest library, and obtain a partial copy.

(4)   Use of quotations

A publicized work may be quoted if such use is compatible with fair practice, and is within a reasonable scope for the purpose of quotation, such as for media reporting, criticism or research.[27]

This provision does not provide that a person may "quote" the publicized work, but rather that such person can "use it with quotations." This means not only that a person may quote another person's work in his/her own work, but also that such work can be used (e.g., reproduced or exhibited) with another person's quoted work.

In order for use in quotations to be permitted, the following requirements must be met: (1) the work to be quoted has been publicized; (2) a person must quote the work; (3) the use in quotations must be compatible with fair practice; and (4) the use must be within a reasonable scope of the purpose of quoting, such as for media reporting, criticism or research.

---

[23] Article 1-3(1) of the Copyright Law Implementing Ordinance, as covered in Copyright Law 31, lists various libraries and material reference institutions. Library reading rooms of primary, middle and high schools, as well as material reference rooms in companies are not included.

[24] Copyright Law, Art. 31(1).

[25] Copyright Law, Art. 31(2).

[26] Copyright Law, Art. 31(3).

[27] Copyright Law, Art. 32(1).

II   Provisions on the limitations of a copyright

As for the requirement (1) above, whether the work has been publicized is determined based on Article 4 which defines publication of a work.

As for requirement (2) above, although there is no explicit language provided in the Copyright Law, the following two elements would be required in order to find that the person "quotes" the work: (1) another person's work which was quoted and the work which quoted it are clearly distinguishable; and (2) given the quantity and the quality of the work which quoted another person's work, the work which quoted another person's work is the primary part, and the work is a subordinate part.[28]

The use in quotations must be compatible with "fair practice" in requirement (3) is defined to the extent of whether such use follows the general practice, because fair practice differs depending on the type of the work, the industry to which the work belongs, and the era or period when the use occurs . For example, in the case of a literary work, it is the general practice that quotation marks are used to distinguish text of a work from another person's work.

As for requirement (4), "the use must be within a reasonable scope for the purpose of quoting, such as for media reporting, criticism or research," and whether the use is "within a reasonable scope" is determined by comparing the whole quantity and quality of another person's work with those of the work which was quoted by considering the purpose of quotation. Media reporting, criticism and research are examples which would fall under the reasonable scope for the purposes of quotation.

(5)   Use for education and examination questions

A publicized work may be published in an educational book to the extent that it is considered necessary for the purpose of school education.[29]

However, in such case, a person who publishes the educational book must notify the author of the use and pay compensation to the copyright holder.[30] The same will apply in the case of broadcasting or wire broadcasting a work in a school-oriented broadcast programming or wire broadcast programming.[31]

Additionally, a teacher or a student who attends a class at a non-profit school may reproduce a publicized original work to the extent necessary for using it in the class.[32]

---

[28] Supreme Court decision of 28 March, 1980, *Minshu*, Vol. 34, No. 3, p. 244.
[29] Copyright Law, Art. 33(1).
[30] Copyright Law, Art. 33(2).
[31] Copyright Law, Art. 34.
[32] Copyright Law, Art. 35(1).

UNIT 11   Copyright Law (4)

No compensation needs to be paid to the copyright holder in this case.

Furthermore, a person may reproduce a work in an examination paper to the extent necessary for school admission examinations and other examinations to test knowledge or skills.[33] A person who reproduces an original work for profit-making purposes must pay compensation to the copyright holder.[34]

(6)   Use for people with disabilities

Reproducing a publicized original work in Braille is permitted in order for people with a visual disability to be able to enjoy it.[35] Moreover, those who conduct a business in relation to the welfare of individuals with a visual disability (to be specified by a cabinet order) are permitted to reproduce a work in a necessary manner in order for people with a visual disability to use it.[36] An example is the creation of an audio book. A similar provision applies to people with a hearing disability.[37]

However, if a copyright holder, a publishing right holder, or their licensee provides a work to the public in the manner as mentioned above, the copyright limitation above would not apply to protect others who reproduce the work, so that the copyright holder can maintain the incentive to proactively provide the work by means suitable for people with disabilities.[38]

(7)   Performances which do not make a profit

A publicized original work may be publicly shown, performed, screened or recited if such performance is not to make a profit, no money is collected from the audience and spectators, and the performer or reciter receives no remuneration,[39] for example, at school-held art festivals or choral competitions.

Note that adaptation is not permitted for such performances,[40] and that the limitation of the copyright above only applies where people perform the original work without any adaption. Further, even if no money is collected for watching the performance itself, but entrance fees for the venue or institution are collected, then this limitation does not apply since the performance would not be considered free-of-charge.

---

[33] Copyright Law, Art. 36(1).
[34] Copyright Law, Art. 36(2).
[35] Copyright Law, Art. 37(1).
[36] Copyright Law, Art. 37(3).
[37] Copyright Law, Art. 37-2.
[38] Copyright Law, Art. 37(3); Copyright Law, Art. 37-2.
[39] Copyright Law, Art. 38(1).
[40] See Copyright Law, Art. 43.

II   Provisions on the limitations of a copyright

(8)   Use for media reporting

An editorial published in a newspaper or magazine which relates to current events and issues in politics, the economy or society, may be reprinted in another newspaper or magazine, or may be broadcasted or wire-broadcasted.[41] However, such editorials may not be used where it is indicated that such use is prohibited.[42]

Also, political speeches delivered in public or public statements made in the course of judicial proceedings may be used in any way, except if they are used to make a compilation of speeches or statements by the same author.[43] Such exception is found, for example, where an author makes a collection of speeches made by a particular politician.

Furthermore, when conducting media reporting of current events by a photograph, film or broadcast, an original work of which the event is a part of, or a work of which the course of the event can be seen or heard in the media report is usable within a reasonable scope for the purpose of media reporting.[44]

Taking into consideration that the freedom of the press is protected under the Constitution as a freedom of expression and is regarded as the key basis to support democracy, this limitation is provided in order to promote seamless media reporting based on such freedom.

(9)   Provisions relating to artistic works

A copyright holder of an artistic or photographic work has an exclusive right to exhibit it.[45] On the other hand, because the originally created version of an artistic or photographic work could be sold as a tangible object that is independent of the copyright, if the person who purchases the ownership right of that creation does not have the right to exhibit it, he/she could not exhibit it to the public.

This would result in a situation where nobody would want to purchase artwork and, as a result, it would negatively impact the sale of artwork. Therefore, Article 45 of the Copyright Law provides that an owner of an originally created version of an artistic or photographic work, or a person who obtained the owner's consent may publicly exhibit that version, which limits the copyright holder's right.[46] However, if the owner intends to

---

[41] Copyright Law, Art. 39(1).
[42] Copyright Law, Art. 39(1).
[43] Copyright Law, Art. 40(1).
[44] Copyright Law, Art. 41.
[45] Copyright Law, Art. 25.
[46] Copyright Law, Art. 45(1).

UNIT 11　Copyright Law (4)

permanently exhibit the originally-created version at an outdoor place which is open to the general public, the copyright holder's authorization is required.[47] Further, once the artwork is (with the copyright holder's authorization) permanently installed at an outdoor place which is open to the general public, people may use such artwork, except for certain cases (e.g., reproducing the original work for the sole purpose of selling them).[48] As the artwork may be the subject matter of a photograph or sketch, it is not appropriate for a copyright holder to exercise his/her right against photographing or sketching the artwork.

(10)　Provisions relating to computer programs or the Internet

An owner of an authorized copy of a computer program (an original work) may reproduce the program (e.g., install or make a backup copy of the program) to the extent necessary for using the computer program.[49]

Further, Article 47-4 allows a temporary reproduction for the purpose of maintenance or repair. If maintenance or repair will be performed on a device which has a function that can reproduce a program by using a built-in recording medium such as a mobile phone, the work recorded on the built-in recording medium may be temporarily saved onto another device, and then restored to such device after the repair.

Moreover, there are provisions on the limitations of a copyright in relation to use of the Internet, such as acts of backing up a work as a preventive measure against loss of information on the Internet,[50] which balances the protection of a copyright and the seamless use of the Internet.

Ⅲ　General provisions on limitations of a copyright

We have taken a general overview of the provisions on the limitations of a copyright as provided specifically in the Copyright Law. The legislation for limiting a copyright is also generally recognized in other countries. There are different ways to limit a copyright. One way is to provide limitations of a copyright for specific acts of use with individual provisions, as in the case of Japan. The other way is to provide limitations of a copyright in the form of general provisions which, either provided with or without

---

[47] Copyright Law, Art. 45(2).
[48] Copyright Law, Art. 46.
[49] Copyright Law, Art. 47-3.
[50] Copyright Law, Art. 47-5; Copyright Law, Arts. 47-6 to 47-7.

148

Ⅲ　General provisions on limitations of a copyright

individual provisions, would comprehensively take into consideration the purpose of use, the nature of the work, or how to use it. A representative example of legislation which provides general provisions is the fair use provision in Article 107 of the U.S. Copyright Law.[51]

There are also opinions in Japan which argue that the "fair use" type of general provisions should be introduced so that the Copyright Law can deal with social and economic changes. Provisions in relation to the incidental use of an original work which were introduced in the 2012 amendment of the Copyright Law were discussed in connection with the appropriateness of introducing general provisions. However, in the 2012 amendment, these provisions were provided as specific limitations of a copyright.

---

[51] U.S. Copyright Law (Code § 107) provides the following:
"Notwithstanding the provisions of sections 106 and 106A, the fair use of a copyrighted work, including such use by reproduction in copies or phonorecords or by any other means specified by that section, for purposes such as criticism, comment, news reporting, teaching (including multiple copies for classroom use), scholarship, or research, is not an infringement of copyright. In determining whether the use made of a work in any particular case is a fair use the factors to be considered shall include:
(1) the purpose and character of the use, including whether such use is of a commercial nature or is for nonprofit educational purposes;
(2) the nature of the copyrighted work;
(3) the amount and substantiality of the portion used in relation to the copyrighted work as a whole; and
(4) the effect of the use upon the potential market for or value of the copyrighted work.
The fact that a work is unpublished shall not itself bar a finding of fair use if such finding is made upon consideration of all the above factors."

Copyright Law (5)

- Moral rights of an author

I Moral rights of an author

1 Definition of moral rights of an author

In UNIT 10, we reviewed that an author who created an original work has a copyright as an economic right. However, Article 17 of the Copyright Law states that the author also has the moral rights of an author in addition to a copyright. In this UNIT 12, we will discuss the author's moral rights provided under the Copyright Law.

The moral rights of an author are rights for protecting their moral interests. Composers and painters compose music or draw a painting to express their sentiments. That is, original works are created through the expression of authors' thoughts and sentiments. In that sense, we can say that works are reflections of the authors' personalities. If so, the authors' moral interests can be impaired depending on how the original works are handled. The authors' moral rights work in order to protect the author's feelings and preferences.

The moral rights of an author consist of the following three rights:[1] (1) the right to make an original work public;[2] (2) the right of attribution;[3] and (3) the right to integrity.[4]

As with the case of a copyright infringement, the author may seek an injunction[5] and compensation for damages[6] against a person who infringes the abovementioned rights.

---

[1] Note that, in addition to these three rights, an exploitation of a work infringing an author's honor or reputation would be deemed the infringement of the moral rights pursuant to Article 113(6) of the Copyright Law. Refer to Part V of UNIT 12.
[2] Copyright Law, Art. 18.
[3] Copyright Law, Art. 19.
[4] Copyright Law, Art. 20.
[5] Copyright Law, Art. 112.
[6] Civil Code, Art. 709.

UNIT 12   Copyright Law (5)

2   Relationship with copyrights

Copyrights and moral rights of an author basically exist independently. As already discussed, a copyright, in principle, lasts for up to 50 years after the author's death.[7] Copyrights may be transferred.[8] On the other hand, since the moral rights of an author are to protect an author's inherent moral interests, they cannot be transferred.[9] Further, if the author dies, his/her moral rights lapse.[10] Therefore, there could be a case where a copyright and moral rights of an author belong to different people, for example, a case where a writer assigned the copyright of his/her work to a publisher.

3   Author's consent

Since a purpose of moral rights is to protect authors' preferences, it is understood that there will be no infringement of the author's moral rights as long as he/she gives consent.

II   Right to make an original work public

1   What is the right to make an original work public?

It is critical for authors to determine whether, when, and how to make an original work public.

For example, e-mails and letters to family or friends could be original works. However, in general, those e-mails and letters are not made public even if the author of such emails and letters is a celebrity. Authors should determine whether the emails and letters are to be made public. Also, a writer might have the intention to make a work public on a certain anniversary. In addition, the writer might have a preference to publicize the work in a specific magazine. These should also be decided by the authors.

The right to make an original work public gives authors a right of control over how their work is made public.

---

[7] Copyright Law, Art. 51(2). Refer to Part III of UNIT 10.
[8] Copyright Law, Art. 61.
[9] Copyright Law, Art. 59.
[10] Please note, however, that, as discussed below, the author's interests are protected even after his/her death to the extent provided by Article 60 of the Copyright Law.

2 Contents of the right to make an original work public

(1) Outline

Article 18(1) of the Copyright Law states, "The author of an original work not yet made public (this includes a work made public by the copyright owner or the licensee without the author's consent) has the right to make available or present that work to the public." As stipulated, the right to make an original work public focuses on works that are not yet made public, and therefore, there is no longer the right to make the original work public once it is published.

In addition, the right to make an original work public for a work covers derivative works based on the original work.[11] Therefore, for example, if a film work which is based on a novel (original work) that has not been published is released, the film's creator would be required to obtain the novelist's consent.

(2) "Made public"

Pursuant to Article 4(1) of the Copyright Law, an original work is deemed to be made public if it is "published" (i.e., depending on its nature, a considerable number of copies of the work that are reasonably sufficient to meet a public demand were distributed to the public),[12] or the work is "presented" to the public through a stage performance, or other similar opportunities.[13]

Although a work is deemed to be made public if it is published as a book or is publicly available on the internet, there are some cases where it is difficult to determine whether the work has been made public.

(3) To make available or present to the public

With respect to a work that has not yet been made public, an author has the right to "make it available" (tangible acts of making it public - e.g., selling printed material) and to "present it" (intangible acts of making it public - e.g., musical performance) to the public. Therefore, if you publish or play in public someone's work that has not been made public without the author's consent, it will infringe the author's right to make an original work public.

For example, in a case where a person who received from a famous novelist

---

[11] Copyright Law, Art. 18(1).

[12] Copyright Law, Art. 3(1).

[13] Besides these conducts, Article 4(2) of the Copyright Law and thereafter provide certain provisions regarding publications.

UNIT 12   Copyright Law (5)

(*Yukio Mishima*) a letter which was not made public and made its contents available to the public by referring to the letter in the recipient's own work, the court held that the recipient infringed the novelist's right to make a work public since his conduct fell under "to make available to the public."[14]

3   Limitations on the right to make an original work public

As described above, as long as an author consents to making a work public, there would be no issues on infringement of such right since the purpose of the right to make an original work public is to protect the author's moral interests.

In this regard, under the Copyright Law, the author's consent is presumed in certain cases where there would be harm to a third party if the author exercises the right to make an original work public. Specifically, if an author transfers a copyright of the work which was not yet made public, it is presumed that the author consented that the work would be made available or presented to the public through the exercise of the right transferred. For example, where an author assigns the right of on-screen presentation to a third party, it would be inappropriate for the author to exercise the right to make an original work public and prevent it from being screened.[15] Therefore, in such case, it will be presumed that the author has consented to the on-screen presentation. In addition, if an author transfers ownership of an original artistic or photographic work which was not yet made public, it is presumed that the author consented to the work's presentation to the public through an exhibition of the work.[16] This is because a person who obtained the ownership of the original artistic or photographic work should be able to make available to the public by exhibiting it. Furthermore, in the case of a cinematographic work, it is presumed that the director, etc. who is an author of the work consented that the cinematographic work would be made available or presented to the public through the exercise of the copyright of the work by its maker who obtains the copyright of such cinematographic work in accordance with Article 29 of the Copyright Law.[17]

However, if there is an agreement contrary to the presumptions provided under the Copyright Law above, such agreement will prevail. In the example above where the

---

[14] Tokyo High Court decision of May 23, 2000, *Hanrei Jiho*, No. 1725, p. 165 (a case involving the protection of an author's moral rights after his death in accordance with Copyright Law, Art. 60).

[15] Copyright Law, Art. 18(2)(i).

[16] Copyright Law, Art. 18(2)(ii).

[17] Copyright Law, Art. 18(2)(iii). Refer to Section 12(2) of UNIT 9.

author assigns the right of an on-screen presentation to a third party, if the author and the third party copyright holder agreed that the work shall not be made public, such agreement would prevail. Furthermore, there are cases in which the author is presumed to give consent to making a work public[18] or in which the right to make an original work public will not be granted[19] when there is need for the disclosure of administrative information by administrative agencies or the management of official documents.

Ⅲ Right of attribution

1 What is the right of attribution?

It would be essentially important for an author to clarify who created the original work. It is easy to imagine that if a musical composition is published without the author's consent under a name other than the author's, this act would infringe on the author's moral interests. In addition, whether indicating a true name, pen name, or handle name (pseudonym) as the author's name, or anonymously publishing an original work is related to the author's preferences, and therefore, these matters should be left to the author's discretion.

The right of attribution is a right to control the indication of an author's name on such works.

2 Contents of the right of attribution

Article 19(1) of the Copyright Law states, "The author of an original work has the right to decide whether to use the author's true name or pseudonym to indicate the name of the author on the originally-made work or in connection with the work at the time it is made available or presented to the public, or to decide that the author's name will not be indicated in connection with that work..."

As previously mentioned, the author has the right to decide whether to use the true name or pseudonym as the author's name when the work is published, or to decide not to indicate the author's name. Therefore, if the author wished to make the work public under a pen name, even if the author's real name is indicated on the work, this would infringe on the author's right of attribution since the author did not desire to disclose

---

[18] Copyright Law, Art. 18(3).
[19] Copyright Law, Art. 18(4).

UNIT 12   Copyright Law (5)

his/her true name. Furthermore, the name selected by the author must be indicated "as the author's name." Therefore, if the author's name is indicated only as an editorial supervisor or a collaborator, this would generally infringe the author's right of attribution.

There are various ways to indicate an author's name including printing it on the cover of a book, stamping the artist's signature and seal on a painting, and introducing the composer's name during the introductory portion of a musical performance. Apart from indicating on the original work, since it is required to indicate an author's name "at the time when the work is made available or presented to the public," the right of attribution does not apply unless the work itself is made available or presented to the public. Therefore, even if you incorrectly refer to an author's name when posting on your weblog a list of books you read, there is no infringement of the right of attribution since the reference to the incorrect name was not made at the time when the work itself was presented to the public.

The right of attribution of an author of an original work covers how the author's name of the original work should be indicated when its derivative work is made available or presented to the public.[20] Accordingly, in the case of making a novel into a film, a name which the novelist selected must be indicated as the author's name of the original work underlying the cinematography.

3   Limitations on the right of attribution

Although an author has the right of attribution, it is practically difficult to confirm with him/her when indicating the author's name each time the work is exploited. Therefore, Article 19(2) of the Copyright Law states that once an author indicates a certain name as the author's name, a licensee who intends to exploit the work, in principle, may indicate the author's name in accordance with how the author had indicated. This is because the use of the author's name once selected and indicated by the author would not infringe on his/her moral interests. Note that Article 19(2) of the Copyright Law also states that the above provision does not apply when the author has manifested otherwise. However, it does not mean that a licensee who intends to exploit the work needs to seek the author's confirmation each time, but instead means that the user should follow the specific instructions made by the author, if any.

[20] Copyright Law, Art. 19(1).

IV Right to integrity

In addition, it is also practically difficult that the author's name must be indicated every time when the work is made available or presented to the public. For example, if background music is broadcasted in a medley style in a coffee shop, it is practically difficult to announce all of the lyric writers and the composers of the tracks when playing the music. Therefore, the indication of the author's name may be omitted under certain conditions (i.e., (1) "if the omission of the author's name is unlikely to harm his interests in relation to his authorship in light of the purpose and method of exploiting the work ;" and (2) "if such omission would not violate fair practices").[21] However, these exceptions apply to limited cases, and therefore, the author's name may not be omitted, for example, in a case where it could be falsely recognized (i.e., the case of violation of requirement (1) above), or where a certain way of indicating the author's name has been fairly and customarily established (i.e., the violation of the requirement (2) above).[22]

Furthermore, there are additional limitations in connection with disclosure of administrative information by administrative agencies as well as the management of official documents[23].

IV Right to integrity

1 What is the right to integrity?

An author is a person who created a work. If any addition to the work not originally written by the author is made without the author's consent or a serious dramatic work is rewritten into a comedy or obscene work without consent, it would infringe on the author's moral interests and reputation. Thus, it is important for the author to keep the integrity of his/her work. The right to integrity is a right to protect the integrity of the author's work.

2 Contents of the right to integrity

(1) Overview

Article 20(1) of the Copyright Law states, "The author of a work has the right to

---

[21] Copyright Law, Art. 19(3).
[22] For example, as it is fairly and customarily established for an author's name to be indicated in the form of a telop in the case of television broadcasting, the author's name cannot be omitted.
[23] Copyright Law, Art. 19(4).

157

UNIT 12   Copyright Law (5)

preserve the integrity of that work and its title, and is not to be made to suffer any distortion, mutilation, or other modification thereto that is contrary to the author's intention." The right to integrity prevents not only an unauthorized modification of a work (e.g., to add a touch of paint to a painting or to rewrite the latter half of a novel), but also an unauthorized alternation of the title even if it is not recognized as a work protected by a copyright. Therefore, a change of the title without the author's consent would constitute an infringement of the right to integrity even if it does not constitute copyright infringement.

A purpose of the right to integrity is to prevent an unauthorized modification that is contrary to the author's intention. Please note that as long as any modification is contrary to the author's intention, it constitutes an infringement of the right to integrity irrespective of whether the results of the modification are good or bad. Therefore, even if an unauthorized modification enhances the public reputation, it would infringe on the right to integrity as long as it is contrary to the author's intention.

(2)   Actual examples

It has been generally understood that the right to integrity has considerable impact.

For example, a court held that, where there were changes of punctuation marks in an essay when the essay was reprinted on a magazine, such changes infringed the right to integrity as long as the changes were contrary to the author's intention.[24]

There is another court case involving a dating simulation game, where its game story was altered by use of a special save data of a memory card so that a certain game character appeared at a time in which she would not have appeared originally. The Supreme Court held that such alternation infringed the right to integrity over game images since the sequence of the game images displayed on a game screen went beyond those originally set by the game program and data.[25]

In addition, there is also another court case with respect to using a photograph for the purpose of a parody. The Supreme Court found that the photograph infringed on the right to integrity of the original work (i.e., photographic work of a snowy mountain and skiers) by producing a montage photograph in which a picture of a tire was superimposed on the original photograph.[26]

---

[24] Tokyo High Court decision of December 19, 1991, *Chitekisaishu*, Vol. 23, No. 3, p. 823.
[25] Supreme Court decision of February 13, 2001, *Minshu*, Vol. 55, No. 1, p. 87.

IV Right to integrity

PARODY MONTAGE CASE   (LEFT: Original work,   RIGHT: Alleged infringing work)

Although the significance of the right to integrity, for example, it would be unreasonable to a licensee who is authorized to make a novel into a film to be criticized on the ground that the licensee's film production infringes the right to integrity of the original novel. Therefore, in general, such argument would not be accepted.[27]

3 Limitations on the right to integrity

Considering the great impact provided by the right to integrity, the Copyright Law provides limitations on it under certain circumstances.

First, a work may be altered to an extent that is unavoidable from the perspective of school educational purposes, such as printing it in a textbook[28]. This provision allows, for example, changing the Chinese characters (*kanji*) of a work to simpler Japanese *hiragana* characters so that elementary school students can read it (provided that it is done within the limitations on copyright regarding the exploitation of a work in a textbook).[29] There is also a limitation on the extension, rebuilding, etc. of architecture.

---

[26] Supreme Court decision of March 28, 1980, *Minshu,* Vol. 34, No. 3, p. 244.
[27] Note that, in such case, it is a practical way to make an agreement with the author not to argue his/her right to integrity.
[28] Copyright Law, Art. 20(2)(ⅰ).
[29] Refer to Section 2(5), Part Ⅱ of UNIT 11.

UNIT 12 Copyright Law (5)

Since the architecture has more aspects of a practical product, the author's right to integrity will be limited if there is a conflict with the extension or rebuilding of the architecture (e.g., in the case of modification of architecture as an architectural work or a wall painting as an artistic work).[30] Furthermore, there is a special limitation on a computer program work, such as debugging or version upgrading of a computer program.[31] This limitation is established based on the idea that practicality is generally important for a computer program and the author's honor, reputation or personality would not be relatively reflected in the computer program. As a result, the user may, without the author's consent, fix a bug or modify a computer program to fit to a different computer, or make an improvement to increase the processing speed.

In addition to the modifications in the specific cases mentioned above, as a general limitation, Article 20(2)(iv) of the Copyright Law states that "a modification which is found to be unavoidable in light of the nature of a work and the purpose and circumstances of its exploitation" is also allowed. It is generally understood that this exception applies only to limited cases (e.g., in cases where an extremely high- or low-pitched part of a musical work could not be recorded due to a technical problem so that the work was not be reproduced perfectly, or in cases where the music could not be perfectly reproduced due to poor performance). Please note, however, that there is criticism regarding such limited interpretation and which argues that such exception should apply to more cases.[32]

V The exploitation of a work in a manner that is prejudicial to the honor or reputation of the author

1 What is the exploitation of a work in a manner that is prejudicial to the honor or reputation of the author?

In addition to the three types of moral rights explicitly provided under the Copyright Law, the Copyright Law categorizes certain acts as an infringement of the moral rights of an author. Article 113(6) of the Copyright Law states, "The exploitation of a work

---

[30] Copyright Law, Art. 20(2)(ii).
[31] Copyright Law, Art. 20(2)(iii).
[32] See Nobuhiro Nakayama, "Chosakuken Hou (Copyright Law)," 2nd edition, 2014, pp. 516-518, and Ryo Shimanami, et al., "Chosakuken Hou Nyumon (Copyright Law in Japan)," 2nd edition, 2016, p. 130.

in a way that is prejudicial to the honor or reputation of the author is deemed to constitute an infringement of the author's moral rights." According to the above provision, a certain act which does not fall under a specific type of the moral rights infringement can be regarded as the infringement of the author's moral rights if the work is exploited by way of harming the author's honor or reputation. This provision complements the protection of the moral interests of an author by preventing a work from being exploited in such a way that the author's intention is distorted or the artistic value of the work is spoiled.

For example, a case where a religious painting is exploited for advertisement of an obscene facility, or where a magnificent musical work is exploited for the punchline of a sketch comedy.

2 Honor or reputation

Unlike the other moral rights, Article 113(6) requires that the author's honor or reputation be infringed upon. In this respect, the provision above focuses not on the author's subjective feelings (i.e., if he feels that his honor or reputation was damaged), but on whether any act which would infringe the author's social honor or reputation was conducted.

VI Protection of moral interests after the author's death

1 Protection of moral interests after the author's death

An author's moral rights are exclusive rights which protect the author's moral interests. Therefore, in principle, the moral rights of an author lapse upon one's death. However, the Copyright Law provides protections for the author's moral interests to a certain extent even after the author's death. Article 60 of the Copyright Law states that "even after the author becomes non-existent, it is prohibited for a person that makes available or presents the author's work to the public to engage in an act that would be prejudicial to the moral rights of the author as if the author existed."[33] This protection covers not only the three moral rights of an author explicitly provided under the Copyright Law, but also the exploitation of a work prejudicial to the author's honor or reputation as

---

[33] Note that this provision provides "becomes non-existent" not "dies" because a legal entity can be the author in the case of a work for hire.

UNIT 12 Copyright Law (5)

described above.

2 Contents of protection

It is prohibited to conduct any act which infringes an author's moral rights even after the death of the author. Furthermore, the protection is granted without a term limit. However, there are several limitations compared to a case where the author is alive. First, the protection works only when a work is made available or presented to the public. For example, the protection is not granted even if a person modifies an author's painting by himself at home after the author's death (although such modification would infringe the right to integrity while the author is alive). In addition, the protection does not work "if an act conducted is found not to contravene an author's will in light of the nature and extent of the act as well as changes in social circumstances and other conditions." It is not clear in which specific cases an act is regarded as not to contravene the author's will. However, whether the moral rights of an author are infringed upon will be determined by taking into account various circumstances including the nature and extent of the act as well as changes of social circumstances.[34]

3 Who claims protection?

Protection based on the above provision continues to be effective for eternity. However, the protection cannot be inherited, and it is necessary to allow someone to claim this protection to prevent any infringement acts. The Copyright Law allows certain bereaved family members to seek an injunction and measures for restoring the author's honor (although they may not seek compensation for damages).[35]

However, in principle, only limited bereaved family members (i.e., spouse, child, parent, grandchild, grandparent, or sibling) of the author are eligible for such claim. Therefore, after their death, the work can be protected only by criminal penalties.[36] In the case of dissolution of a legal entity, the rights are exclusively protected by criminal penalties after dissolution.

---

[34] For example, it would be allowed that an author's diary which was not made public becomes made publicly available without his/her consent after hundreds of years from the author's death.
[35] Copyright Law, Art. 116.
[36] A fine up to five million yen in accordance with Copyright Law, Art. 120.

Design Law

I Overview of the Design Law

1 What is the Design Law?

(1) Importance of a design

A wide variety of designs exist in the world. When just looking at our personal belongings, there are various articles, such as stationery, tableware, home electronics, and packaging, which have a variety of shapes and patterns.

Since a design is an important factor for improving an article's function or appearance, the design of an article also needs to be protected.

(2) Purpose of the Design Law

The Design Law is a legal system for protecting a design as an intellectual property. Article 1 of the Design Law provides that its purpose is to encourage the creation of designs through promoting the protection and utilization of designs, which thereby contributes to the development of industries. The Design Law gives protection to a "design" (explained below in more detail) by granting a design right and promoting the utilization of the design so as to encourage creation of excellent designs and enhance the development of the industry.

2 Difference and similarity with the Patent Law

As mentioned above, the Design Law aims to enhance the development of an industry by protecting a design. The Patent Law, as mentioned in the other units, also aims to enhance the development of an industry by protecting an invention. In this section, we will review the difference and similarity between both laws.

(1) Invention and design

As the Design Law protects a design, the subject matter for protection differs from that of the Patent Law. Both laws aim to protect designs or inventions which are newly created by humans. Further, a design provides a wide variety of roles. Therefore, in the case of an industrial design of a machine component, the subject matter for protection

UNIT 13   Design Law

would be substantially identical to an invention of such component. However, the Patent Law protects only an invention but does not protect a design. Also, as explained below, a design is not technology itself but an article's external appearance. Therefore, a design sometimes overlaps, and sometimes does not overlap, an invention.

(2) Need of registration

Similar to the Patent Law, protection cannot be given to a design which is merely created. To obtain the exclusive right to the design, the design needs to be filed with the JPO in a predetermined format and then examined and registered. Therefore, in the Design Law, unlike the Copyright Law, protection is not automatically given to a design when it is merely created.[1]

(3) Exclusive right

Similar to a patent right, a design right is an exclusive right. Therefore, even though a person creates a design independently from and without imitating another person's registered design, such act may constitute infringement.

(4) Duration of protection

Similar to a patent right, there is a limitation on the duration of protection of a design right. However, unlike a patent right, the duration of the design right is 20 years from the date when the design is registered (and not from the date of application).[2]

3   Protection under the Unfair Competition Prevention Law

In addition to a design right obtained through application, examination and registration, a design of an article is also protected by the Unfair Competition Prevention Law which prohibits imitation of the form.[3]

The Unfair Competition Prevention Law prohibits, as an act of unfair competition, the acts of assigning, leasing, displaying for a purpose of assigning or leasing, exporting and importing goods which imitated a certain form of another person's goods. Further, a person whose business interests have been damaged by unfair competition can (i) request an injunction[4], and (ii) seek compensation for damages incurred if the unfair competition act was conducted negligently or with intent.[5]

---

[1] Refer to Section 3, Part I of UNIT 1.
[2] Design Law, Art. 21(1).
[3] Unfair Competition Prevention Law, Art. 2(1)(iii).
[4] Unfair Competition Prevention Law, Art. 3.
[5] Unfair Competition Prevention Law, Art. 4.

II What is a design?

The Unfair Competition Prevention Law is similar to the Design Law in terms of protecting a design of an article; however, unlike the Design Law, the design can be protected without application and examination procedures. On the other hand, the Unfair Competition Prevention Law: (i) only covers counterfeit goods (i.e., goods which were created based on the form of another person's goods and are substantially identical to such goods;[6] and (ii) applies only for three years from the date the goods were first sold in Japan.[7]

II What is a design?

The Design Law protects a "design," which according to Article 2(1) of the Design Law must satisfy the following four requirements:

(1) being the form "of an article;"

(2) being an article's "shape, patterns or colors, or any combination thereof" which are collectively called "form;"

(3) bringing about an aesthetic impression "through the eye" (visual observation) and

(4) bringing about "an aesthetic impression."

1 Form "of an article"

(1) Design of an article

One of the characteristic features of the Design Law is the scope of the design to be protected. Specifically, the Design Law only protects a design of an article.

An "article" must be a tangible object. Therefore, for example a design of a gas, liquid or powder that has no fixed shape would not be protected under the Design Law. Also, since a design of light such as a laser or fireworks is not a design of an article, it is also not protected.

(2) Being transactional and a partial design

An article must be independently transactional or saleable. For example, considering an automobile or a fountain pen which are independently saleable articles, the tires of an automobile and the tip of a fountain pen are not finished products; however, since they are independently saleable, they would also be considered an "article."

---

[6] Unfair Competition Prevention Law, Art. 2(5).
[7] Unfair Competition Prevention Law, Art. 19(1)(V)(a).

In addition, there are cases where the partial design of an article is innovative and significant, but the part of the article itself is not independently transactional; e.g., the shape of an automobile's roof or the shape of a grip of a fountain pen. There is a partial design protection system which protects such partial designs. As shown below, the partial design of an article can be registered.

(Examination Guidelines for Design, 71.7.1.2.1)

The above example shows where the registration of a handle of scissors, which is unlikely saleable by itself, is requested as a partial design. The portion for which protection is sought is shown in the solid lines and the blade of the scissors for which protection is not sought is shown in the broken lines.

2 "Form" of an article

The elements of a design to be protected are limited to "the shape, patterns or colors or any combination thereof"[8] and are collectively considered the "form" of an article. Other elements of a design such as glossiness and texture are not protected by the Design Law. Only the shape, patterns and colors of an article are protected by the Design Law. Since every article has a shape, the following four types of designs are protected: (i) an article's shape; (ii) combination of an article's shape and a pattern; (iii) combination of an article's shape and color; and (iv) combination of an article's shape, pattern and color.

3 Visual observation

Since the Design Law protects an external appearance of the design, the design to be protected must be visually observed through the eye.

A design that is too small and cannot be observed by the naked eye is excluded from protection unless it is common practice to view the design under magnification when selling the article. In particular, this issue would arise in the case of precision machinery

---

[8] Design Law, Art. 2(1).

II   What is a design?

component. For example, in the case of an industrial design of an extremely small connector terminal, a court held that the design cannot be registered because it could not be perceived by the naked eye and it was not common practice to make a magnified observation in a catalog when selling the connector terminal.[9]

Also, the article's inner structure which cannot be observed from the outside may not be protected by the Design Law. Therefore, for example, even if an innovative driving unit is incorporated into a robot toy, the driving unit would not be recognized as a design of the robot toy unless it could be observed from the outside. However, if the inner structure can be observed from the outside under normal use conditions, it would be recognized as a design. For example, the keyboard of a piano cannot be observed from the outside when the lid of the piano is closed. However, when playing the piano, the design of the keyboard can be naturally observed from the outside because the lid of the piano is open. Therefore, the design of the keyboard can be recognized and protected as a design (of a piano).

4   Aesthetic impression

Finally, it must be noted that the Design Law focuses on an aesthetic impression. Although an aesthetic impression has little function as a requirement, this requirement is to exclude from protection a form which only has a technical implication.

5   Design of a graphic image

It would be difficult to consider the operational screen design of a smartphone as a design of the smartphone itself, and therefore, an operational screen design may not be considered to be a form of an article.

However, a graphic image on a screen is an essential element of today's electronic devices. Most electronic devices (e.g., personal computers and smartphones) and home electronics are provided with a liquid crystal screen to display a lot of information. On the liquid crystal screen, various designs of graphic images are used so that the devices can be efficiently used or a user can recognize at a glance how to use the device. Thus, the design of the graphic image displayed on a screen is significant in terms of user-friendliness of the device.

---

[9] Intellectual Property High Court decision of March 31, 2006, *Hanrei Jiho*, No. 1929, p. 84.

UNIT 13   Design Law

In light of the circumstances where the demand for protection of a graphic image design is increasing, in current Design Law practice, there are two types of designs of a graphic image which are protected by the Design Law.[10]

(1)   Graphic image necessary for an article's function

A graphic image of an article that is subject to the Design Law will be protected if it satisfies the following requirements: (i) the image displayed is necessary for the article's function; and (ii) the image is recorded in such article.

A typical example is a liquid-crystal clock. The graphic image of the clock which shows the time that is displayed on a liquid-crystal screen is essential to fulfill the function of the liquid-crystal clock. Therefore, such graphic image could be protected as the form of the liquid-crystal clock.

(2)   Graphic image used for article's operation

Also, a graphic image of an article that is subjected to the Design Law will be considered to be the form of an article if it satisfies the following requirements: (i) the image is provided for use in the article's operation in order to enable the article to perform its function; (ii) the image is displayed on the article or on an article used in combination with the article; and (iii) the image is recorded in the article.[11] Unlike the graphic image described in the preceding paragraph, an operational screen used to fulfill the article's function would be protected.

For example, an operational screen of a smartphone used to fulfill the calendar function, and the operational screen of an HDD recorder to perform programmed recording (although the image is normally displayed on a connected monitor) would also be protected.

On the other hand, a video game screen, for example, cannot be protected under the Design Law since it does not fall under either type of the graphic images to be protected as mentioned above in that image on the screen is an image of the game software, which is content that is independent of the article itself.

According to the recent revision of Examination Guidelines for Design, a computer may constitute a new article with specific function where it is integrated with software (a computer with additional function). In this case, a graphic image of a software that has been recorded in the article shall be handled as if may constitute the form of a

---

[10] *See* Examination Guidelines for Design, Part VII, Chapter IV.
[11] Design Law, Art. 2(2).

part of the new article. This revision would provide some protection for graphic images of application software.

Ⅲ Requirements for design registration

1 Requirements for registration

Similar to the Patent Law where an invention must satisfy the patent requirements to obtain a patent for the invention,[12] a design must satisfy certain requirements in order to be registered.

2 Industrial applicability

If the article for which a design is used cannot be manufactured on a large scale by means of industrial production, protection of such design would not contribute to the development of industry, and thus, would not meet the purpose of the Design Law. Therefore, in order for a design to be registered, the design must be "industrially applicable."

The industrial applicability does not necessarily mean that the article has to be manufactured in a plant. However, the article needs to be manufactured on a large scale by an industrial production method (including the handicraft industry). Therefore, a one-off article such as a painting or carving would not be protected under the Design Law since it was not supposed to be manufactured on a large scale. Also, a design created by using a shape of natural products without modification by humans (e.g., a design created by using the shape of a natural stone), would not be protected because such article cannot be manufactured on a large scale.

3 Novelty

(1) Publicly-known design

There is no need to protect a publicly-known design by giving a design right. Since a publicly-known design already exists in the world, it is not necessary to enhance its creation. Further, if a design right, which is an exclusive right, was given to the publicly-known design, this could inhibit the development of related industries. This concept is

---

[12] Refer to UNIT 3.

UNIT 13   Design Law

similar to that of the Patent Law.

Accordingly, a publicly-known design, which at the time of applying for a design registration was: (i) publicly known; or (ii) described in a distributed publication or made publicly available through an electronic telecommunication line, cannot be registered.[13]

(2) Design similar to a publicly-known design

In addition to a design which is identical to a publicly-known design, a design which is similar to a publicly-known design cannot be registered.[14] This is based on the idea that a design which is similar to a publicly-known design has no value for protection, and therefore, a design right should not be granted for such design.

The table shown below indicates how to determine the similarity of designs.

	Identical article	Similar article	Dissimilar article
Identical form	Identical design	Similar design	Dissimilar design
Similar form	Similar design	Similar design	Dissimilar design
Dissimilar form	Dissimilar design	Dissimilar design	Dissimilar design

Since a design is an article's form, when determining the similarity of a design, both the article and the form need to be similar. If either an article or form is dissimilar, such design would be regarded as a dissimilar design. For more detail, please see the paragraph concerning the exercise of a design right in Section 2, Part VI of this UNIT 13.

(3) Exception to the lack of novelty

The Design Law also provides an exception which is similar to the exception to a lack of novelty in the Patent Law.[15] For example, even if a design was displayed in a trade fair and became publicly known prior to its application for registration, there still would remain a possibility that such design would not lose its novelty if certain conditions are met.[16]

---

[13] Design Law, Art. 3(1)(i) and (ii).
[14] Design Law, Art. 3(1)(iii).
[15] Patent Law, Art. 30; Refer to Section 7, Part III of UNIT3.
[16] Design Law, Art. 4.

III Requirements for design registration

4 Not easily created

Where a person ordinarily skilled in the art of a design can easily create a design based on a publicly known form, such design cannot be registered.[17] Even where the design has novelty, if a person skilled in the art can easily create the design, there is no need to encourage the creation by giving it protection. On the contrary, if a design right, which is an exclusive right, was given to such design, this could inhibit the development of related industries. Therefore, the Design Law requires that a design not be easily created from the publicly known form (and not from the publicly known design as in the requirement for novelty).

Therefore, in the case where only the pattern is publicly known, although the pattern is not a publicly known "design" (since the pattern itself is not an article), if the person skilled in the art can easily create a design by applying the pattern to a certain article, the design registration could not be made due to not meeting the requirement of being "not easily created."

5 First-to-file system

As with a patent right, a design right is an exclusive right and thus cannot be granted to more than one person. Therefore, the first-to-file principle is also employed in the Design Law.[18] When several applications are filed for an identical or similar design, only the first applicant is entitled to obtain the design registration (where two or more applications are filed on the same date, it is handled in a manner similar to the Patent Law[19]).

6 A design of a later application which is identical or similar to a part of a design of a prior application will be excluded from protection

In the Design Law, as with the Patent Law, a registered design is to be published in a design gazette. Therefore, when an automobile's design is registered, the whole design of an automobile including the tire portion is published in a design gazette. As a result, in addition to a subsequently filed design of an automobile which is identical or

---

[17] Design Law, Art. 3(2).
[18] Design Law, Art. 9; Refer to Part V of UNIT 3.
[19] Refer to Section 2(1), Part V of UNIT 3.

UNIT 13   Design Law

similar to the registered design, the subsequently filed design of a tire which is identical or similar to the tire portion of the registered design would have no novelty and be denied.

On the other hand, even if the automobile's design was already filed, if the design of the tire is filed before the automobile's design is published through a design gazette, the design of the tire would not lose novelty.[20] Also, the first-to-file principle is applied only when the filed design is identical or similar to another design. Therefore, since an automobile and a tire are dissimilar in terms of its article and form, both of the above designs appear to be registered.

However, it is not appropriate to grant a design right to a tire design, which will become known to the public when the automobile's design is published in the gazette, only because the gazette of the automobile's design had not yet been published. Further, there are complicated issues concerning the scope of rights if a design right of an automobile and a design right of a tire are owned by different people.

Accordingly, the Design Law provides that a design of a subsequently filed application that is identical or similar to a part of a design of a prior application cannot be registered.[21] Thus, in the preceding case, a subsequently filed design of a tire which is identical or similar to the tire portion of an automobile will be rejected.

7   Unregistrable design

The following designs are not registrable: (i) a design which would likely injure public order or morality; (ii) a design which would likely cause confusion with an article of another person's business; and (iii) a design solely consisting of a shape that is essential to ensure the functions of the article.[22] The following are examples of the above designs, respectively: (i) a design that represents another country's national flag; (ii) a design that simply represents another person's famous mark; and (iii) a shape of a reflector of a parabolic antenna or a shape standardized to secure its compatibility.

IV   Person who is protected

A person who is to be protected under the Design Law is determined in a manner

---

[20] Unlike the Patent Law, there is no application publication system in the Design Law.

[21] Design Law, Art. 3-2.

[22] Design Law, Art. 5.

V Application and examination / trial

similar to the Patent Law. Also, a misappropriated application and an employee design are also handled similarly to those of the Patent Law.[23]

V Application and examination / trial

The procedures of application and examination / trial are similar to those in the Patent Law. Therefore, in this paragraph, only an outline of the procedures is explained.[24]

1 Application

For a design registration, together with the application, the drawings, in principle, must be submitted to the Commissioner of JPO.[25] Unlike the Patent Law, there are no description articles such as claims, and the scope of the right is determined only based on the statements in the application and drawings.

Although each design must be described in its own application,[26] if a certain set of articles has one coordinated design as a whole; e.g., a set of tableware, this set of articles may be accepted as a "design for a set of articles."[27]

Unlike the Patent Law, as there is no publication of application system in the Design Law, a design in a pending application for design registration is not available to the public until it is published in a design gazette. Additionally, by following a certain procedure, an applicant may request that the drawings and the statement mentioned in the application of a registered design not be published in a design gazette for a certain period, which is known as the "secret design" system.[28] The secret design system may allow the applicant to keep the design secret and retain protection as a design right until, for example, the timing of a product announcement.

2 Examination

Similar to the Patent Law, an examiner examines whether or not the respective requirements for registration are met. If no reason for refusal is found, the examiner must

---

[23] Refer to UNIT 4.
[24] Refer to UNIT 5.
[25] Design Law, Art. 6(1).
[26] Design Law, Art. 7.
[27] Design Law, Art. 8.
[28] Design Law, Art. 14.

UNIT 13   Design Law

render a decision to grant a design right.

3   Trial

The Design Law allows for a trial against a decision of refusal and a trial for invalidation of design registration.[29]

However, it does not provide a trial for correction, and a trial for invalidation of a registration of extension is also not provided.

On the other hand, the Design Law provides a trial against the examiner's decision to reject an amendment,[30] which enables one to obtain a prompt determination on whether an amendment is acceptable.

VI   Design right and exercise of it

1   Contents of design right

Similar to a patent right, a design right is an exclusive right to work the design for a business (such as the manufacture, use, or assign the article of the design for a business).[31] The design right covers the work of a design which is identical or similar to a registered design.[32]

The duration of a design right is a period of 20 years from the date of its registration.[33]

2   Exercise of design right

The holder of a design right has the right to seek an injunction[34] and compensation for damages[35] against another party's work of a design which is identical or similar to a registered design without the consent of the holder. This paragraph will discuss design right infringement by focusing on the similarity of designs.

---

[29] Design Law, Arts. 46 and 48.
[30] Design Law, Art. 47.
[31] Design Law, Art. 2(3).
[32] Design Law, Art. 23.
[33] Design Law, Art. 21(1).
[34] Design Law, Art. 37.
[35] Civil Code, Art. 709.

VI Design right and exercise of it

(1) Similarity of articles

To determine that a registered design is similar to a design of an article at issue, the article of the registered design and the article at issue must be similar.

Whether the articles are similar is determined based on their usage and function. If the article of the registered design has a common usage and function with the article at issue, the articles will be determined to be similar. On the other hand, if the article of the registered design has no common usage and function with the article at issue, the articles will be determined to be dissimilar. There was a cosmetic puff case where the similarity between a powder puff and a germanium silicon brush was an issue. In the above case, the court held that the general function of the powder puff is putting foundation on the face, but the powder puff also has the usage and function of cleansing the face, and thus, the germanium silicon brush which was used for cleansing and massaging the face was similar to the cosmetic puff.[36]

(2) Similarity in form

In addition to the similarity of the article, the form of the registered design and the form of the article at issue must be similar. In general, the registered design and the design of an article at issue are to be identified, and then an essential part of the registered design is identified. In principle, when the essential part of the registered design is in common with the design of the article at issue, the similarity in form between the designs is recognized, which would constitute an infringement of the design right.

The similarity between the designs must be determined through the eye of a consumer.[37] Therefore, the essential part of a design is a part which would draw the strong attention of a consumer. For example, regarding a design of a television, a consumer would pay attention to the form of the front face of the television but would not pay much attention to the form of the rear face of the television. Therefore, the essential part of a design of a television is in general found in the front face. Thus, when a design has only the form of the rear face in common with another design, this would not be considered similar forms of a design.

Also, consumers would not pay attention to a widely-known form. Therefore, a widely-known form is hardly recognized as an essential part of a design. Accordingly, if a design has only a widely-known form in common with another design, it would not be

---

[36] Osaka District Court decision of December 15, 2005, *Hanrei Jiho*, No. 1936, p. 155.
[37] Design Law, Art. 24(2).

recognized that the form of the design is similar.

Let's see a specific example.

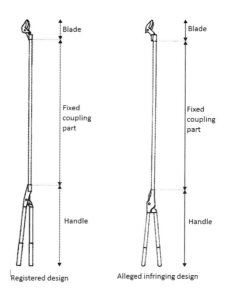

In the *"long-handled branch cutter"* case, the similarity between the above designs was at issue.[38]

The court held that "the consumers of a long-handled branch cutter would focus on the shape of the blades ... the ratio of the length of the fixed coupling part or the length of the handle with respect to the entire length of the branch cutter and the shape of the handle." Also, the court determined that the shape of the handle was not an essential part because the shape of the handle was simple and had already been publicly known. The defendant in the case argued that the shape of the joint part was also an essential part (since the shape of the joint part of the alleged infringing design was different from that of the registered design, if the shape of the joint part was acknowledged as an essential part, the alleged design would be considered dissimilar and the claim of infringement would be denied). However, the court denied the above argument by stating that the consumers of a long-handled branch cutter would not focus on the shape of the joint part. Thus, the

---

[38] Osaka District Court decision of December 16, 2010 (2010 (*Wa*) No. 4770).

court held that "the essential part of the present registered design is the shape of the blades and the ratio of the length of the fixed coupling part or the length of the handle with respect to the entire length of the branch cutter," and thus, the alleged design infringed upon the registered design.

3 Infringement by utilizing a registered design

The similarity between designs can be directly comparable as in the case above, however, there are some cases where a registered design is included in another party's design.

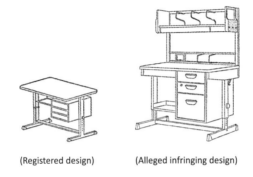

(Registered design)   (Alleged infringing design)

The desk for studying shown on the left side is the registered design. The desk with a shelf shown on the right side is the alleged infringing design. The alleged infringer was using a design of a desk provided with a shelf. When comparing the two designs, they both would be recognized as dissimilar designs. However, the desk part of the alleged infringing design is similar to the registered design. Where a registered design is incorporated into another design as a part of the design, the alleged infringing design utilizes the registered design, and therefore, there would be an infringement of the registered design.[39]

4 Indirect infringement

Similar to the Patent Law, the Design Law also sets forth a provision concerning indirect infringement.[40] However, unlike the Patent Law, the Design Law classifies only the

---

[39] See Design Law, Art. 26; Osaka District Court decision of December 22, 1971, *Mutaisaishu*, Vol. 3, No. 2, p. 414.

UNIT 13   Design Law

following business type acts as indirect infringement: (1) an act such as producing or assigning a product which is used exclusively to produce an article of a registered design or similar design thereof; and (2) an act of possessing an article of a registered design or similar design thereof for the purpose of assigning, leasing or exporting it.

5   Defense

The concept of a defense in the Design Law is referred to in Part Ⅲ of UNIT 7 regarding the infringement of a patent right. Specifically, a prior use right, invalidity defense and exhaustion of a design right are defenses which may be asserted in a design infringement suit.

The Design Law also has a provision regarding a non-exclusive license based on a prior application, which is specific for the Design Law.[41]

Ⅶ   Utilization of design right

Similar to a patent right, a holder of a design right is allowed to do the following acts: work the design; transfer the design right; establish an exclusive license for the design right; grant a non-exclusive license for the design right; and establish a pledge over the design right.[42]

---

[40] Design Law, Art. 38; Refer to Section 3, Part Ⅱ of UNIT 7.

[41] Design Law, Art. 29-2.

[42] Refer to UNIT 6.

Unit 14: Trademark Law

I Outline of Trademark Law

1 Protection of trademarks

A trademark is an identification mark used to distinguish one's own goods or services provided by a business from those provided by another business. Specifically, a trademark is a mark which has a function to distinguish one's own goods or services from those of another person. Thus, a trademark embodies a business' commercial reputation which the business has obtained through its commercial efforts.

Where the trademark, which embodies the commercial reputation of a business, is used by another person without permission of the business the benefits which the business should receive from a consumer due to its reputation are taken away by another person. Thus, if the use of a trademark by another person without permission is not prohibited, a business would not put forth any efforts to increase its business reputation.

The Trademark Law is to protect trademarks and ensure that the commercial reputation of the people who use trademarks is maintained, and it is thereby intended to contribute to the development of the industry and protect the consumers' interest.[1]

As understood from the above, the scope of protection of the Trademark Law differs from that of the Patent Law, Copyright Law and Design Law. The Patent Law and other laws are creative laws which protect the results of creative activity of individuals. On the contrary, the Trademark Law is a labelling law which protects the marks which embody a commercial reputation.[2]

2 Functions of trademarks

Trademarks have the function of distinguishing one's own goods or services from those of another person, and the following three functions are derived from this function.

(1) Function of indicating the origin: Function of indicating that certain goods or

---

[1] Trademark Law, Art. 1
[2] Refer to Section 3, Part I of UNIT 1.

UNIT 14   Trademark Law

services for which the same trademark is used have the same origin.

(2)   Function of guaranteeing the consistency of the quality: Function of indicating that goods or services for which the same trademark is used have the same quality.

(3)   Function of promoting and advertising: By frequent use of a trademark, the trademark is remembered by the consumer so as to increase and induce the consumption of the goods or services.

3   Scope of protection

The Trademark Law protects "trademarks". A "trademark" is any word(s), figure (s), symbol(s) or three-dimensional shape(s) or colors, or any combination thereof, sounds and others (to be set forth in a cabinet order) which are: (1) used in connection with a goods of a person who commercially produces the goods (a "goods trademark"); or (2) used in connection with a service of a person who commercially provides the service (a "service trademark")[3].

Conventionally, as a trademark, a word trademark, a figurative trademark, a symbolic trademark or a three-dimensional trademark, or any combination thereof had been within the scope of protection. In accordance with the revision of the Trademark Law in 2014, sounds were added to the constituent of the trademark, so that a sound trademark is now within the scope of the protection. Additionally, color trademarks, dynamic trademarks, hologram trademarks and positional trademarks were added to the scope of the protection.

However, aromatic trademarks, tactile trademarks and taste trademarks do not fall within the scope of protection. If these trademarks need to be protected in the future, they will be added in accordance with a cabinet order.

Even where a mark is not protected as a "trademark," as mentioned below, it is also possible to receive protection as an "indication of goods or business" under the Unfair Competition Prevention Law.

---

[3] Trademark Law, Art. 2, (1)

I   Outline of Trademark Law

| Scope of the protection of the Trademark law |

NO. 618689
Word trademark; consisting only of character(s), including *hiragana*, *katakana*, roman characters, numbers, and foreign languages.

No. 4239513
Figurative trademark; consisting only of figure(s), including graphic figure(s), stylized figure(s), a combination of figures and figured word(s), etc.

No. 449081
Symbolic trademark; consisting only of symbol(s), including emblem(s), trade name(s), symbolic alphabet(s) or Japanese characters, etc.

No. 4182141
Three-dimensional trademark; consisting of a three-dimensional shape; including an advertising doll, container for goods, shape of goods, etc.

No. 5930334
Color trademark; consisting only of color(s); consisting of one color or a combination of colors without a border or outline.

No. 5190340
Combined trademark; consisting of a combination of at least two elements of a word, symbol, figure, three-dimensional shape, and color.

No. 5804299
Sound trademark; consisting of music, sound, natural tones and others which is auditorily sensible, including a trademark only consisting of musical elements, linguistic elements, and a combination thereof.

No. 5842088
Dynamic trademark; in which a word, figure, etc., change with the lapse of time.

No. 5804315
Hologram trademark; in which a word, figure, etc., change in a holographic or by other methods.

No. 5804314
Positional trademark; where the position of a word, figure, etc., is to be provided on the goods is specified.

UNIT 14   Trademark Law

4   Requirement of protection (requirement for registration)

(1)   Outline

In order to receive the protection of a trademark, an application for registration of the trademark for which protection is sought should be filed. In order to register the trademark, the requirement of the protection (requirement for registration) is to be satisfied. A trademark cannot be registered if it falls under one of the following three cases.

(1)   Trademark which is not capable of distinguishing one's own goods or services and those of another person;[4]

(2)   Trademark which cannot be registered from the perspective of public interest;[5] or

(3)   Trademark which cannot be registered from the perspective of private interest.[6]

The JPO will conduct an examination to determine whether the trademark falls under any of the above cases (1), (2) and (3), and if such trademark does not fall within the above cases, the JPO will render a decision that the trademark is to be registered. Upon payment of the registration fees, the trademark right is registered and a trademark right is created.[7]

Where a trademark falls under any of the above cases (1), (2) and (3), the application for a trademark registration will be refused. Where a trademark which is registered in error which falls into any of the above cases (1), (2) and (3), such registration is revocable.[8] Thus, where the Invalidation trial decision becomes final and binding, the trademark right shall be deemed not to have existed retroactively[9].

---

[4] Trademark Law, Art. 3(1) for each item.
[5] Trademark Law, Art. 4(1), items (ⅰ) to (ⅶ), (ⅸ), (ⅹⅵ) and (ⅹⅷ).
[6] Trademark Law, Art. 4(1), items (ⅷ), (ⅹ), (ⅺ), (ⅻ), (ⅹⅳ), (ⅹⅴ), (ⅹⅶ) and (ⅹⅸ).
[7] Trademark Law, Art. 18.
[8] Trademark Law, Art. 46(1)(ⅰ).
[9] Trademark Law, Art. 46-2

I Outline of Trademark Law

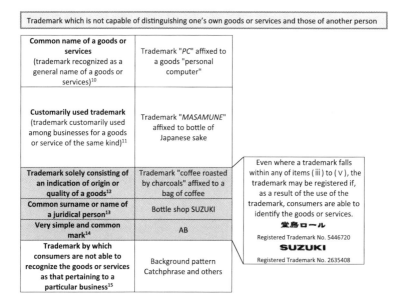

(2) Trademark which is not capable of distinguishing one's own goods or services and those of another person

Since a trademark is a mark for distinguishing one's own goods or services and those of another person, a trademark which is not capable of distinguishing one's own goods or services from those of another person may not be registered.[16] However, in accordance with Article 3(2), a trademark which falls within Article 3(1)(ⅲ) to (Ⅴ) may be registered where the trademark is capable of distinguishing one's own goods or services and those of another person by use.

(3) Trademark which cannot be registered from the perspective of public interest

From the perspective of the public interest, trademarks listed in the following chart, e.g., trademarks which may give rise to a confusion with the indication used by a nonprofit organization, cannot be registered.[17]

---

[10] Trademark Law, Art. 3(1)(ⅰ).
[11] Trademark Law, Art. 3(1)(ⅱ).
[12] Trademark Law, Art. 3(1)(ⅲ).
[13] Trademark Law, Art. 3(1)(ⅳ).
[14] Trademark Law, Art. 3(1)(Ⅴ).
[15] Trademark Law, Art. 3(1)(ⅵ).
[16] Trademark Law, Art. 3(1), for each item.
[17] Trademark Law, Art. 4(1)(ⅰ) to (ⅶ), (ⅸ), (ⅹⅵ) and (ⅹⅷ).

UNIT 14   Trademark Law

> **Trademark which shall not be registered due to public interest**

	Example of marks	Example of marks which shall not be registered
Trademark identical with or similar to the indications used by a nonprofit organization and others (Art. 4(1)(i) to (vi) and (ix))	Chrysanthemum (item (i)) Mark of IAEA (item (iii)) Mark of Red Cross (item (iv))	- Trademark identical with or similar to the national flag and others of Japan or foreign countries (Art. 4(1)(i)); - Trademark identical with or similar to the badge of the Union to the Paris Convention (Art. 4(1)(ii)); - Trademark identical with or similar to the badge of the United Nations and other international organizations (Art. 4(1)(iii), except for the case mentioned in above cases Art. 4(1)(iii)(a)(b)); - Trademark identical with or similar to the emblem or title of the red cross with a white background (Art. 4(1)(iv)); - Trademark identical with or similar to an official hallmark or sign indicating control or warranty by the national or local government (Art. 4(1)(v)); - Trademark identical with or similar to the famous mark indicating the state, local authorities or organizations thereof, or nonprofit organizations (Art. 4(1)(v)); and - Trademark identical with or similar to the mark of a prize awarded at an exhibition (Art. 4(1)(ix)).
Trademark which is likely to cause damage to public policy (Art. 4(1)(vii))	- "Dr. ○○"	- Trademark having a structure with words and figures which are too extreme, obscene, discriminative or offensive - Trademark which use is prohibited by law - Trademark which is offensive to a national of a specific country or a trademark against international faith
Trademark which is likely to mislead as to the quality of the goods/services (Art. 4(1)(xvi))	Trademark as "○○ gastrointestinal agents" for a cold remedy as a designated goods	Trademark likely to mislead as to the quality of the goods/services in relation to the trademarks
Trademark consisting of features/ characters which the trademark must be comprised of as provided by Cabinet Order	- spherical ball - colors and sounds naturally arising from goods and others	- Tire of a car which must be round - Black color as a color of charcoal - Sound generated when pouring a carbonated drink into a glass

(4)   Trademark which cannot be registered from the perspective of private interest

Trademark which is likely to infringe the right of another person cannot be registered. This includes:

(1)   Trademarks containing the portrait or the name/title of another person;[18]

(2)   Trademarks identical with or similar to another person's well-known

---

[18] Trademark Law, Art. 4(1)(viii)

184

I   Outline of Trademark Law

trademark;[19]

(3)   Trademarks identical with or similar to another person's prior registered trademark which registered trademark had been filed prior to the filing date of the application for registration of such identical or similar trademarks;[20]

(4)   Trademarks identical with a registered defensive mark (defined below) of another person;[21]

(5)   Trademarks identical with or similar to the name of a plant variety registered in accordance with the Plant Variety Protection and Seed Law;[22]

(6)   Trademarks which are likely to cause confusion in the source or origin of goods or services;[23]

(7)   Trademarks comprised of a mark indicating the place of origin of wines or spirits;[24] and

(8)   Trademarks using another person's famous trademark for unfair purposes.[25]

However, among the above cases, trademarks that fall under cases (1), (2), (6) and (8) will not be refused unless such trademarks fall under any of these cases at the time of filing of an application as well as at the time of the grant of the trademark registration.[26]

(a)   Trademarks containing the portrait or the name/title of another person

A trademark containing the portrait or the name, title, etc. of another person cannot be registered.[27] This provision is for the protection of the moral rights of another person. However, with the approval of the person, his/her moral rights will not be infringed upon, and the trademark may be registered.[28]

(b)   Trademarks identical with or similar to another person's well known trademark

A trademark identical with or similar to another person's well known trademark (a trademark widely recognized among consumers) that is used in connection with goods or services identical with or similar to those of another person cannot be registered.[29] This

---

[19] Trademark Law, Art. 4(1)(Ⅹ)
[20] Trademark Law, Art. 4(1)(ⅹⅰ).
[21] Trademark Law, Art. 4(1)(ⅹⅱ).
[22] Trademark Law, Art. 4(1)(ⅹⅳ).
[23] Trademark Law, Art. 4(1)(ⅹⅴ).
[24] Trademark Law, Art. 4(1)(ⅹⅶ).
[25] Trademark Law, Art. 4(1)(ⅹⅸ).
[26] Trademark Law, Art. 4(3).
[27] Trademark Law, Art. 4(1)(ⅷ).
[28] Trademark Law, Art. 4(1)(ⅷ), *See* parenthesis.
[29] Trademark Law, Art. 4(1)(Ⅹ).

UNIT 14   Trademark Law

provision is for the protection of the vested interest in the trademark in which another person has been built a certain reputation, and for the prevention of a confusion of the origin of the goods or services.

(c) Trademarks identical with or similar to another person's prior registered trademark which had been filed prior to the filing date of an application for registration of such identical or similar trademarks

A trademark identical with or similar to another person's prior registered trademark which had been filed prior to the filing date of an application for registration of such trademark cannot be registered if such a trademark is used in connection with goods or services identical with or similar to the designated goods or designated services relating to the registered trademark.[30]

Trademark Law applies the principle of prior application (i.e., "first-to-file"). The principle of prior application is a principle in which the first application filed would be entitled to the trademark right.[31] If an application is filed for a trademark which is identical with or similar to a registered trademark which application for registration had been filed prior to the application for the identical or similar trademark, such identical or similar trademark should not be registered due to the principle of prior application.

(d) Trademarks identical with a registered defensive mark of another person

A trademark identical with a registered defensive mark of another person, if such a trademark is used in connection with designated goods or designated services relating to the defensive mark registration cannot be registered[32].

The defensive mark (*Bogohyosho*) is a system for the enhanced protection of a famous registered trademark.[33] If a famous registered trademark is registered as a defensive mark in connection with goods and services not similar to the goods or services used by the trademark user, such user can prevent an identical trademark from being registered by another person. The use of the trademark identical with the registered defensive trademark for the designated goods or designated services is deemed to be an infringement of the trademark right and is thus prohibited.[34]

---

[30] Trademark Law, Art. 4(1)(xi).
[31] Trademark Law, Art. 8(1).
[32] Trademark Law, Art. 4(1)(xii).
[33] Trademark Law, Art. 64.
[34] Trademark Law, Art. 67(1).

I Outline of Trademark Law

(e) Trademarks identical with or similar to the name of a plant variety registered in accordance with the Plant Variety Protection and Seed Act

A trademark identical with or similar to the name of a plant variety registered in accordance with the Plant Variety Protection and Seed Law and used in connection with seeds or seedlings of the plant variety or for goods or services similar to the plant variety cannot be registered.[35]

In accordance with the Plant Variety Protection and Seed Law, any person who commercially transfers seeds or seedlings of a registered plant variety shall be obligated to use the name of the registered plant variety and be prohibited from using the name of any plant varieties when he/she transfers seeds or seedlings of a plant variety other than the registered plant variety or similar plant variety.[36] The purpose of the Trademark Law, Article 4(1)(xiv) is to prevent a trademark right from being generated by the registration of a trademark identical with or similar to the name of the seeds and seedlings of the registered plant variety or goods or services similar to such plant variety.

(f) Trademarks which are likely to cause confusion in the source or origin of goods or services

A trademark which is likely to cause confusion in connection with the goods or services pertaining to a business of another person cannot be registered.[37]

Since the trademarks which are likely to cause confusion in the source of origin may indeed confuse the consumers and such confusing trademark does not have its contemplated function to distinguish one's own goods or services from those of another person and therefore, this provision prohibit such confusing trademarks from being registered.

The "confusion" set in forth in Item (XV) accordingly contemplates the situation where the goods or services are of the origin of another person, when the trademark which application for registration has been filed is used for the "designated" goods or services (confusion in the narrow sense). The "confusion" set forth item (XV) also contemplates the situation where consumers may misunderstand that a certain economical or organizational relationship exists between the goods or services of the applicant and those of another person (even though there is no misidentification in origin

---

[35] Trademark Law, Art. 4(1)(xiv).
[36] Plant Variety Protection and Seed Act, Art. 22.
[37] Trademark Law, Art. 4(1)(XV).

UNIT 14   Trademark Law

of goods or services in the strict sense (confusion in the broad sense). Item (XV) thus meets the situation, for example, where consumers are misled or confused to misconceive that the goods or services are produced or sold by the user of the famous trademark or a person who has an economical or organizational relationship to him even though the trademark identical with or similar to an another person's famous trademark is used for the goods or services which is not similar to goods or services for which the famous trademark is used.

(g)   Trademarks comprising of a mark indicating the place of origin of wines or spirits

A trademark comprising of a mark indicating (1) the place of origin of wines or spirits in Japan which has been designated by the Commissioner of the JPO and is being used on wines or spirits produced in a region other than the place of origin, or (2) a mark indicating the place of origin of wines or spirits in a member country of the World Trade Organization which is prohibited by the member from being used on wines or spirits produced in a place other than the place within the region of the member, cannot be registered if such a trademark is used in connection with wines or spirits produced in the a region other than the place of origin.[38]

(h)   Another person's famous trademark used for unfair purposes

A trademark identical with or similar to a trademark famous in Japan or abroad, if such trademark is used for unfair purposes cannot be registered.[39] This provision is necessary to prevent the trademarks famous in Japan or abroad from being used for unfair purpose.[40]

5   Similarity in trademarks and similarity in goods or services

Similarity in trademarks and in goods or services is important concepts of the Trademark Law. In accordance with Article 4(1)(xi)), a trademark identical with or similar to another person's prior registered trademark which had been filed prior to the filing date of an application for registration of the identical or similar trademark, cannot be registered in order to use for same or similar goods or services. Accordingly, if the trademark which application for registration had been filed is not identical with, but similar to, the prior registered trademark, such trademark may not be registered. Also, if the designated goods

---

[38] Trademark Law, Art. 4(1)(xvii).
[39] Trademark Law, Art. 4(1)(xix).
[40] Refer to UNIT 15.

188

I　Outline of Trademark Law

or services are not identical with, but similar to, those of the prior registered trademark, such trademark may not be registered as well.

Trademark Law, Article 37 (i) which provides injunction rights regarding trademark provides that a person who uses a trademark identical with or similar to the prior registered trademark for goods or services identical with designated goods or services and goods or services similar to the designated goods or services infringe the trademark right. Therefore, even if the trademark used is not identical with the prior registered trademark but is similar to it, and even if the goods or services for which the trademark is used is not identical with the designated goods or services but is similar to them, the trademark right would be infringed upon.

In the Trademark Law, there is no specific provision concerning the scope of "similarity" in trademarks or goods or services, except for Article 2(6) which provides cases where goods or services may be similar and Article 6(3) which provides that the "categories of goods or services" are not perceived as the scope of similarity in the goods or services. Therefore, the determination of "similarity" is a matter of interpretation.

Generally, the similarity with a trademark is determined by looking at whether there is confusion in the source or origin of goods or services that is likely to be caused when both trademarks in comparison are used for identical or similar goods or services. For such purpose, the appearance, pronunciation and the concept of the trademark are often considered as the elements to be evaluated in determining similarity. Market practice is also considered. For the purpose of "similarity" of goods or services, whether there could be confusion in the source or origin by use of same or similar trademark for goods or services in issue will be considered.

6　Filing an application for registration of trademark and opposition against registered trademark

(1)　Procedure for filing and application for registration of trademark

In order to acquire a trademark right, an application must be filed with the Commissioner of the JPO. When filing an application the following must be stated in the application form: (1) the name or title and domicile or residence of the applicant; (2) the trademark for which registration is sought; and (3) the goods or services for which the trademark is used (i. e., the "designated goods" and "designated services") and the category of the goods or services in accordance with the Trademark Law Enforcement

189

UNIT 14   Trademark Law

Order.[41]

When an application is filed, the JPO conducts a formalities examination to determine whether there are any deficiencies in the required formalities. Subsequently, the examiner will conduct a substantive examination to determine whether there are any reasons for refusal.[42] One of the reasons for refusal includes that the requirements for registration are not satisfied.

If there is no reason for refusal, the examiner will render a decision that the trademark is to be registered. On the other hand, if there is a reason for refusal, a notification which states the reason(s) for refusal will be rendered to the applicant, and the applicant is given an opportunity to provide a (written) opinion.[43] The applicant submits a written argument and/or an amendment in response to this notification, and the examiner will render a decision that the registration is to be granted if he/she determines that the application no longer has any reason for refusal. If the applicant does not respond, or if the examiner determines that the reason for refusal was not overcome despite the applicant's response, a decision of refusal will be rendered.

An applicant who objects to a decision of refusal may request a trial to oppose the decision.[44]

In the Trademark Law, the "Publication of Application" system is adopted. Thus, the contents of the application are published in the trademark gazette immediately upon filing of an application.[45]

(2)   Opposition against a registration

When a trademark application is determined to satisfy the requirements for registration, such trademark, is registered upon payment of registration fees.

However, since the examination conducted by the examiner is not always perfect, there may be cases in which a decision that the trademark is to be registered in error. Accordingly, as an opportunity to review the registration, there is a system for opposition against the registration.

After the trademark is registered, a trademark gazette publishing the registered trademark for designated goods or services, etc., will be issued. During the period of two

---

[41] Trademark Law, Art. 5(1).
[42] Trademark Law, Art. 15.
[43] Trademark Law, Art. 15-2.
[44] Trademark Law, Art. 44.
[45] Trademark Law, Art. 12-2.

I Outline of Trademark Law

months following the issuance of the trademark gazette, an opposition may be filed by anybody based on the reasons for opposition listed in the Trademark Law, Article 43-2. The reasons for opposition are almost the same as the reason for invalidation.

The examiner will render a decision that the registration is to be maintained where he/she determines that the registered trademark has no reasons for opposition.[46] On the other hand, the examiner will render a decision that the registration is to be cancelled where he/she determines that the registered trademark has reason(s) for opposition.[47] If the decision to cancel the trademark right has become final and binding, such trademark will be deemed to have not existed from the beginning.[48]

7 Trials and actions against trial decisions

(1) Trials

Under the Trademark Law, there are the following trial procedures which are used as a means to appeal against an administrative disposition, such as a decision of refusal, registration of trademark, etc., made by the JPO. In principle, a trial is concluded with a trial decision.

---

[46] Trademark Law, Art. 43-3(4).
[47] Trademark Law, Art. 43-3(2).
[48] Trademark Law, Art. 43-3(3).

UNIT 14   Trademark Law

Name of Trial	Outline
(1) Trial against a decision of refusal (Art. 44)	Trial to lodge an appeal against an examiner's decision of refusal
(2) Trial against a decision of dismissal of an amendment (Art. 45)	Trial to lodge an appeal against an examiner's decision of dismissal of amendment
(3) Trial for invalidation of a trademark right (Art. 46)	Trial to retroactively extinguish a trademark right. If the trial decision to invalidate the trademark right is final and binding, the trademark right is retroactively extinguished.
(4) Trial for cancellation of trademark registration which has not been used (Art. 50)	Trial for cancellation of the registration of a trademark which has not been used. A part of the designated goods or services may be included in the scope of the cancellation.
(5) Trial for cancellation of trademark registration which has been used by the trademark right holder for unfair purposes (Art. 51)	Trial for cancellation of the registration of a trademark which has been used by the trademark right holder for unfair purposes. If the request is accepted, the entire trademark registration will be cancelled.
(6) Trial for cancellation of a trademark which has been used for unfair purposes as a result of transfer of the trademark (Art. 52-2)	Trial for cancellation of the registration of a trademark which has been used by the trademark right holder for unfair purposes as a result of transfer of the trademark. If the request is accepted, the entire trademark registration will be cancelled.
(7) Trial for cancellation of a trademark which has been used by a licensee for unfair purposes (Art. 53)	Trial for cancellation of the registration of a trademark which has been used by a licensee for unfair purposes. If the request is accepted, the entire trademark registration will be cancelled.
(8) Trial for cancellation of a trademark which has been registered by a representative for unjust purposes (Art. 53-2)	Trial for cancellation of the registration of a registered trademark which has been registered by a representative for unjust purposes. If the request is accepted, the entire trademark registration will be cancelled.

If the trial decision to invalidate a trademark right becomes final and binding in an invalidation trial as listed under (3)[49], such trademark right will be deemed to have not existed from the beginning[50].

If the trial decision for cancellation of the registration of a trademark which has not been used becomes final and binding in a trial listed under (4)[51], the trademark right will be deemed to have been extinguished at the date of filing of the appeal for cancellation.[52] On the other hand, if the decision for cancellation becomes final and

---

[49] Trademark Law, Art. 46.
[50] Trademark Law, Art. 46-2(1).
[51] Trademark Law, Art. 50.

I   Outline of Trademark Law

binding in a trial for cancellation listed under (5) to (8), the trademark right will become extinguished for the future thereafter.[53]

The invalidation trial listed under (3) and the trial for cancellation listed under (4) are frequently used for as countermeasures against infringement litigation and are therefore subsequently mentioned in Sections 4 and 5, Part Ⅱ of this UNIT.

(2) Actions against a trial decision

A party who is not satisfied with a trial decision may file an action opposing such trial decision with the Intellectual Property High Court, which is a special branch of the Tokyo High Court[54]. This would also apply to a decision to revoke the registration in the opposition (procedure) against a registration.

8   Trademark rights and infringement of a trademark right

(1) Trademark rights

As mentioned above, when a trademark registration is granted, a trademark right is created upon payment of registration fees.[55] The duration of a trademark right ends 10 years from the establishment registration date. However, the trademark right may be renewed by registration of renewal.[56]

(2) Exclusive right and prohibitive right

A trademark right is an exclusive right to use a registered trademark in connection with designated goods or services.[57] This monopolistic right to use is referred to as an "exclusive right."

Accordingly, another person who uses a trademark *identical* with the registered trademark for goods or services *identical* with the designated goods or services without permission from the trademark right holder infringes on the trademark right.

Under the Trademark Law, to effectively utilize the exclusive right, another person who uses a trademark *similar* to the registered trademark for goods or services *identical* with the designated goods or services and a trademark *identical* with or *similar* to the registered trademark for goods or services *similar* to the designated goods or services

---

[52] Trademark Law, Art. 54(2).
[53] Trademark Law, Art. 54(1).
[54] Trademark Law, Art. 63(1), Law for Establishment of the Intellectual Property High Court, Art. 2(2).
[55] Trademark Law, Art. 18(1) and (2).
[56] Trademark Law, Art. 19.
[57] Trademark Law, Art. 25.

193

UNIT 14   Trademark Law

without permission from the trademark right holder also infringes on the trademark right.[58] The right to prohibit the use of a trademark within a similar scope is referred to as a "prohibitive right."

(3)   Limitation on the effect of a trademark right

As mentioned above, the trademark right is an exclusive right to use the registered trademark in connection with the designated goods or services and to exclude another person from using the trademark in an identical/similar scope. However, if the trademark right could be exercised without exception, a smooth economic activity may be interrupted. Thus, the Trademark Law in Article 26 provides that the legal effect of the trademark right is limited in certain cases. An alleged infringer may not be liable for trademark right infringement by successfully asserting and proving that the trademark he/she has been using falls within such exceptions under the Trademark Law, Article 26(1). Under the Trademark Law, Article 26(1), the trademarks of which legal effect is limited are listed below.

(1)   Trademarks indicating one's own name, title, etc., in a commonly used manner:[59]

The right of a registered trademark identical with or similar to one's own name is not effective to the extent that the trademark is used to indicate himself/herself. Here, the term "title" denotes the name of a juridical entity such as a company.

(2)   Trademarks indicating a common name, a certain quality of goods or services in a commonly used manner, or customarily used tradename:[60]

The right of a registered trademark consisting of a word or other similar expressions which indicate a common name or a certain quality of goods or services is not effective where it is used as a common name or expression of quality or it is a customarily-used trademark.

(3)   Trademarks solely consisting of characteristics or features which are indispens-able for a certain goods, etc., which characteristics or features are designated by a cabinet order:[61]

An application for registration of a trademark solely consisting of characteristics

---

[58] Trademark Law, Art. 37(i).
[59] Trademark Law, Art. 26(1)(i).
[60] Trademark Law, Art. 26(1)(ii) to (iv).
[61] Trademark Law, Art. 26(1)(v).

194

I   Outline of Trademark Law

or features which are indispensable for a certain goods etc. which characteristics are designated by Cabinet Order will be refused in accordance with the Trademark Law, Article 4(1)(xviii). Even if a trademark is registered in error, the trademark right is ineffective if another person uses the trademark.

(4)   Trademarks which are not used in such a manner that consumers can acknowledge that the trademark in issue is used for the goods or services in relation to someone's business:[62]

The Trademark Law provides certain remedies against trademark infringement with the trademark holder because the use of trademark usually disturbs the function of the trademark to distinguish one's own goods or services from those of another person or the function to indicate the origin thereof. If so, such remedies against trademark infringement are not applicable to a trademark "which is not used in such a manner that the consumers can acknowledge that the trademark in issue is used for the goods or services in relation to someone's business("Trademark use worthiness theory" *Shohyo-teki-shiyo-ron*). At the revision of the Trademark Law in 2014, the concept of "Trademark use worthiness theory" that has been generally supported in the precedents and prevailing views among the scholars has been explicitly introduced as the above provision.

(4)   Infringement of a trademark right

Another person who "uses" a registered trademark without permission within the scope of the exclusive or prohibitive trademark right infringes upon such trademark right.

Therefore, in the trademark infringe cases, whether the alleged infringer "used" the holder's trademark is an issue. The concept of the "use" of a mark is defined in the Trademark Law, Article 2(3), and in accordance with said provision, the acts listed below in Table 3 apply to the "use" of the trademark.

---

[62] Trademark Law, Art. 26(1)(vi).

UNIT 14   Trademark Law

"Use" of a mark		Specific examples
Use of a mark in goods	An act of affixing a mark to a goods or a package of a goods (Art. 2(3)(ⅰ))	- An act of indicating a mark on a goods - An act of integrating electromagnetic information of the trademark into an interface for an actuation so as to make visible
	An act of assigning, delivering, displaying for the purpose of assignment or delivery, exporting, importing of goods or a package of a goods to which a mark is affixed, or providing such goods or package of goods through an electrical telecommunication channel (Art. 2 (3) (ⅱ))	- An act of selling a goods to which a mark is affixed - An act of distributing electronic information property such as a program through network
Use of a mark in a service	Act of affixing a mark to an item to be used by a person who receives a service when the service is provided (Art. 2(3)(ⅲ))	- An act of affixing a mark to a vehicle body of a railway vehicle - An act of affixing a mark to a passbook of a bank
	An act of providing a service by using an item to which a mark is affixed, to be used by a person who receives the service when the service is provided (Art. 2(3) (ⅳ))	- An act of transportation service by using a truck to which the mark of a company is affixed
	An act of displaying an item (including an item to be used by a person who receives the service when the service is provided) to which a mark is affixed, to be used for providing a service for the purpose of providing a service (Art. 2(3)(Ⅴ))	- An act of affixing a mark to an item to be used for providing a service: An act of setting up a coffee machine to which a mark is affixed to the coffee shop - An act of affixing a mark to an item to be used by a person who receives a service when the service is provided: An act of displaying a coffee cup to which a mark is affixed in a coffee shop
	An act of affixing a mark to an item pertaining to the provision of the service to a person who	- An act of affixing a label with a mark to an item pertaining to a process/repair to be conducted

196

	receives the service when the service is provided (Art. 2(3)(ⅵ))	by a processor/repairperson
	An act of providing a service by displaying a mark on an image viewer when the service is provided through an image viewer by an electromagnetic device to provide the service (Art. 2(3)(ⅶ))	- An act of affixing a mark to a display affiliated with an image viewer at the time of providing a service - An act of affixing a mark to an image viewer on which the operation of an image delivery service or a sound delivery service is conducted through the image viewer
Advertising-like use of a mark in a goods or service	An act of displaying or distributing an advertisement, a price list or a trading document in relation to goods or a service, to which a mark is affixed, or providing information on such content to which a mark is affixed by an electromagnetic device. (Art. 2(3)(ⅷ))	- An act of using a mark in printed matters such as magazines, newspapers, signboards, advertisements, advertising figures, television advertising ,etc.
Use a sound mark	An act of making a sound mark for the purpose of assigning/delivering goods or providing a service (Art. 2(3)(ⅸ))	- An act of making a sound mark at the opening of a movie.
Further acts designated by Cabinet Order (Art. 2(3)(ⅹ))		———

However, if the use by the alleged infringer does not involve use of a trademark under "Trademark use worthiness theory," the effect of the trademark right shall be limited in accordance with the Trademark Law, Article 26(1)(ⅵ).[63]

(5) Indirect infringement

As discussed, person who uses a trademark within the scope of the exclusive or prohibitive right of the trademark infringes upon such trademark right. The Trademark Law further regards certain acts preliminary to the infringing acts as an infringement of a trademark right (indirect infringement).[64]

---

[63] Refer to Section 8(3), Part Ⅰ of this UNIT.
[64] Trademark Law, Art. 37(ⅱ) to (ⅷ).

UNIT 14   Trademark Law

(6) Defense against infringement allegation

Even in the use of a trademark which is identical with or similar to a registered trademark for a goods or service which is identical with or similar to the designated goods or service, the alleged infringer does not infringe upon the trademark right if he/she has a justifiable reason.

In a trademark right infringement action, the alleged infringer is allowed to present the following justifiable reasons:

(1)   Prior use right ;[65]

(2)   Trademark Law Article 26;[66] and/or

(3)   invalidity defense.[67]

Reasons (1) and (3) will be described later in Sections 2 and 3, Part II of this UNIT. Also, separate from an infringement action, a claim may be filed with the JPO to extinguish a trademark right of a trademark right holder.

(7) Remedies against infringement

The trademark right holder may claim an injunction of infringement against a party who infringes on his/her trademark right.[68] Furthermore, he/she may claim compensation for damages sustained due to the infringement.[69] A claim for injunction may be made against a non-intentional or non-negligent infringer, whereas a claim for compensation can only be recovered from an intentional or negligent infringer. However, the negligence of the infringer is presumed in the infringing act.[70] This framework is identical to that of patent infringement cases.

(8) Utilization of trademark rights

The ways to utilize a trademark right include the trademark right holder using his/her own trademark, assigning the trademark right, establishing a license or a trademark pledge, etc.

Similar to the exclusive and non-exclusive licenses of a patent right,[71] types of licenses for trademarks include an exclusive or non-exclusive license. An exclusive licensee

---

[65] Trademark Law, Art. 32.
[66] Refer to Section 8(3), Part I of this UNIT.
[67] Trademark Law, Art. 39 referring to Patent Law, Art. 104-3.
[68] Trademark Law, Art. 36.
[69] Civil Code, Art. 709.
[70] Trademark Law, Art. 39 referring to Patent Law, Art. 103.
[71] Refer to Section 3, Part II of UNIT 6.

has the right to exclusively use a registered trademark similar to the trademark right holder[72] and a non-exclusive licensee only has the right to use a registered trademark.[73]

II Defense against a claim of infringement

1 Defense in an infringement litigation and procedures at the JPO

The measures to defend against a trademark right infringement claim includes submission of a counterargument as a defense in an infringement litigation and filing of a trial at the JPO to extinguish the trademark right.

The following sections will explain the right to use a trademark based on prior use[74] and the counterargument for invalidation[75] which the alleged infringer can present at the infringement litigation. Additionally, an invalidation trial and a trial for cancellation of a trademark which has not been used will be described as procedures to be taken at the JPO.

2 Prior use right

Prior use right is the protection of well-known unregistered trademarks in which a reputation has been built. When the trademark right holder claims an injunction or compensation for damages by exercising the trademark right to a party, the party may assert the right to use a trademark based on prior use as a defense.

Prior use right has the following requirements:[76]

(1) The prior user had used the trademark identical with or similar to the registered trademark in connection with goods or services identical with or similar to the designated goods or services in Japan prior to the date of filing of an application for the trademark registration;

(2) The prior user had not been using the trademark for the purpose of unfair competition;

(3) The trademark of the prior user had been well-known at the time of filing of the

---

[72] Trademark Law, Art. 30(2).
[73] Trademark Law, Art. 31(2).
[74] Trademark Law, Art. 32.
[75] Trademark Law, Art. 39 referring to Patent Law, Art. 104-3.
[76] Trademark Law, Art. 32.

199

UNIT 14   Trademark Law

application for the trademark registration; and

(4) The prior user had been continuously using the trademark.

3   Invalidity defense

If it is determined that the trademark right is to be invalidated at a trial for invalidation, the trademark right holder may not exercise his/her trademark right against the adverse party.[77]

Under the Trademark Law, there is a trial to invalidate a trademark which will be mentioned in the next section. The validity of the trademark right can be disputed in the invalidation trial, while in a trademark right infringement litigation, the validity of the trademark right can be examined as well. In a trademark right infringement litigation, the alleged infringer may argue that there is a reason for invalidation of the trademark right. If this defense is accepted, the trademark right holder may only have a limited ability to exercise the trademark right, and a claim for injunction and compensation will be rejected. This argument is generally referred to as the defense for invalidation. As compared to a JPO trial decision to invalidate a trademark right in an invalidation trial (which is generally available to any party), the determination of the invalidation of a trademark used as a defense in an infringement litigation will only be effective among the parties of the litigation.

4   Trials for invalidation

An invalidation trial is to retroactively extinguish a trademark right for which there are reasons for invalidation. Typically, an examiner will conduct an examination of the application for registration of a trademark, and if the examiner determines that the trademark satisfies the requirements for registration, a trademark right will be created by registration of the establishment of the trademark.[78] However, there are cases in which a trademark right is created in error, because the examination conducted by the examiner is not always accurate. Since such trademark should not continue to be valid, a request for an invalidation trial may be filed in order to extinguish the trademark right based on certain reasons for invalidation.[79] Only an interested party may file a request for an

---

[77] Trademark Law, Art. 39 referring to Patent Law, Art. 104-3(1).
[78] Trademark Law, Art. 18(1).
[79] Trademark Law, Art. 46(1).

II Defense against a claim of infringement

invalidation trial.[80] Where the decision of invalidation is final and binding, the trademark right will be deemed not to have existed from the beginning.[81] Therefore, the trial decision of invalidation will be legally effective against any party.

In principle, the reasons for invalidation are the same as those for refusal. Items set in forth in Article 3 and Article 4(1) constitute the reasons for refusal as well as the reasons for invalidation. For some of the reasons for invalidation, a request for an invalidation trial cannot be filed after a lapse of five years from the date of registration of the establishment of the trademark right.[82]

5 Trial for cancellation of trademark registration which has not been used

In a trial for cancellation of a trademark which has not been used, a third party may file a request for a trial for cancellation of the registration of a registered trademark which has not been used continuously for three years and more by the trademark right holder in connection with the designated goods or services.[83] The request for the trial may be filed by any person only and for a part of the designated goods or services. If the designated goods of the registered trademark are; e.g., "A and B," and the registered trademark has not been used for goods B, but only for the goods A, the trial may be filed for rescinding the registration with respect to goods B.

If a trademark is registered, an exclusive and monopolistic right to use it is created, even if the registered trademark has not been used. However, such an exclusive and monopolistic right for trademarks which are not used may disturb public interests. Furthermore, the ability to select a trademark by a party other than the trademark right holder will be unreasonably restricted. Therefore, the system for rescinding the registration of a registered trademark which has not been used for a certain period was created.

However, trademarks which have not been used will not always be cancelled. If the trademark right holder proves a justifiable reason for not using the trademark, the trademark could be exempted from cancellation.[84] The "justifiable reason" in such a case

---

[80] Trademark Law, Art. 46(2).
[81] Trademark Law, Art. 46-2(1).
[82] Trademark Law, Art. 47.
[83] Trademark Law, Art. 50(1).
[84] Trademark Law, Art. 50(2).

UNIT 14   Trademark Law

would be a totally unavoidable reason.

Ⅲ   Protection under the Unfair Competition Prevention Law

1   Outline

In accordance with the Trademark Law, trademarks or marks commercially used in goods or services, will be protected. Also, trademarks are protected under the Unfair Competition Prevention Law Article 2 (1) (ⅰ) and (ⅱ) as indications of goods etc. (hereinafter referred as "indications of goods"). The "indication of goods" includes "a name, a trade name, a trademark, a mark, a container or packaging for goods pertaining to a person's commerce, or any other indication of a person's goods or business."[85]

In order to be protected under the Unfair Competition Prevention Law, specific procedures such as a registration which are required for the Trademark Law are not needed. Instead, the "indication of goods" must be well-known or famous. Furthermore, while the trademark right is effective nationwide, the protection in accordance with the Unfair Competition Prevention Law, Article 2(1)(ⅰ) and (ⅱ) is limited to the area where the indication of goods is well-known or famous. Namely, in accordance with the Unfair Competition Prevention Law Article 2(1)(ⅰ) and (ⅱ), the indication of goods etc. which embodies a commercial reputation will be protected within the area where the reputation is established. On the other hand, in accordance with the Trademark Law, regardless of whether or not the trademark embodies a commercial reputation, nationwide protection will be given by registration in advance, so that the trademark right holder is able to create and maintain the reputation by using the trademark.

A person whose business interests are damaged pursuant to any of the unfair competition acts set forth in Article 2(1) of the Unfair Competition Prevention Law, may claim an injunction of the act and compensation for damages.[86]

2   Act which gives rise to confusion with a well-known indication of goods, etc.

In accordance with the Unfair Competition Prevention Law, Article 2(1)(ⅰ), an

---

[85] Unfair Competition Prevention Law, Art. 2(1)(ⅰ); Refer also to UNIT 15.
[86] Unfair Competition Prevention Law, Art. 3 and 4.

202

Ⅲ Protection under the Unfair Competition Prevention Law

act of using an indication identical with or similar to a well-known indication of goods of another person and an act which gives rise to confusion with goods or the business of another person are defined as an act of unfair competition.

The term "confusion" according to Article 2(1)(ⅰ) is similar to the Trademark Law, Article 4(1)(XV).This confusion includes the case where third parties believe a person B who uses an indication identical with or similar to a well-known Indication of goods, etc. of a person A must be identical to the person A (confusion *sensu stricto*). Further, this confusion includes the case where third parties believe that the person A and the person B are economically or organizationally affiliated with each other (confusion *sensu lato*).

Even if the act at issue falls under item (ⅰ), a claim for injunction or compensation for damages will not be allowed for the common use of a common name or a widely-recognized indication of goods or business in a normally used manner.[87]

3 Act of unauthorized use of a famous indication of goods, etc

In accordance with the Unfair Competition Prevention Law, Article 2(1)(2), an act of unauthorized use of an indication identical with or similar to a famous indication of goods of another person is defined as an unfair competition act. The use of a famous indication of goods, etc. for goods or services irrelevant to such goods may not eventually give rise to confusion. However, even without confusion, the use in such a manner may constitute an unjust free-ride over the famous indication of goods which is attractive for the customer. If such use is allowed to continue, the value of the goods which are distinguished by the famous indication of goods would be diluted and the positive impression of the indication of goods would also be affected. Thus, in such a case where the indication of goods becomes famous rather than well-known, the indication of goods would be protected by item (ⅱ) even without confusion.

Similar to item (ⅰ), even if the act falls under item (ⅱ), a claim of injunction or compensation for damages would not be accepted against the use of a common name or a widely-used indication of goods or business in a normally used manner.[88]

---

[87] Unfair Competition Prevention Law, Art. 19(1)(ⅰ).
[88] Unfair Competition Prevention Law, Art. 19(1)(ⅰ).

Unit 15: Unfair Competition Prevention Law

I Introduction to the Unfair Competition Prevention Law

1 Purpose of the Unfair Competition Prevention Law

Article 1 of the Unfair Competition Prevention Law provides, "The purpose of this law is to provide measures, etc. for the prevention of unfair competition and for the compensation of damages caused by unfair competition, in order to ensure fair competition among undertakings and proper implementation of international agreements related thereto, and thereby contribute to the sound development of the national economy."

Based on the principle of freedom of business, free competition among undertakings is a basic rule. However, there are some unfair competition acts, such as the unauthorized use of or misappropriation of another person's work results which had been achieved by much effort. These unfair competition acts would impact not only an undertaking' private interests but also the public's interest in maintaining fair competition, which would interrupt the sound development of the economy. Therefore, the purpose of the Unfair Competition Prevention Law is to prevent such excessively unfair competition acts to protect the fair competition among undertakings, and thereby to contribute to the sound development of the national economy.

Acts of unfair competition are listed in Article 2(1). A person whose business interests have been damaged or are likely to be infringed upon by unfair competition acts can request an injunction of such act.[1] Moreover, a person whose business interests have been intentionally or negligently damaged by unfair competition acts can claim for compensation of incurred damages.[2]

Further, under the Unfair Competition Prevention Law, certain criminal penalties are provided in relation to some types of unfair competition acts.[3] The commercial use of a

---

[1] Unfair Competition Prevention Law, Art. 3.
[2] Unfair Competition Prevention Law, Art. 4.

UNIT 15   Unfair Competition Prevention Law

foreign state's national flag,[4] commercial use of a mark of an international organization,[5] and provision of wrongful gain to foreign public officials[6] are also subject to criminal sanctions, even though they are not categorized as an act of unfair competition.

2   Characteristic of Unfair Competition Prevention Law

(1)   Limitative listing of unfair competition

Article 2(1) of the Unfair Competition Prevention Law provides a definition of the "unfair competition," and lists 16 unfair competition acts. Any act which does not fall within the 16 types of unfair competition provided in Article 2(1) would not be recognized as an unfair competition act and thus not be restricted.

We can easily recognize what acts fall under the definition of unfair competition if they are specifically listed in the law, which provides for legal stability and predictability. However, if a new type of unfair competition act arises due to the changing of the times, such act cannot be immediately restricted unless the law is amended to add such act to the definition of unfair competition. In this regard, there have been discussions about introducing a catch-all clause which would comprehensively restrict unfair competition acts.[7] However, at this juncture, the Unfair Competition Prevention Law (which was fully revised in 1993 and amended thereafter) categorizes unfair competition acts in a limited manner.

(2)   Regulation of activities

Among the interests protected by the Unfair Competition Prevention Law, and as similar to the Trademark Law, for example, the Unfair Competition Protection Law protects well-known or famous indication of goods[8] which will protect the commercial reputation of businesses that is embodied in such indication. Also, similar to the Design Law or Patent Law, the Unfair Competition Protection Law protects the characteristics of goods which would fall under a "design"[9] and protects trade secrets[10] to protect the work results of

---

[3] Unfair Competition Prevention Law, Art. 21.
[4] Unfair Competition Prevention Law, Art. 16.
[5] Unfair Competition Prevention Law, Art. 17.
[6] Unfair Competition Prevention Law, Art. 18.
[7] For example, the German Unfair Competition Prevention Law states in Article 3(1) that "an unfair commercial trading is not admissible."
[8] Unfair Competition Prevention Law, Art. 2(1)(i) and (ii).
[9] Unfair Competition Prevention Law, Art. 2(1)(iii).
[10] Unfair Competition Prevention Law, Art. 2(1)(iv) to (x).

206

I   Introduction to the Unfair Competition Prevention Law

individuals' creative activities. Based on this perspective, the Unfair Competition Prevention Law plays a role in protecting intellectual property, and is therefore a part of the intellectual property laws such as the Patent Law, the Trademark Law and others.

However, the Patent Law or the Trademark Law protects intellectual property by granting certain rights, whereas the Unfair Competition Prevention Law prohibits certain types of use of intellectual property as unfair competition acts. In other words, the Patent Law or the Trademark Law are laws which grant certain statutory intellectual property rights (i.e. entitlement law), while the Unfair Competition Prevention Law is a law which regulates a person's activities.[11]

(3)   Limitations for a person who is eligible to exercise a right of injunction and a right to claim compensation for damages

The Unfair Competition Prevention Law aims at ensuring fair competition among undertakings. In that sense, similar to the Antitrust Law, it takes part in the preservation of fair competition. However, the Antitrust Law allows the Fair Trade Commission, an administrative agency, to issue a cease and desist order and at the same time, grants certain rights such as a claim of an injunction order to an individual (including consumers) whose private interests have been damaged. On the other hand, in principle, the Unfair Competition Prevention Law only provides civil protections (except for protections to specific types of acts), and a person who may seek an injunction and compensation for damages is limited to a person whose business interests have been or would likely be damaged.

Although the definition of the term "business" mainly includes profit-making businesses, a non-profit business would also be included in the definition as long as such business makes a settling of its accounts. Accordingly, a public service corporation as well as a special non-profit organization are entitled to seek an injunction or compensation for damages. On the other hand, consumer organizations or consumers who are irrelevant to the business may not seek an injunction or compensation for damages under the Unfair Competition Prevention Law. Furthermore, generally, trade associations do not serve their own business, and are therefore, not entitled to seek an injunction or compensation for damages.

---

[11] Refer to Section 3, Part I of Unit 1.

207

UNIT 15   Unfair Competition Prevention Law

3   Overview of unfair competition acts

The Unfair Competition Prevention Law defines in Article 2(1) the following 16 activities as an unfair competition act.

Unfair competition acts concerning the indication of goods or form of goods, etc.:

1   an act which gives rise to confusion of an entity of a well-known "Indication of goods, etc." which means "something which indicates goods or business;"[12]

2   an act of unauthorized use of a famous indication of goods, etc.;[13]

3   an act of imitating a certain form of goods;[14]

Unfair competition acts concerning trade secret:

4   an act of wrongfully acquiring a trade secret and an act of disclosing or using the wrongfully acquired trade secret;[15]

5   an act of acquiring, using or disclosing a trade secret by a subsequent acquirer who knew or was grossly negligent in not having known at the time of the acquisition the trade secret was initially wrongfully acquired;[16]

6   an act of using or disclosing a trade secret by a subsequent acquirer who, after the acquisition of the trade secret, became to know or was grossly negligent in not having known that the trade secret was initially wrongfully acquired;[17]

7   an act of using or disclosing a trade secret presented by the owner for the purpose of making a profit or causing damages;[18]

8   an act of acquiring, using or disclosing a trade secret by a subsequent acquirer who knew or was grossly negligent in not having known that the trade secret was initially wrongfully disclosed;[19]

9   an act of using or disclosing a trade secret by a subsequent acquirer who, after the acquisition of the trade secret, became to know or was grossly negligent in not having known that the trade secret was initially wrongfully disclosed;[20]

---

[12] Unfair Competition Prevention Law, Art. 2(1)(i).
[13] Unfair Competition Prevention Law, Art. 2(1)(ii).
[14] Unfair Competition Prevention Law, Art. 2(1)(iii).
[15] Unfair Competition Prevention Law, Art. 2(1)(iv).
[16] Unfair Competition Prevention Law, Art. 2(1)(v).
[17] Unfair Competition Prevention Law, Art. 2(1)(vi).
[18] Unfair Competition Prevention Law, Art. 2(1)(vii).
[19] Unfair Competition Prevention Law, Art. 2(1)(viii).
[20] Unfair Competition Prevention Law, Art. 2(1)(ix).

I Introduction to the Unfair Competition Prevention Law

10 an act of assigning a product resulting from a wrongful use;[21]

Other unfair competition acts:

11 an act of providing devices which disable technological restrictions which restrict the viewing of images, the hearing of sounds, the running of programs, or the recording of images, etc.;[22]

12 an act of providing devices and the like which disable technological restrictions which restrict anyone other than specific persons, such as a contracting party, from viewing images, hearing sounds, running programs, or recording images allows specific people, such as a contracting party to view or record images, or run programs, etc.;[23]

13 a wrongful act in relation to domain names;[24]

14 an act which gives rise to misleading quality and the like;[25]

15 an act which defames business reputation;[26] and

16 an act of using a trademark by an agent etc.representative without permission.[27]

Due to limited book volume, the below explanation focuses on unfair competition acts involving trade secret, and provide brief explanation on other unfair competition acts. Acts numbered 1 (set forth in Art 2(1)(i)) and 2 (set forth in Art 2(1) (ii)) above are to protect a company's reputation and honor accumulated in certain indication of goods, and therefore, these provisions have common features with the Trademark Law, where a trademark will be protected by creating the trademark right (refer to Part Ⅲ of Unit 14 (Trademark Law)). Further, act no. 3, which is a prohibited act of imitating a certain form of a product, will comprehensively protect the form of a product by sharing roles with the Design Law (refer to Section 3, Part I of Unit 13).

Considering the fair and safe trading between the parties, the Unfair Competition Prevention Law, in certain cases, exempts the application of provisions on injunctive relief, compensation for damages, and penalties even if the party conducts an unfair competition act.[28] These exemptions will be reviewed later.

---

[21] Unfair Competition Prevention Law, Art. 2(1)(X).
[22] Unfair Competition Prevention Law, Art. 2(1)(Xi).
[23] Unfair Competition Prevention Law, Art. 2(1)(Xii).
[24] Unfair Competition Prevention Law, Art. 2(1)(Xiii).
[25] Unfair Competition Prevention Law, Art. 2(1)(Xiv).
[26] Unfair Competition Prevention Law, Art. 2(1)(XV).
[27] Unfair Competition Prevention Law, Art. 2(1)(Xvi).
[28] Unfair Competition Prevention Law, Art. 19.

UNIT 15　Unfair Competition Prevention Law

Ⅱ　Unfair competition acts concerning trade secrets

1　Overview

Companies need to keep confidential valuable information acquired by their efforts in business activities in order to prevent another party from imitating it. If such information is technical information, the companies may seek protections under the Patent Law etc. However, there are some cases where the protections under the laws of industrial property are inappropriate, since in such case, the information will be disclosed to the public. Furthermore, business information such as a customers' name list or a customer service manual for sales promotion will not be protected by the laws of industrial property. Accordingly, it is important for companies to keep confidential the information acquired by their efforts in order to protect such information against the imitation.

However, it is not easy to completely keep information confidential. A typical example is an industrial spy, but there have been recently issues on, in particular, an employee's leakage or unauthorized use of trade secret information when the employee changes jobs.

Therefore, the Unfair Competition Prevention Law includes unfair activities in relation to trade secrets as one of the unfair competition acts to prohibit the wrongful acquisition, use and disclosure of trade secret information acquired through a company's business efforts.

2　Definition of trade secret

Under Article 2(6) of the Unfair Competition Prevention Law, a trade secret means "technical or business information useful for business activities, such as manufacturing or marketing methods, that are kept secret and are not publicly known." The information to be protected as a trade secret must satisfy the following three requirements:

(1)　Information must be kept secret;

(2)　Information must be technical or business information useful for business activities (i.e., utility); and

(3)　Information must not be publicly known.

Ⅱ　Unfair competition acts concerning trade secrets

(1)　Being kept secret

A trade secret must be "kept secret" (or controlled as a secret) because a person who will acquire, use or disclose the trade secret cannot easily determine beforehand whether the information would be a trade secret nor predict whether his/her own conduct would fall within an unfair competition act.

Generally, in order to satisfy the requirement of being kept secret, it is not sufficient that the owner of the trade secret simply recognizes that the subject information is a secret. It is required that employees or customers easily recognize the owner's intention to keep the information confidential by clearly presenting such intention through an economically reasonable measure on confidential compliance, depending on the specific situation.[29]

Typical examples are (ⅰ) a document bearing an indication of "secret," "confidential," or "prohibited to be disclosed" and strictly stored in the company's safe, and (ⅱ) information which only restricted employees may have access to or which is subject to a confidentiality obligation provided under the company's internal rules. Nevertheless, there are no uniform standards on to what extent and how the information is handled to determine if it being kept confidential, and according to case precedents, the nature of the information, the manner in which the information is being kept, and the company's size, etc. shall be taken into consideration. For example, a court held that even though a company did not have a manual on how to control trade secrets, had no rule that a stamp of "confidential" should be put on any printed documents, and did not enter into a non-disclosure agreement with their customers to which the information was disclosed, the information was kept secret by considering the facts that only limited employees may have access to it, and that the employees may have objectively recognized that the information at issue was a trade secret.[30]

(2)　Utility

Information to be protected as a trade secret must be "technical or business information useful for business activities" since the use of information which is not useful for business activities would not need to be restricted as an unfair competition act.

---

[29] "Annotation to the Unfair Competition Prevention Law," revised version (2015), p. 41, edited by the office for the intellectual property policy of the Minister of Economy, Trade and Industry ("Annotation") (http: //www. meti. go. jp/policy/economy/chizai/chiteki/unfair-competition. html#chikujo).

[30] Nagoya District Court decision of March 13, 2008, *Hanrei Jiho*, No. 2030, p. 107.

UNIT 15   Unfair Competition Prevention Law

Article 2(6) lists a production method and a marketing method as examples of technical or business information useful for business activities. A product design, manufacturing process, or know-how in manufacturing are considered as examples of the production method. A customers' name list, a sales manual and a procurement list are considered as examples of the marketing method. This information has been obtained by spending costs and are useful for the business activities for production, sales and provision of services.

The requirement of utility will be satisfied if the information is considered to be potentially useful in the future, even if it is not currently used in business activities. Moreover, not only the information which can be positively useful for business activities, but also the negative information such as unsuccessful experimental data could be deemed useful information since it would be valuable for business activities in that it may save costs and time or prevent further failures.

On the other hand, information kept by companies may include information in relation to tax evasion or a bribe as well as their executive officer's personal scandal. If such information would widely spread to the public, the company's reputation would be negatively affected and their business performance may decline. However, considering the purposes of the Unfair Competition Prevention Law, the trade secrets that are protected must contribute to the development of the national economy. As the information above has an illegal nature and is not useful or appropriate to be protected, it is not considered to be a trade secret. A court held that information in relation to a bid for a public work which was wrongfully acquired was not useful and was not deemed a trade secret under the Unfair Competition Prevention Law.[31]

(3)   Not being publicly known

A trade secret requires "not being publicly known" since it is not necessary to protect information which is openly known and widely spread in society, and if the protection was granted to such information, it would unreasonably interrupt the free access and availability of information.

"Not being publicly known" means that information is not generally accessible from outside of the owner's control, such as the information concerned has not been stated in a publication. Even if any person other than the owner knows the information, it

---

[31] Tokyo District Court decision of February 14, 2002 (2000 (*Wa*) No. 9499).

II   Unfair competition acts concerning trade secrets

is not considered to be publicly known as long as a confidentiality obligation is imposed on them, regardless of the number of people since the information is still under the control of the owner. On the other hand, if only a single person who is not under the owner's control knows the information, then it becomes publicly known.

Also, information which is included in a product generally available in the market can be obtained by analyzing such product, which is called "reverse engineering." It is not wrongful conduct to obtain a trade secret through "reverse engineering." However, does the information which can be obtained by the reverse engineering satisfy the requirement of "not being publicly known?"

Efforts and costs for the "reverse engineering" may vary. If it is easy to reverse-engineer a product in the market, the owner could have foreseen at the time of placing the product on the market that the information would be known to the public. In such case, there is no need for such information to be treated as a trade secret, and the owner should not be entitled to trade secret protection. In this regard, a court held that information which could easily be acquired by analyzing a sold product without spending many costs would not satisfy the requirement of not being publicly known.[32]

On the other hand, if it is difficult to reverse-engineer a product, the information contained in the product is worth being protected and will be regarded as non-public information since the owner of the information can still have priority over the competitor by retaining ownership of it. A court held that even if it is possible to reverse-engineer a product in the market, if experts would need to spend a lot of time and money to analyze the product, then the information obtained will be considered non-public information.[33]

3   Unfair competition acts

The Unfair Competition Prevention Law categorizes seven unfair competition acts in relation to trade secrets.[34] The seven categories of the unfair competition acts are mainly classified into the following three types:

Type I: The Act of wrongfully acquiring a trade secret from its owner and following acts by subsequent acquirers in the process of distributing the trade secret[35]

---

[32] Intellectual Property High Court decision of July 21, 2011, *Hanrei Jiho*, No. 2132, p. 118.
[33] Osaka District Court decision of February 27, 2003 (2000 (*Wa*) No. 10308, 2012 (*Wa*) No. 2833).
[34] Unfair Competition Prevention Law, Art. 2(1)(iv) to (X).
[35] Unfair Competition Prevention Law, Art. 2(1)(iv) to (vi).

UNIT 15   Unfair Competition Prevention Law

Type Ⅰ includes industrial espionage as a typical example of the wrongful acquisition of the trade secret.

Type Ⅱ : The Act of wrongful use and disclosure of a trade secret legally provided by its owner and following acts by subsequent acquirers in the process of distributing the trade secret.[36]

Type Ⅲ : Acts in the process of distributing a product which was result from a wrongful acts provided by the Types I and II above.[37]

---

[36] Unfair Competition Prevention Law, Art. 2(1)(ⅶ) to (ⅸ).
[37] Unfair Competition Prevention Law, Art. 2(1)(Ⅹ).

214

II Unfair competition acts concerning trade secrets

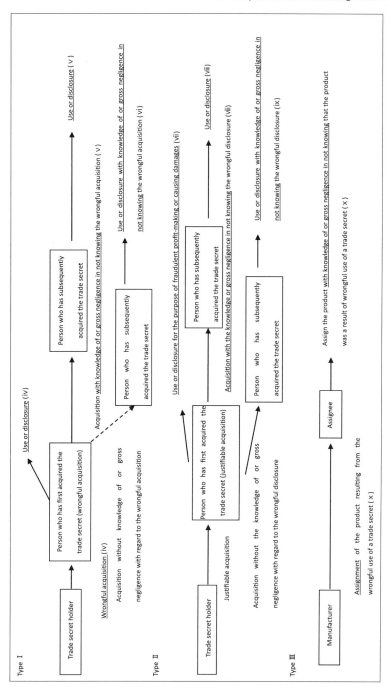

UNIT 15   Unfair Competition Prevention Law

(1)   Wrongful acquisition of a trade secret and disclosure or use of the wrongfully acquired trade secret[38]

An unfair competition act under Article 2(1)(ⅳ) is an act of acquiring a trade secret by theft, fraud, duress, or other wrongful means from its owner (act of a wrongful acquisition), and an act of use or disclosure of the wrongfully acquired trade secret. The term "use" means the use of the trade secret for one's own business activities, and "disclosure" means (ⅰ) to make the trade secret publicly known, or (ⅱ) to present it to a specific person while keeping the trade secret confidential to the public.

(2)   Subsequent acquirer's acquisition of a trade secret with knowledge or gross negligence in not knowing that such trade secret was wrongfully acquired, or use or disclosure of the trade secret wrongfully acquired[39]

An unfair competition act under Article 2(1)(Ⅴ) is an act of acquiring, using or disclosing a wrongfully acquired trade secret by a subsequent acquirer with knowledge or gross negligence in not knowing that the trade secret was wrongfully obtained.

The term "with knowledge" refers to the case where a person has learned that a trade secret was wrongfully acquired. The term "gross negligence" refers to the case where a person could have easily learned of the wrongful acquisition of the trade secret by exercising his/her duty of care which is generally required for transactions (even if he/she has no knowledge about the wrongful acquisition), and which can be almost equivalent to "having learned" of the wrongful acquisition.

(3)   Subsequent acquirer's use or disclosure of an acquired trade secret with knowledge or gross negligence in not knowing subsequent to its acquisition that the trade secret was initially wrongfully acquired[40]

Article 2 (1) (Ⅴ) of the Unfair Competition Prevention Law prohibits the acquisition, use or disclosure of a trade secret with knowledge or gross negligence in not knowing that the trade secret was wrongfully obtained. Therefore, Article 2(1)(Ⅴ) does not apply if a person acquired a trade secret without knowledge or gross negligence in not knowing that the trade secret was wrongfully acquired. On the other hand, Article 2(1)(ⅵ) defines as unfair competition an act of using or disclosing an acquired trade secret with knowledge or gloss negligence in not knowing that the trade secret was initially wrongfully

---

[38] Unfair Competition Prevention Law, Art. 2(1)(ⅳ).
[39] Unfair Competition Prevention Law, Art. 2(1)(Ⅴ).
[40] Unfair Competition Prevention Law, Art. 2(1)(ⅵ).

II Unfair competition acts concerning trade secrets

obtained by a *bona fide* acquirer.

(4) Use or disclosure of a trade secret presented by its owner for the purpose of fraudulent profit-making or to damage the owner of the trade secret[41]

An unfair competition act under Article 2(1)(ⅶ) is an act of using or disclosing a trade secret legally presented by its owner for the "purpose of making a fraudulent profit" or to "damage the owner of the trade secret." The purpose of fraudulent profit-making means to make a fraudulent profit in a manner which is against public policy or the principles of good faith, including the purpose of making wrongful profit for a third party. The purpose of damaging the owner of the trade secret means to make unreasonable and tangible or intangible damages such as damages to the owner's property, or causing a loss of his/her reputation. In this respect, it is not required that any actual damage is caused as a result.[42]

(5) Subsequent acquirer's acquisition, use or disclosure of a trade secret with knowledge or gross negligence in not knowing that the trade secret was wrongfully disclosed[43]

An unfair competition act under Article 2(1)(ⅷ) is an act of acquiring a trade secret through wrongful disclosure (including (ⅰ) disclosure for a purpose of making an illegal profit or causing damage to the owner of a trade secret provided under Article 2(1) (ⅶ) above or (ⅱ) disclosure through violation of a confidentiality obligation) after having learned of, or being grossly negligent in not having learned of these wrongful disclosure acts, as well as an act of using or disclosing the trade secret obtained in the above manner.

The term "confidentiality obligation" includes, but is not limited to, that explicitly provided in the laws for professionals, such as lawyers, certified accountants, or certified tax advisers as well as that provided under a contract.

(6) Subsequent acquirer's use or disclosure of a disclosed trade secret with knowledge or gross negligence in not knowing that subsequent to its acquisition, the trade secret was initially wrongfully disclosed[44]

An unfair competition act under Article 2(1)(ⅸ) is an act of using or disclosing an acquired trade secret with knowledge or gross negligence in not knowing that the trade

---

[41] Unfair Competition Prevention Law, Art. 2(1)(ⅶ).
[42] *See* Annotation, *supra* note 29, p. 80, 81.
[43] Unfair Competition Prevention Law, Art. 2(1)(ⅷ).
[44] Unfair Competition Prevention Law, Art. 2(1)(ⅸ).

UNIT 15   Unfair Competition Prevention Law

secret was initially wrongfully disclosed.

(7)   Assignment of a product resulting from wrongful use[45]

An unfair competition act under Article 2(1)(X) is an act of transferring a product resulting from the wrongful use of a technical secret (i.e., a product infringing a trade secret), or an act of transferring the product by a person with knowledge or gross negligence in not knowing that the product was created by the wrongful use. This provision was newly implemented in 2015 in order to improve the deterrence against infringing acts by restricting the transfer of products which infringe a trade secret.

4   Statute of limitations

Under the Unfair Competition Prevention Law, an owner of a trade secret is entitled to request an injunction against a person who conducts an unfair competition act in relation to a trade secret as a remedy against such unfair competition act.[46] However, if the right to request an injunction is awarded in a case where a person continues, for a long time period, to produce, sell, or research and develop products in which another person's trade secret is contained (i.e., such production, sale or research and development would fall within the unfair competition act), it would seriously affect the infringing party's employment or business relationships, and as a result, the injunction would negatively impact the legal stability.

Accordingly, from the perspective of stabilizing social and legal relationships, Article 15 of the Unfair Competition Prevention Law provides a (i) three-year statute of limitations, and (ii) twenty-year period of exclusion[47] with respect to the right to request an injunction against the unfair competition acts in relation to the trade secrets. Therefore, unless the owner of the trade secret seeks injunctive relief within three years after he/she knew (i) the existence of the unfair competition act in relation to the trade secret and (ii) the person who had performed the unfair competition act in relation to the trade secret, the right to request an injunction will be extinguished, and no request for injunction will be accepted thereafter.

---

[45] Unfair Competition Prevention Law, Art. 2(1)(X).

[46] Unfair Competition Prevention Law, Art. 3.

[47] A holder of the trade secret may no longer exercise a right to seek injunctive relief if twenty years have elapsed from the time of the unfair competition act conducted, regardless of whether the owner does not recognize the existence of the unfair competition act or the person who performed the wrongful act.

II   Unfair competition acts concerning trade secrets

Further, Article 4 provides a right to seek compensation for damages to business profits caused intentionally or by (gross) negligence. However, Article 4 also provides, in its proviso, that once the right to seek an injunction is extinguished in accordance with Article 15, the right to seek compensation for damages above will not be exercisable with respect to the damages incurred due to use of the trade secret thereafter.

5   Exemptions

Articles 19(1)(vi) and (vii) of the Unfair Competition Prevention Law provide exemptions from the unfair competition acts concerning trade secrets.

As mentioned above, even if a person had no knowledge, or no gross negligence in not knowing that a trade secret was initially wrongfully acquired or disclosed, if he/she, subsequent to the acquisition of the trade secret, learns of or has gross negligence in not having learned of such wrongful acquisition or disclosure, such person's use or disclosure of the trade secret would constitute an unfair competition act.[48] However, although these provisions contributes to the protection of the owner of the trade secret, unexpected damages may be caused to a person who has acquired the trade secret in consideration of substantial amounts, and as a result, the safety of the trade would be harmed.

Accordingly, Article 19(1)(vi) provides that if a person who obtained a trade secret through a transaction without the knowledge or gross negligence in not knowing the wrongful acquisition or disclosure, uses or discloses the trade secret within the scope authorized under such transaction (e.g., within the period term or regional scope provided under a license agreement), certain provisions such as the right to seek an injunctive relief or compensation for damages, or the imposition of a penalty would not apply.

Also, as stated above, the assignment of a product which infringes on another party's trade secret falls under an unfair competition act.[49] However, once the statutory limitations period provided under Article 15 has elapsed, the holder of the trade secret may no longer exercise the right to seek injunctive relief against the wrongful use. If so, it would be inequitable if the prohibition of the assignment of a product resulting from the wrongful use of the trade secret would continue to be effective. Therefore, Article 19(1) (vii) provides that relevant remedies such as the right to seek injunctive relief or compensation for damages, or the imposition of a penalty would not apply to the

---

[48] Unfair Competition Prevention Law. Art. 2(1)(vi) and (ix).
[49] Unfair Competition Prevention Law, Art. 2(1)(x).

UNIT 15   Unfair Competition Prevention Law

assignment of a product resulting from the wrongful use of a trade secret after the right to request an injunction against such wrongful use has been extinguished.

Ⅲ   Other unfair competition acts

1   Provision of devices which disable technological restrictions

Articles 2(1)(xi) and (xii) define an act of providing devices which disable technological restriction measures as unfair competition act, so as to legally support the technical control taken by the contents providers, such as copy protection control or access control.

Article 2(1)(xi) specifies the act of providing devices or programs which disable technological restriction measures restricting the viewing of images, etc. Article 2(1)(xii) specifies the act of providing devices or programs which restrict anyone other than specific persons, such as a contracting party, from viewing images, etc.

The term "technological restriction measures" means measures to restrict an unauthorized duplication of images and accessibility by electromagnetic methods in accordance with Article 2(7). For example, the micro-vision system which restricts the recording of the contents, and the scramble system for the chargeable satellite broadcasting.

The remedies such as a right to seek an injunctive relief or compensation for damages, or imposition of a penalty will not apply if a person intends to use the devices or programs which disable technological restriction measures for the purpose of examination or research.[50]

2   Wrongful act in relation to domain names

An unfair competition act provided under Article 2(1)(xiii) is "the act of acquiring or holding a right to use a domain name that is identical with or similar to another person's specific indication of goods, etc. (a name, trade name, trademark, mark, or any other indication of goods or services pertaining to a person's business), or the act of using the above domain name for the purpose of making a fraudulent profit or causing damages to another person."

---

[50] Unfair Competition Prevention Law, Art. 19(1)(viii).

Ⅲ Other unfair competition acts

In principle, a domain name can be acquired on a first to file basis, and no substantial examination is conducted for the acquisition. Thus, we have often seen cases where a domain name identical with or similar to another person's trade name or trademark is acquired so as to take advantage of such person's reputation or to resell the domain name at an unreasonably expensive price. Article 2(1)(xiii) prohibits such acts in order to protect fair competition.

3 Misleading indication for quality, etc.

An unfair competition act provided under Article 2(1)(xiv) is the act of making an indication which would mislead a product's place of origin, quality, contents, manufacturing process, purpose of use, or quantity, or a service's quality, contents, purpose, or quantity.

Whether a certain indication would be misleading is generally determined by comprehensively taking into account various factors, such as the contents of the indication or business situation, which depend on each specific case. Also, even if the indication is not actually misleading, it is sufficient as long as the indication would likely mislead the consumer.

Article 19(1)(i) states an exemption from Article 2(1)(xiv) above which provides that a right to request for injunction, etc., are not applicable if a common name or a customary indication for goods or business is used in a commonly prevailing manner. One example is indicating "French bread" on baguettes made in Japan.

4 Defamation of business reputation

An unfair competition act provided Article 2(1)(xv) is an "act of making or circulating a false statement that damages a competitor's reputation of its business." This is a typical unfair competition since making or circulating a false statement directly impacts a business' reputation and could cause fatal damages on the targeted business.

For example, Article 2(1)(xv) would apply if a holder of a certain intellectual property right (e.g., a patent) makes an announcement to the public or its competitor's customers that the competitor's product infringes on the holder's IP right, and it is later found that the competitor's product has not infringed on the holder's IP right or that the holder's IP right is invalidated. In such case, the competitor's reputation was damaged as a result of the false statement made by the holder of the IP right which alleges the

UNIT 15   Unfair Competition Prevention Law

competitor's patent infringement, and therefore Article 2(1)(XV) would apply.

There are cases in which courts held that if the announcement to the competitor's customers was made as part of exercising an intellectual property right such as a patent, it would be considered justifiable. However, even if the announcement was made as part of exercising the right, if the contents or the method of the announcement was beyond that socially acceptable, and as a result, the announcement was considered made for the purpose of damaging the competitor's reputation, or prevailing over the competitor in business with its customers or in the market, then such announcement would be considered an unfair competition act.[51]

5   Unauthorized use of trademark by agent

An unfair competition act provided under Article 2(1)(XVi) is an act of using, without justifiable grounds, a trademark of another person in a foreign country (country of the Union established by the Paris Convention, a member of the World Trade Organization, or a contracting party to the Trademark Law Treaty) by the trademark holder's agent or representative, or a person who was, within one year of the act, its agent or representative.

Originally, under the principle of territorial jurisdiction, the trademark will become effective only in a country in which the trademark is registered. However, Article 2 (1)(XVi) above aims at internationally improving the protection of the trademark holder.

Articles 19(1)(i) and (ii) of the Unfair Competition Prevention Law provides an exemption from Article 2(1) (XVi) above. Article 19(1)(i) has been discussed in the previous section relating to "misleading indication of quality." As for Article 19(1)(ii), it focuses on the exemption for use of a person's own name without a wrongful purpose.

---

[51] Tokyo High Court decision of August 29, 2002, *Hanrei Jiho*, No. 1807, p. 128.

Index

abstract ⋯ 69

act of making a work transmittable ⋯ 132

action against a trial decision ⋯ 7

aesthetic impression ⋯ 167

agent ⋯ 222

amendment ⋯ 71~

anonymous or pseudonymous work ⋯ 136

Antitrust Law ⋯ 207

application for registration (Design Law) ⋯ 173

application for registration (Trademark Law) ⋯ 189

applied art ⋯ 112

architectural work ⋯ 113

article ⋯ 165

artistic work ⋯ 112,133

author ⋯ 12,117

author's honor or reputation ⋯ 161

automatic public transmission ⋯ 131

award granting non-exclusive license ⋯ 90

being kept secret ⋯ 211

biological invention ⋯ 25

broadcasting ⋯ 131

calendar year method ⋯ 136

cinematographic work ⋯ 113

claims ⋯ 6,67~

common expression ⋯ 108

compulsory license ⋯ 90

computer program (Copyright Law) ⋯ 114,160

computer program (Patent Law) ⋯ 18,22

223

Index

confidentiality obligation ···217

confusion···203

confusion in the source or origin of goods or services ·······························187

copyright ···13〜,127

Copyright Law ···12〜

copyrightable ···105〜

counterargument by correction ···102

craftsmanship ··112

creation ·· 25

creation law ···3

creator doctrine···117

critical significance·· 44

database ··116

debug ···160

decision of cancellation ·· 75

decision of maintenance··· 75

decision of refusal ·· 71

decision to grant a patent ·· 70

defamation of business reputation ···221

defensive application·· 48

derivative work···115,153,156

description in publication·· 36

design··165〜

design for a set of articles ···173

Design Law···10〜,163〜

design of a graphic image···167

design right ···174

detailed explanation of the invention ·· 66

diagrammatical works··113

disclosure of administrative information ···155,157

discovery ·· 25

distribution system ··133

doctrine of equivalents ·· 95

224

Index

domain name	220
downloading	130
drawing	69
educational book	145
employee	57
employee invention	57~
employer	57
employment regulation	61
enablement requirement	23,66
entitlement law	3
essential feature	95~
essential part	175
examination	69~
examination paper	146
exception to the lack of novelty	38~,170
exclusive license	84
exhaustion	103~,134
ex-parte trial	76
expression	107
fair practice	144,157
fair use provision	149
final notification of reasons for refusal	72
finding of the gist of an invention	38
fine art	112
first notification of reasons for refusal	72
first-to-file system	44~,171,186
first-to-invent system	45
form of an article	166
free invention	60
function of guaranteeing the consistency of the quality	180
function of indicating the origin	179
function of promoting and advertising	180
general provision	148

225

Index

idea ··· 107
identification mark law ·· 3
imitation ··127,164
inclusion ··· 142
incomplete invention·· 24
indirect infringement··96〜,177,197
industrial applicability (Design Law)·· 169
industrial applicability (Patent Law)·· 30
industrial property·· 3
infringement by utilizing a registered design ···················· 177
infringement of a trademark right···································· 195
intellectual property··· 1
international exhaustion ··· 134
inter-partes trial·· 77
invalidity defense ···101〜
invention ···4,17〜
invention of a chemical substance ······························· 24
inventive step ··41〜
inventive step of a use invention ································· 43
inventor ·· 52
joint copyright ···121
joint invention··· 52
joint work ···119
laws of nature ··· 18
license ··· 83
license by agreement ··· 83
licensee··· 83
limitation of a copyright ··· 139
limitation on the effect of a trademark right ················ 194
limitation on the right of attribution ·························156〜
limitation on the right to integrity······························159〜
limitation on the right to make an original work public ····154〜
limitative listing ··· 206

226

Index

literal infringement	94
literary work	110
Made public	153
maker of the cinematographic work	118,154
management of official documents	155,157
media reporting	147
medical invention	31
misappropriated application	53～
monopolistic non-exclusive licensee	86
moral right of an author	13,151～
multiple claims system	67
musical work	111
non-exclusive license	85
non-substantive examination principle	69
not being publicly known	212
not easily created	171
notification of reasons for refusal	70
novelty	32～,169～
numerically limited invention	43
original work	115,133,135,153,154,156
originality	108
parody	158
partial design	166
patent application	65～
Patent Law	4～
patent opposition	75
patent right	8～
patentability	29～
people with disabilities	146
performance which do not make a profit	146
period of exclusion	218
person skilled in the art	41,66,171
photographic work	110

227

Index

principle of no formalities ·· 127

prior use right ··· 100~,199

private use ··· 140

process invention ·· 18

process invention by which a product is produced ························· 18

product invention ·· 17

protection of moral interests after the author' s death ················· 161~

pseudonym ··· 155

public ··· 129

public transmission ·· 131

publication of application ······································· 74~,173,190

publicly ··· 34

publicly-known ··· 35

publicly-worked ··· 35~

published ··· 153

purpose of damaging the owner of the trade secret ··················· 217

purpose of making a fraudulent profit ·· 217

quotation ··· 144

reasonable benefit ··· 62~

reasonable value ··· 63

regulation of activities ··· 206

reproduce ··· 129

reproducibility ··· 23

request for examination ·· 6,70

requirements for registration (Design Law) ······························· 169~

requirements for registration (Trademark Law) ························· 182~

reverse engineering ··· 213

right of attribution ··· 155~

right of distribution ··· 133

right of exhibition ··· 133

right of on-screen presentation ··· 130

right of original author in relation to exploitation of a derivative work ··············· 135

right of performance ··· 130

228

Index

right of pledge ⋯⋯⋯⋯⋯⋯⋯⋯⋯⋯⋯⋯⋯⋯⋯⋯⋯⋯⋯⋯⋯⋯ 89

right of public transmission ⋯⋯⋯⋯⋯⋯⋯⋯⋯⋯⋯⋯⋯⋯⋯ 131

right of recitation ⋯⋯⋯⋯⋯⋯⋯⋯⋯⋯⋯⋯⋯⋯⋯⋯⋯⋯⋯⋯ 132

right of rental ⋯⋯⋯⋯⋯⋯⋯⋯⋯⋯⋯⋯⋯⋯⋯⋯⋯⋯⋯⋯⋯⋯ 134

right of reproduction ⋯⋯⋯⋯⋯⋯⋯⋯⋯⋯⋯⋯⋯⋯⋯⋯⋯⋯ 129

right of transfer of ownership ⋯⋯⋯⋯⋯⋯⋯⋯⋯⋯⋯⋯⋯⋯ 134

right of translation and adaptation etc ⋯⋯⋯⋯⋯⋯⋯⋯⋯ 135

right to integrity ⋯⋯⋯⋯⋯⋯⋯⋯⋯⋯⋯⋯⋯⋯⋯⋯⋯⋯⋯ 157～

right to make an original work public ⋯⋯⋯⋯⋯⋯⋯⋯ 152～

right to obtain a patent ⋯⋯⋯⋯⋯⋯⋯⋯⋯⋯⋯⋯⋯⋯⋯ 5,51

right to translate ⋯⋯⋯⋯⋯⋯⋯⋯⋯⋯⋯⋯⋯⋯⋯⋯⋯⋯⋯ 135

rights of an author ⋯⋯⋯⋯⋯⋯⋯⋯⋯⋯⋯⋯⋯⋯⋯⋯⋯ 13～

secret design ⋯⋯⋯⋯⋯⋯⋯⋯⋯⋯⋯⋯⋯⋯⋯⋯⋯⋯⋯⋯ 173

secret prior art ⋯⋯⋯⋯⋯⋯⋯⋯⋯⋯⋯⋯⋯⋯⋯⋯⋯⋯ 47～

selection invention ⋯⋯⋯⋯⋯⋯⋯⋯⋯⋯⋯⋯⋯⋯⋯⋯⋯⋯ 43

serial publication ⋯⋯⋯⋯⋯⋯⋯⋯⋯⋯⋯⋯⋯⋯⋯⋯⋯⋯⋯ 138

similarity in form ⋯⋯⋯⋯⋯⋯⋯⋯⋯⋯⋯⋯⋯⋯⋯⋯⋯⋯⋯ 175

similarity in trademarks ⋯⋯⋯⋯⋯⋯⋯⋯⋯⋯⋯⋯⋯⋯⋯⋯ 188

similarity of articles ⋯⋯⋯⋯⋯⋯⋯⋯⋯⋯⋯⋯⋯⋯⋯⋯⋯ 175

similarity of designs ⋯⋯⋯⋯⋯⋯⋯⋯⋯⋯⋯⋯⋯⋯⋯⋯ 174～

single claim system ⋯⋯⋯⋯⋯⋯⋯⋯⋯⋯⋯⋯⋯⋯⋯⋯⋯ 67

software-related invention ⋯⋯⋯⋯⋯⋯⋯⋯⋯⋯⋯⋯⋯ 21～

specification ⋯⋯⋯⋯⋯⋯⋯⋯⋯⋯⋯⋯⋯⋯⋯⋯⋯⋯ 6,66～

statute of limitations ⋯⋯⋯⋯⋯⋯⋯⋯⋯⋯⋯⋯⋯⋯⋯⋯ 218

statutory license ⋯⋯⋯⋯⋯⋯⋯⋯⋯⋯⋯⋯⋯⋯⋯⋯⋯⋯ 60

sub-divided rights ⋯⋯⋯⋯⋯⋯⋯⋯⋯⋯⋯⋯⋯⋯⋯⋯ 13,128

substantive examination principle ⋯⋯⋯⋯⋯⋯⋯⋯⋯⋯ 69

support requirement ⋯⋯⋯⋯⋯⋯⋯⋯⋯⋯⋯⋯⋯⋯⋯⋯ 68

technical idea ⋯⋯⋯⋯⋯⋯⋯⋯⋯⋯⋯⋯⋯⋯⋯⋯⋯⋯ 22～

technical scope of a patented invention ⋯⋯⋯⋯⋯⋯⋯ 94

technological restriction ⋯⋯⋯⋯⋯⋯⋯⋯⋯⋯⋯⋯⋯⋯ 220

term for the protection of a work ⋯⋯⋯⋯⋯⋯⋯⋯⋯⋯ 136

thoughts or sentiments ⋯⋯⋯⋯⋯⋯⋯⋯⋯⋯⋯⋯⋯⋯ 106

Index

title･･158

trade secret ･･･210

trademark･･･180

Trademark Law ･･11,179～

trademark right ･･･193

trademark which is not capable of distinguishing one=s own goods or services and those of another person ･･･183

transfer of patent right ･･･ 82

trial･･7～,76～,173,191～

trial against a decision of refusal ･･･････････････････････････････71,77

trial against the examiner's decision to reject an amendment･･････････ 174

trial decision of correction･･････････････････････････････････････ 80

trial decision of invalidation ･･････････････････････････････････ 78

trial for correction ･･ 78～

trial for invalidating a patent･･･････････････････････････････････ 78

trial for invalidating the registration of extension ･･････････････････ 80

trial for invalidation ･･ 78

true name ･･･155

Unfair Competition Prevention Law･･･････････････15～,164,202,205～

unity of invention ･･･67,73

unpatentable invention ･･････････････････････････････････････ 49

unregistrable design･･･172

use invention ･･･ 26

use it with quotations ･･144

utility ･･211

Utility Model Law ･･･ 9～

utilization of the laws of nature ･･････････････････････････････ 18～

version upgrade･･160

visual observation ･･166

well-known ･･202

wire-broadcasting ･･･131

work for hire･･ 12,122

working for experimental or research purposes ･･････････････････ 99

230

Index

wrongfully acquired ·· 216
wrongfully disclosed ·· 217

カバーデザイン 株式会社廣済堂

Intellectual Property Law in Japan
日本知的財産法

2017年（平成29年）12月27日 初版 発行

編 者	茶園 成樹
©2017	CHAEN Shigeki
発 行	一般社団法人 発明推進協会

発 行 所　一般社団法人 発明推進協会
　　　　　所在地　〒105-0001 東京都港区虎ノ門2-9-14
　　　　　電　話　03-3502-5433（編集）03-3502-5491（販売）
　　　　　ﾌｧｸｼﾐﾘ　03-5512-7567（販売）

印　刷　株式会社 丸井工文社　　Printed in Japan
乱丁・落丁本はお取り替えいたします。
ISBN 978-4-8271-1301-3 C3032
本書の全部または一部の無断複写複製を禁じます（著作権法上の例外を除く）。
本書は「知的財産法入門第2版」(茶園成樹著　有斐閣2017年) を翻訳したものです。

発明推進協会 HP：http://www.jiii.or.jp/